THE AMERICAN PENAL SYSTEM

This thoughtful examination of incarceration in the United States from the 1980s to the current time offers for consideration a transparent and humane correctional model for the future. Author Helen Clarke Molanphy employs an interdisciplinary approach encompassing sociology, penology, memoir, philosophy, and history.

Featuring the work of researchers as well as penal theorists of the Enlightenment era, literati who have written about crime and punishment, inmates, social justice activists, and journalists, the author incorporates first-hand interviews with participants in the landmark *Ruiz v. Estelle* lawsuit, which found incarceration in the Texas Department of Corrections to be cruel and unusual punishment in violation of the Eighth Amendment. Synthesizing lessons learned from years of studying the American prison system through contact with inmates, correctional authorities, legislators, and prisoner advocates, Molanphy offers a narrative of crime and punishment, degradation, and dehumanization, but with hope pointing to future correctional reforms. The book not only catalogs human rights abuses and the pain inflicted by corrupt penal systems, but also provides a roadmap for an enlightened society to conceive of ways to reduce mass incarceration and provide humane treatment of inmates.

This reflective survey of the pervasive issues that afflict the prison industrial complex offers a compelling analysis of the past and possible future of the US penal system for students of criminal justice, corrections, penology, and the sociology of punishment.

Dr. Helen Clarke Molanphy is political science emeritus professor at Richland College in Dallas, Texas. She has taught sociology and criminal justice courses at various institutions including Southern Methodist University, the University of Texas at Dallas, Adams State University, the Santa Fe University of Art and Design, and the Santa Fe Community College. Molanphy is the author of a family memoir, *Over P.J. Clarke's Bar: Tales from New York's Famous Saloon*, using her maiden name, Helen Marie Clarke. She resides in Santa Fe, New Mexico, with her husband, John Molanphy.

"This book is an excellent survey of the pervasive issues that plague the American Prison System, and it eloquently interrogates valuable solutions for those very problems."

Dr. Tyrell Connor, *Associate Professor, SUNY New Paltz*

THE AMERICAN PENAL SYSTEM

Transparency as a Pathway to Correctional Reform

Helen Clarke Molanphy

Cover image: © Getty Images

First published 2022
by Routledge
605 Third Avenue, New York, NY 10158

and by Routledge
4 Park Square, Milton Park, Abingdon, Oxon, OX14 4RN

Routledge is an imprint of the Taylor & Francis Group, an informa business

© 2022 Helen Clarke Molanphy

The right of Helen Clarke Molanphy to be identified as author of this work has been asserted in accordance with sections 77 and 78 of the Copyright, Designs and Patents Act 1988.

All rights reserved. No part of this book may be reprinted or reproduced or utilised in any form or by any electronic, mechanical, or other means, now known or hereafter invented, including photocopying and recording, or in any information storage or retrieval system, without permission in writing from the publishers.

Trademark notice: Product or corporate names may be trademarks or registered trademarks, and are used only for identification and explanation without intent to infringe.

Library of Congress Cataloging-in-Publication Data
Names: Molanphy, Helen, author.
Title: American penal system : transparency as a pathway to correctional reform / Helen Clarke Molanphy.
Description: New York, NY : Routledge, 2022. | Includes bibliographical references and index.
Identifiers: LCCN 2021056563 (print) | LCCN 2021056564 (ebook) | ISBN 9781032248240 (hardback) | ISBN 9781032248219 (paperback) | ISBN 9781003280279 (ebook)
Subjects: LCSH: Imprisonment--United States--History. | Prison administration--United States--History. | Corrections--United States--History. | Criminal justice, Administration of--United States--History.
Classification: LCC HV9466 .M65 2022 (print) | LCC HV9466 (ebook) | DDC 365/.973--dc23/eng/20220126
LC record available at https://lccn.loc.gov/2021056563
LC ebook record available at https://lccn.loc.gov/2021056564

ISBN: 978-1-032-24824-0 (hbk)
ISBN: 978-1-032-24821-9 (pbk)
ISBN: 978-1-003-28027-9 (ebk)

DOI: 10.4324/9781003280279

Typeset in Bembo
by KnowledgeWorks Global Ltd.

CONTENTS

Preface   *vii*

PART I
The Texas Department of Corrections   **1**

  1 Texas Control Model   3

  2 Jailhouse Lawyers   8

  3 *Ruiz v. Estelle*   13

  4 Texas Prison Administrators   18

  5 Texas Today   24

PART II
Demographics of American Prisons   **29**

  6 The Unschooled   31

  7 The Young and the Old   36

  8 The Female Inmate   41

  9 Poor People of Color   46

  10 The Political Prisoner   52

PART III
Major Problems in Corrections — 57

11 Guard Brutality and Corruption — 59

12 Wrongfully Convicted — 65

13 Treatment of Mentally Ill Inmates — 71

14 Prison Labor — 76

15 Privatization of Corrections — 81

PART IV
Toward Ending Mass Incarceration — 87

16 Legislative Agendas — 89

17 The Supreme Court and the US Department of Justice — 95

18 Reducing Recidivism — 100

19 Alternative Models — 105

20 Restorative Justice — 111

Epilogue — *116*
Bibliography — *124*
Index — *127*

PREFACE

The inspiration for *The American Penal System: Transparency as a Pathway to Correctional Reform* began on a spring afternoon in 1978 when I stepped from a taxi into the courtyard of the Cerezo Jail in Juarez, Mexico, for what was to be my first time visiting a correctional institution. As a new instructor of criminal justice studies at the Government and Law High School in Dallas, Texas, I was accompanied by the director of internships, Carol Flynn, who had invited me to join her at an El Paso, Texas, criminology conference. Carol exited the taxi and walked with me into the dusty yard of an old adobe building in which yellow-beaked chickens pranced around and traditionally clothed Catholic nuns tended to female prisoners' children. Meanwhile, two severe-looking guards, armed with a heavy-duty rifles resting on their shoulders, were pacing back and forth in front of the jail entrance.

When one of the guards asked why we were there, Carol responded that the jail director was expecting us for an interview arranged by Ann Richards, then the director of the Texas Juvenile Justice Department, but soon to become the governor of the state. With that, the guard led us through worn wooden doors into the facility where we were met by a slight, pleasant-looking inmate, with trustee status, who guided us to the director's office. During our hour with the director, he addressed the problem of gang violence at Cerezo, as well as the deprived backgrounds of most of the inmates. When Carol and I left the director's office, we rounded a bend in the hallway and were approached by the same inmate. He handed me a note, and said, "You two ladies are from Texas, so please read this. It's about my experience in your state's prison."

With his note in my hand, I walked with Carol through several Juarez streets as little children begged us for a few cents. Locating a taxi, we settled inside and read the prisoner's words:

> When I arrived at the Ellis unit I was placed in the Diagnostic Center where I was brainwashed. The guard who brought me to my cell referred to me as "greaser" and told me that my ass was his and he didn't want "no shit" from me. I had to give him a good day's work or else.
>
> The Texas Department of Corrections is one of the most brutal joints in the United States. Physical brutality is an everyday thing. So is homosexuality because sex deprivation is one of the worst features of prison life. TDC inmates are subject to beatings, head knockings, ass-kickings and even killings by the guards. I personally saw several senseless beatings in the cotton fields.

> Sending all those youngsters, all these first offenders to the TDC, is the worst crime that society can commit. Most of these youngsters are not hardened criminals but once they reach TDC they are on their way to becoming some of the worst individuals in any society. They are raped by inmates and beaten by guards.[1]

Disturbed by what the prisoner had written, his message became the opening salvo to my doctoral dissertation on the Texas prison system. In 1980, when it was time to write my dissertation for the humanities doctoral degree from the University of Texas at Dallas, I was fortunate to acquire articles written in the 1930s by Houston police reporter Harry McCormick from Anne Williams, an editor at the *Dallas Times Herald*.

While digesting McCormick's important historical work on the brutal conditions in the Texas prison system in that era, I learned that the Texas Department of Corrections (TDC) was being sued for "cruel and unusual" punishment under the Eighth Amendment of the US Constitution. In 1980, Fifth Circuit Court Judge William Wayne Justice had reached his conclusions about TDC violations in *Ruiz v. Estelle*, a class-action civil rights lawsuit that was the result of a near decade of legal struggle between eight inmates and the TDC administration. At that point, I went to my files and reread the Cerezo inmate's note on his harrowing experience in the Texas prisons. His information, plus Harry McCormick's news reports and the *Ruiz v. Estelle* case, helped me formulate a dissertation topic, "The Idea of Punishment: Texas Prison System as a Case Study," that was approved by my UTD professors.

In the four decades since my doctoral research was completed in 1982, we have witnessed the emergence of mass incarceration. About 2.3 million Americans, largely poor and of minority backgrounds, are imprisoned and seven million more persons are on probation or parole. Due to a lower crime rate, a slight decline in our prison population has occurred, but America still incarcerates 25% of the world's prisoners, while representing only 5% of the world's population. Our country also has a high ratio of prisoners per capita, over 700 per 100,000; elsewhere in the western industrial world, the per capita average is 150 persons per 100,000. In addition, conditions in our correctional facilities often fall below the standards set in many other western democracies. Widespread inhumane treatment, as well as high recidivism rates, raise serious questions about the efficacy of our current penal system.

People of all political persuasions are admitting that the American prison system is in crisis, broken physically, economically, and morally. Criminologists argue about the main cause of mass incarceration, with crime, drug laws, harsh sentencing, and prosecutorial fervor at the top of the list. Over the past 30 years, the number of incarcerated persons in American prisons and jails has increased by 500% with the annual cost of the prison industrial complex well over $80 billion dollars.

Inmates are housed in 102 federal prisons, 1,719 state prisons, 901 juvenile corrections facilities, 3,163 local jails, 76 Native American jails, as well as in military prisons, immigration detention facilities, civil commitment centers, and prisons in US territories. About 630,000 persons occupy jails, of which only 167,000 have been convicted; the remaining 443,000 are not able to produce bail and have been awaiting trial. State prisons now incarcerate nearly a million and a half persons and over 200,000 inmates fill federal facilities. About 445,000 employees work in our prisons, with 295,000 acting as guards.

Women are a minority in prisons, comprising 103,674 of the millions incarcerated, but their numbers are growing. By race, African Americans are the majority with 581,000 in prison, while there are 350,000 Hispanics, 516,200 Anglos, and 90,000 other incarcerated. Noncitizens make up 26% of all prisoners, with the largest number in state prisons.

About 237,000 inmates are incarcerated in state prisons for drug offenses; 253,000 are there for property crimes, some of which may be related to drugs; and 725,000 inmates have been convicted of violent crimes, such as robbery, assault, manslaughter, murder, and rape.

Approximately half of federal prisoners are imprisoned for drug offenses. These statistics on drug and other nonviolent offenders tell a story; even if we legalized or decriminalized narcotics use and reduced the number of nonviolent offenders sent to prison, American correctional facilities would remain overcrowded, especially in state prisons in which so many persons are incarcerated for violent crimes.[2]

The coronavirus pandemic has highlighted the overcrowding, the lack of adequate sanitation and medical care, the bureaucratic methodology, and the enormous personal and economic costs of our current system. The statistics on the prevalence of this virus in our country mirror the statistics on imprisonment; while we have 5% of the world's population, so far, America has accounted for 25% of the deaths from COVID-19. A very large proportion of illness and deaths from this virus has been borne by American prisoners; statistics indicate that the effect of COVID-19 in prisons is five times that of the free world.

Over the last 40 years, as I taught criminology and penology college-level courses in three states, Texas, Colorado, and New Mexico, I met or learned about dedicated people who disclosed inhumane prison conditions and offered insights on how to create a more just approach to American corrections. Much of this transparency occurred due to efforts of investigative journalists, as well as advocacy groups and members of the bar. Many of these persons faced the enormous power of the prison industrial complex in a David and Goliath scenario.

Besides citing the humane and unconstitutional conditions of the present American correctional model, *The American Penal System: Transparency as a Pathway to Correctional Reform* presents ways in which reforms are being introduced to address mass incarceration, while also ending cruel and unusual punishment. Most analysts agree that real reform can only take place if the number of prisoners decreases substantially.

Part I of this interdisciplinary book showcases efforts at transparency in the Texas penal system, especially through the prisoner lawsuit, *Ruiz v. Estelle*, that aimed at reform of the state's retributive system. Part II examines inhumane conditions as well as prospects for improvement among major demographic groups in our prisons: the unschooled, juveniles, the elderly, minorities, female inmates, and political prisoners. Part III covers problems and possible remedies regarding five major issues in American prisons: guard brutality and corruption, the wrongfully convicted, mentally ill inmates, labor issues, and profiteering in the prison industrial complex. Part IV deals with ongoing efforts to reduce both inhumane treatment and mass incarceration initiated by legislatures, governors, courts, justice departments, and advocacy groups; this section also examines alternative correctional models utilized in Europe, as well as the penological philosophy of restorative justice that is inherent in indigenous cultures.

Much of the general information in *The American Penal System: Transparency as a Pathway to Correctional Reform* is based on extensive research, as well as years of teaching college courses including: constitutional issues related to penal institutions, criminal law, the war on drugs, women in prison, race and class, probation and parole, the media and criminal justice, juvenile justice, and film seminars related to crime and punishment. Citations are from interviews with persons connected to the American prison system, library research, and scholarly books by authors concerned about the crisis in the American penal system. In some instances, citations resulted from attendance at legislative hearings and the use of government documents.

As I was writing this book, I paid attention to television and radio stories, as well as to print sources. I've also participated in several Zoom sessions, run by nonprofit organizations, so some citations, pertaining to recent information on prison conditions, are taken from Internet sources. Communication is changing rapidly and major print and television sources do not report on American prisons as often as alternative media does, a sad reflection on the lack of transparency in the penal system. However, as the reader will see from the bibliography, in the last decade, many scholars have written books on conditions in prison, as well as on penal reform.

Inferno, one of the references utilized for this book, was written by Harvard humanities scholar Robert Ferguson who provided an excellent in-depth description of the barbaric and unconstitutional penal conditions that our taxes pay for. In his prologue, Dr. Ferguson says that he was so disturbed by the amount of brutality in our prisons that he considered giving up his project, but he continued on in the interest of exposing this inhumanity to American citizens. I had similar feelings and, like Dr. Ferguson, I believe that transparency is vitally important for the development of humane penal policies. US Supreme Court Justice Louis Brandeis once said: "Sunlight is said to be the best of disinfectants."

Many thanks to my family for encouraging the writing of this book. I am also grateful to Vanessa O'Loughlin of the writers' resource, writing.ie, in Dublin, Ireland, for her long-time support, and to Ellen Boyne of Taylor and Francis for her devoted guidance. *The American Penal System: Transparency as a Pathway to Correctional Reform* is dedicated to the generous persons who provide transparency in our correctional system and help alleviate the inhumane conditions of the prison industrial complex in which too much unnecessary suffering occurs.

Notes

1 Note from inmate at Cerezo Jail in Juarez, Mexico in 1979
2 United States Department of Justice Report – "Correctional Population in United States, 2017–2018," Prepared by Laura Maruschak and Todd Minton, August 2020

PART I
THE TEXAS DEPARTMENT OF CORRECTIONS

1
Texas Control Model

Well before the 1971 uprising at New York's Attica Correctional Facility, Texas male inmates, living in what was known as "the prison crescent," acted out their discontent. The men resented the harsh supervision of wardens who ran the prison units as a source of cheap labor, as well as the contemptuous and distrustful attitude of most of the guards. As a result, inmates in the prison farm units developed a culture that gave the appearance of conformity, alongside an underground pattern of nonconformity.

The men improvised by brewing "pruno" or "raisin jack" and making "glim boxes," substitutes for lighters. Their homemade "stingers" were used to heat water and, for weapons, they fashioned "shivs." The problem of inadequate cash was solved by counterfeiting. As no rehabilitation existed, the men merely hoped to survive, while they dreamed of escape.

An older Texas Department of Corrections (TDC) inmate said, "There was no such thing as filing a writ in those years. The prisoners had no rights so they rioted."[1]

Prison riots are usually set off by a single event. Wardens dread them, fearing loss of their jobs. Uprisings indicate the system is breaking down and this frightens the public and the politicians. While state governors worry about the loss of their reputations for good management, riots point to prison problems, but they don't hold public interest for long.

In the 1930s, riots in the Texas prisons, referred to as "bucks," were derived from the expression, "bucking the system." These prison "bucks" centered around the scarcity and low quality of the food, the overcrowded conditions in the prison dormitories, and the mistreatment by guards. While TDC Warden Lee Simmons' explanation for "bucks" was inmate idleness and lack of discipline, the official history of the Texas Department of Corrections, *TDC: 30 Years of Progress*, indicated that prisoners were involved in "bucks" due to poor living conditions, along with beatings in the fields.[2]

At that time, many states, especially in the North, did not allow prison industries in order to protect free world workers, but Texas and other southern states did. The TDC daily scheduling of harsh work in the fields and shops, while motivating "bucks," may have limited the opportunity for more widespread protests to take place. In addition, the architectural design of TDC, with its far-flung farm units, acted as a preventative to major uprisings.[3]

During the first half of the twentieth century, other groups besides the prisoners shone a light on the dysfunctional TDC system. Progressive reform entities, such as the 1924 Joint Committee on Prison Reform, urged rehabilitation and, to a limited extent, the Texas legislature backed that agenda. These politicians affirmed that brutality should be abolished and that new programs, such as classification, industrial training, and education, needed to be introduced. While the TDC authorities publicly agreed with the Commission's proposals, they did little to prevent brutality or to lobby for the funds needed to develop these programs.

The Joint Committee went even further by urging the relocation of some Texas prison units to more populated areas and they advocated the construction of a hospital for prisoners suffering from mental illness. The Committee members recommended that, after subtracting the cost of their maintenance, prisoners should be paid for their labor and they urged parole board members to secure work for inmates before their discharge. None of these reforms were adopted by the Texas legislature, but calls for similar changes would be heard in the ensuing decades.[4]

The Texas Joint Committee's progressive proposals were in keeping with the ideas of penologists throughout the country. Rehabilitation, or the reshaping of the criminal into a noncriminal, was being touted as the proper function of a prison system and national reformers critiqued the Texas prison system as a stark example of the "control and punish" style.

In 1931, the National Commission on Law Observance and Enforcement, appointed by President Herbert Hoover and popularly known as the Wickersham Commission, did a study of penal conditions throughout our country. The Commission called the American penitentiary system antiquated and inefficient, and said that these institutions contributed to crime, thus indicating that Texas prisons were not the only ones in need of reform.[5]

In addition to the official reform groups, investigative reporters were extremely important in exposing the poor conditions at TDC. George Waverly Briggs of the *San Antonio Express-News* wrote about the convict leasing and chain-gain system in the South, with the result that this form of slave labor was ended in 1912. One of the places that Briggs described was Sugar Land, an area of mosquito-infested swampland that lies southwest of Houston, Texas, in which barelegged inmates labored in the wet sugarcane fields of the Imperial Prison Farm Camp and often died from disease. Their diet was the same every day: moldy biscuits for breakfast and cold, hard corn bread and black-eyed peas for both lunch and dinner.

Nearly a century later, when the Fort Bend Independent School district near Sugar Land began construction of a vocational center, workmen found the remains of 95 African Americans who labored at the camp; examination of their bodies indicated that these inmates had been tortured in the fields in which their blood ran deep.[6]

In 1931, the same year that the Wickersham Commission wrote its report, the *Houston Press* ran an article, entitled "Ghostwriters," written by an anonymous reporter who stressed how diligent TDC was in prohibiting the flow of news from inside the farm units. This journalist revealed stories of convicts who prepared glowing reports about the prison administration, while brutality was covered up and the availability of marijuana, morphine, denatured alcohol, and homemade prune wine was never mentioned.[7]

Police reporter Harry McCormick of the *Houston Press* was responsible for a large body of work that provided a close look at the horrendous conditions at TDC; from 1931 to 1937, McCormick exposed the brutality by the guards and by some prisoners, this, despite the fact that prison officials worked to suppress all news of killings, torture, and escapes. McCormick challenged the prison administration's daily operations and he was more effective than official governmental bodies, concerned politicians, or civil rights groups because his writing reached more of the public and led to some improvements at the Texas farm units. The basis for McCormick's first story was "kited" out by another *Houston Press* reporter who had gone to prison on a hot-check charge.[8]

Next, McCormick wrote an article, based on information from the prison grapevine, about an inmate who, after leading 30 men in a run for liberty, was shot down in cold blood. Because of McCormick's revelation, Warden Lee Simmons was censored by the TDC prison board for not reporting the death.[9]

Harry McCormick went on to write about John Bailey, a prisoner who was beaten by a sadistic guard after he fell and broke his ankle; the county health officer reported that even if half of what Bailey said was true, the brutality was outrageous. Another McCormick story concerned W. E. Leonard, a burglar who contracted tuberculosis and was forced to work in the fields, despite suffering from a high fever.[10]

One of McCormick's feature articles covered the plight of Charles Johnson, a World War I veteran and a drug addict. Sent to prison for the burglary of a drugstore, Johnson was placed in solitary confinement due to complaints from guards that he refused to work.

An official from the Armed Services found Johnson and wrote:

> Visitors go through the prison for twenty-five cents. But here was a sight that would have been worth an extra fee. It was a ghastly horror. The cell from which Johnston rarely emerged was no larger than a pantry without facilities for bathing...He had a wild stare in his eyes and sat, like a scared thing about to bolt with fear.[11]

Warden Lee Simmons denied McCormick's story and blamed Charles Johnson's condition on his use of drugs. However, when Johnson was examined at the Veterans Administration hospital, doctors found him poorly nourished, emaciated, hallucinating, and suffering from tuberculosis and bronchitis, conditions not induced by drug abuse. After Charles Johnson was declared insane and pardoned by the governor of Texas, Lee Simmons declared, "I'm glad to get rid of prisoners as hard to handle as he was. Johnson was a bad influence on the other prisoners here."[12]

Harry McCormick's story about inmate Clarence Williams followed. When this man attempted to escape from Retrieve Farm and guards discovered him in a tree, they surrounded him with bloodhounds and ordered him to either jump down among the dogs or be shot.

In his news report about Williams, McCormick wrote:

> The boy was covered with a mass of bites. His clothing was nearly stripped from his body. He was forced to march ahead of the horses back to camp. Even old-time convicts shuddered at the sight of the boy. A new man who attempted to cleanse Williams' wounds was whipped. Williams died shouting, "keep them off me, keep them off me."[13]

Later, one of Harry McCormick's sources sent him a copy of Clarence Williams' death certificate in which the attending doctor lied, saying that he did not know what caused the lacerations. More shocking was a report revealing that a guard, who had actually prevented Williams' escape, was discharged from his duties that day. Rather than returning Clarence Williams to his cell, other guards threw the escapee out into the field and set the 25 dogs, housed at Retrieve Farm, against him.

McCormick's source wrote, "They're killing men on these damned farms. They kill them, bury them, and then make out an escape report and the world moves on."[14]

In 1933, M. E. Foster, Harry McCormick's editor at the *Houston Press*, addressing the suppression of news by TDC authorities, wrote,

> Prison officials have not denied the truth of any statement printed by the Press, but some of those in charge have put forth statements that were either evasive or incorrect, as proven by autopsies and prison records.[15]

M. E. Foster reminded Warden Lee Simmons that the prison system belonged to Texans and that Simmons' duty was to keep the taxpayers informed of events, including riots and escapes. The editor told Simmons that he should allow photographers into the prison for executions as a concrete way to show others that crime did not pay.

Near the end of Lee Simmons' tenure, he openly defended his policies and opposed a bill ending corporal punishment at TDC. When the "bat," a three-inch by two-foot leather instrument with a wooden handle and a rawhide thong, was forbidden, Simmons remarked, "Most employees hated to see the "bat" go. The guards are afraid it will lead to loss of control."[16]

In his book, *Assignment Huntsville*, self-published 20 years after his retirement, Lee Simmons spoke of the overcrowding and of the unsafe, unsanitary conditions that he found at TDC and he blamed these on the Texas legislature's fixation on saving money.[17]

Meanwhile, Harry McCormick's personal contact with prisoners at TDC provided him with insights that other journalists did not enjoy. While some of his peers often viewed penological methods, such as indeterminate sentences, probation, and parole, as examples of being soft on criminals, McCormick did not agree. His investigative stories were groundbreaking, leading to needed changes at TDC. In this respect, he resembled nineteenth-century reformers, John Howard and Elizabeth Fry, and early twentieth-century muckrakers, Ida Tarbell and Upton Sinclair.

Texas prisoners appreciated what an advocate they had in Harry McCormick and, at his death in 1968, they established a cancer fund in his memory. TDC Director George Beto eulogized McCormick, saying he had done more for Texas prisoners than any other single individual. In another eulogy, one of McCormick's press colleagues cited convict Raymond Hamilton's praise of the reporter's search for the truth, even after Warden Lee Simmons had barred him from the prison. McCormick's colleague added that Texas Governor James Allred allowed Harry to attend Ray Hamilton's execution because this was the condemned inmate's last request.[18]

From 1962 to 1972, Director O. B. Ellis, who had managed a prison farm in Tennessee, was in charge of TDC. Ellis advocated rehabilitation goals, but he focused on making the prison units cleaner and safer, and he obtained funds for a major building program. The Ellis unit was named for him and became the most tightly run facility in TDC, housing many lifers, recidivists, and those who made trouble. This was a form of poetic justice as O. B. Ellis was always bent on segregating the troublemakers from the rest of the population. The Ellis unit was known to be disciplined and orderly, with few disturbances or gang activity, unlike other units in San Quentin, California, or Joliet, Illinois. However, former inmates at the Ellis unit told of a high level of depression, resulting from anxiety and boredom.[19]

The Texas control principle that O. B. Ellis perfected spread to other state prisons, mainly in the South, but later in the North. This concern for security accounts for many restrictions that continue to mortify American prisoners; examples include infrequent visitation; limited amounts of money spent on inmates for food, housing and clothing; loss of personal property; inadequate medical care; and the insistence on uniforms and serial numbers. The discipline of hard work and daily existence in dark, crowded cells enforces the control principle, while wardens back discipline with threats of more punishment.

Despite the amount of control, over the years, some Texas inmates attempted to escape. As an example, in July of 1974, powerful South Texas heroin kingpin Fred Gomez Carrasco and two other inmates at the Walls Unit in Huntsville seized 11 prison workers and 4 inmates as hostages. The three men, who had permission to work in the prison library, had obtained smuggled pistols and ammunition. Under orders from Director Jim Estelle, TDC officials began negotiations with the convicts, supplying them with their requests of food, clothing, sanitary products, walkie-talkies, and bulletproof helmets; Texas Governor Dolph Briscoe even approved the men's request for an armored getaway car. After 11 days, the convicts made an attempt at escape, moving from the prison library to the waiting vehicle. When prison guards and Texas Rangers blasted them with fire hoses, the three escapees fatally shot two female hostages. Receiving gunfire from the Rangers, Fred Carrasco committed suicide and one of his accomplices was killed. The third man was placed on death row and executed in 1991, 17 years after the hostage-taking.[20]

During this same period, several Texas prisoners, frustrated by the lack of facilitation of 1960s national calls for humane treatment and rehabilitation, decided to take another route. They became jailhouse lawyers and confronted the injustice and unconstitutional conditions in the TDC, making a resounding impact on corrections in America.

Notes

1. Molanphy, Helen Clarke, *Idea of Punishment: Texas Prison System as a Case Study*
2. Ibid.
3. Ibid.
4. Ibid.
5. Ibid.
6. Ibid.
7. Ibid.
8. "Kiting" was a practice used by many of the prisoners and involved stringing information out secretly.
9. Molanphy, Helen Clarke, *Idea of Punishment: Texas Prison System as a Case Study*
10. Ibid.
11. Ibid.
12. Ibid.
13. Ibid.
14. Ibid.
15. Ibid.
16. Ibid.
17. Ibid.
18. Ibid.
19. Ibid.
20. Texas Ranger Hall of Fame and Museum, texasranger.org

2
Jailhouse Lawyers

In 1980, my doctoral research involved interviewing Lawrence Pope, one of the eight plaintiffs in *Ruiz v. Estelle* and a major contributor to the lawsuit. At the time, Pope was a parolee being assisted by Charles and Pauline Sullivan, founders of Citizens United for the Rehabilitation of Errants (CURE), based in Austin, Texas.

Pope was a bank official in Waco, Texas when his partners secretly sold their stock shares to a Dallas swindler. After examiners fired all the bank administrators in 1960, Lawrence Pope borrowed funds to start a business selling bank forms to financial institutions in the hope that his Texas banking acquaintances would provide clients. When these men went back on their promises, Pope, a middle-class man, became a bank robber; following two robberies netting him $7,000, he was arrested by Federal Bureau of Investigation (FBI) agents.

Federal and state courts rejected Pope's insanity plea and, at the age of 42, he received concurrent federal and state sentences of 25 and 50 years. After an unsuccessful attempt to escape, Pope entered the federal prison at Leavenworth, Kansas, and, while there, he filed writs asking federal courts to protect the rights of prison inmates. As a result of his work, civil rights advocate Judge Thurgood Marshall, then a solicitor general, ordered Leavenworth officials to allow prisoners to file pleas.

Because of Pope's advocacy work, federal authorities classified him as a troublemaker and transferred him to the Huntsville unit of the Texas Department of Corrections (TDC), ironically located in his own hometown. At that time, Texas had the largest prison population in the nation; among the 30,000 inmates, at least 40% were repeat offenders and 90% were high school dropouts from impoverished backgrounds. African Americans constituted 50% of the inmates, even though this demographic group represented 20% of the Texas population. Within this maximum-security segregated system, inmates labored in rigid, severely disciplined farm units spread throughout the eastern half of Texas. Despite its tremendous size, TDC cost taxpayers one-fourth of other prison systems.[1]

Lawrence Pope was 52 years of age and suffering from bronchial asthma and diabetes when he was assigned to strenuous duties in the cotton fields at the Ellis Unit. After Pope learned that only one doctor served thousands of prisoners, the lack of health care, plus his Methodist faith and long-time membership in the Boy Scouts, motivated him to use his legal skills again. As a plaintiff in the *Ruiz v. Estelle* case, Lawrence Pope paid a price for his writ-writing because he was often placed for long periods in solitary confinement on a bread and water diet, a punishment that aggravated his chronic diseases.[2]

DOI: 10.4324/9781003280279-3

Until the 1960s, federal courts had refused to accept inmate lawsuits, always referring the cases back to the states in which they originated, but this changed when the Warren Court began accepting litigation from prisoners and their attorneys. In 1964, the US Supreme Court ruled in *Cooper v. Pate* that prisoners had the right to challenge the practices of officials in federal court. By igniting a nationwide civil rights movement for inmates, *Cooper v. Pate* resulted in a number of lawsuits; *Newman v. Alabama* followed *Cooper v. Pate* and established that inmates were entitled to basic medical care, reasonably adequate food, clothing, shelter, sanitation, and personal safety. Given these two decisions, federal courts declared that eight state prison systems in the Deep South violated the "cruel and unusual" punishment clause of the Eighth Amendment; as a result, these institutions were handed over to federal court receivership. Of the thirty-nine states outside the Deep South, four of them, Alaska, Delaware, New Mexico, and Rhode Island, were also placed under a federal court's supervision during that period.

Texas plaintiffs submitted complaints in *Novak v. Beto* and *Cruz v. Beto,* two important cases that preceded *Ruiz v. Estelle*. TDC prisoner Ronald Novak sued Director George Beto in 1970 on the grounds that he was placed in harsh conditions in solitary confinement for seeking legal advice from fellow inmate Fred Cruz. While Novak referenced *Johnson v. Avery* (1969) in which the court ruled that inmates could help one another in legal cases, a Texas court ruled against him after hearing TDC Director George Beto argued that in-house attorneys eliminated the need for inmates writ-writers.

Director Beto also testified that Fred Cruz's legal consultation to Novak constituted a danger to the system and would lead to a prisoner-run institution. When the judge in the case accepted Beto's argument, he added that TDC could determine the conditions of their solitary confinement. While Novak lost in this court, a few years later, an appeals court ruled in his favor, stating that prisoners could seek legal advice without being punished.[3]

Fred Cruz was born into a single mother's household in a ghetto in San Antonio, Texas, then among the poorest cities in our nation. Cruz, a marijuana user, dropped out of school after the eighth grade and turned to robbery to support his heroin habit. In the mid-1960s, Cruz accidentally shot and killed his best friend, and, while he was not charged for this, at age 21, he was given a 35-year sentence for aggravated robbery.

Cruz worked in TDC's Harlem unit for ten hours, six days a week, as a stoop laborer in the sugar cane and cotton farm surrounding the prison. He fit the overall demographic description of Texas inmates: urban, young, product of a broken home, a school dropout, no record of prior employment, and, along with 60% of the prison inmates, a member of a minority group.

While housed in a racially segregated unit, Fred Cruz learned about earlier Mexican-American unsuccessful strikes against the brutal fieldwork at the Harlem unit. He became an admirer of the Chicano movement that denounced discrimination against those of Latino backgrounds, including the farmworkers championed by Cesar Chavez in the 1960s. Cruz also studied the lives of Martin Luther King and Malcolm X and he equated the relocation of Mexican-American urban inmates to rural Texas prison units with the way that slavery had uprooted Africans to America.

Fred Cruz concluded that it was important that Mexican Americans, growing in numbers in TDC, join with African Americans to end injustices. His sense of justice led him to study constitutional law and to start an appeal of his lengthy sentence in the prison "writ room." A voracious reader, Cruz also kept a diary of his daily activities and of his journey to Buddhism, an eastern philosophy emphasizing acceptance and nonviolence.[4]

Cruz, like Lawrence Pope, put up with hard assignments, disciplinary beatings, and solitary confinement to continue his legal work and practice his Buddhism. In 1972, Cruz began preparing his case, arguing that his First Amendment right to religious freedom was usurped by

George Beto when the TDC director denied Cruz the right to correspond with his Buddhist priest and ordered his Buddhist spiritual books to be removed. Whenever Cruz was caught sharing his beliefs with other inmates, the guards tossed him into solitary, with no clothing or bedding, and with only a hole in the middle of the cell for a toilet.[5]

Despite the unlikelihood of his gaining judicial attention, Fred Cruz wrote his legal argument on toilet paper during one of his solitary confinement periods. He cited the First Amendment, calling for religious freedom, as the basis for his right to practice Buddhism and to share his beliefs with his fellow inmates. Cruz was assisted by a Columbia University law school graduate and legal aid attorney, Frances Jalet, who was horrified by conditions in TDC and, as a result, joined with civil rights attorney William Bennett Turner to work on Cruz's case. While an initial court denied Cruz' arguments, when *Cruz v. Beto* was heard by the US Supreme Court, judges ruled in his favor and this landmark case led to the granting of religious freedom to prisoners in other states.[6]

During her work with her inmate client, Frances Jalet fell in love with Fred Cruz, twenty-nine years younger than herself. Jalet successfully appealed Cruz's lengthy prison sentence and, when he was paroled in 1972, the couple were married in Mexico. In the free world, Cruz founded the Texas Jail and Prison Coalition to help minorities behind bars. Failing to find work, he relapsed back to heroin use and his addiction led to the couple's divorce five years later.[7]

It was later revealed that Director Beto went to great lengths to try to stop Frances Jalet-Cruz's consultations with Fred Cruz and David Ruiz. Beto had her fired from three of her legal aid jobs, but Jalet-Cruz took the fourth position in Houston and kept coming through the TDC gates in pursuit of justice.[8]

When Charles Sullivan of CURE introduced me to Lawrence Pope, he had just been released from El Reno federal prison in Oklahoma after being remanded there by the Fifth Circuit Court in order to protect him from retaliation by the TDC administration for his role as a writ-writer. At the time, Pope was 64 years, with an intense visage and pure white hair covering his large head. A generous man, he was eager to help me with my dissertation research.

During our first interview, Charlie Sullivan excused himself to make a phone call, and said, "Tell Helen about the Eight Hoe Squad. I'll be in the next room if you need me."

Lawrence nodded, and said, "Charlie is referring to the field line number for eight of us litigants."

Wheezing from his asthma, Lawrence described retaliation from Director Beto who ordered the eight litigants moved to the unit for mentally disturbed prisoners, thinking that they would be prevented from influencing other potential writ-writers and, more importantly, would give up their legal pursuits. In this unit, with no access to recreational activities or prison programs, the eight men worked six days a week, shoveling manure, or stacking telephone poles and railroad ties. Lawrence Pope said that the worst retaliation was being forced to take psychoactive drugs, such as Thorazine and Librium; he added that the men were often able to slip the pills out of their mouths.

After pouring himself a cup of coffee, Lawrence continued his story. The pain in his eyes was visible as he recalled those days when, in a cynical ploy, these multi-racial writ-writers were double-bunked together, breaking the Texas prison practice of racially segregating inmates. While authorities hoped that the men would turn on each other, Lawrence bragged that they didn't; when one of them was punished, the men insisted that the guards punish all of them.

Wardens made other attempts to break the spirits of jailhouse lawyers and end litigation against TDC. One administrator offered a Mexican-American inmate the option of having forced sex with one of the white writ-writers, if this man would give up his own support of legal action against TDC. The man refused. Another inmate, Emiliano Figueroa, stated in federal court that he had previously lied that David Ruiz tried to rape him when the two men were incarcerated at the Harris County Jail in Houston. Bravely, Figueroa testified that officials promised him freedom for his lies and he added that a prison warden threatened to have him killed if he reneged on his story.[9]

Lawrence described the writ-writers' next challenge when, in the midst of their litigation, three TDC prisoners filed suit against Frances Jalet-Cruz for disturbing the prison environment. Jalet-Cruz could have lost her law license over this accusation, but she caught a lucky break. One of the men suing her refused to testify in court and a second inmate took the stand and declared that he had been persuaded by TDC authorities to sue Jalet-Cruz. The court ruled in Jalet-Cruz' favor, dismissing the charges and ordering TDC to give her a settlement of $25,000 and to pay all her legal defense fees. Director George Beto retired soon after.

During our interview, Lawrence Pope stated that David Ruiz was similar to Fred Cruz, growing up in a Texas barrio as one of the thirteen children of Mexican-American itinerant farmworkers. Nearly illiterate, Ruiz lived with poverty and police mistreatment. At the age of 12, he was placed in a juvenile detention unit for shoplifting and fighting, but, upon release, his unruly behavior continued. David Ruiz worked long hot hours in the cotton fields, claiming that white country boy guards in the juvenile detention facilities called him a "meskin" and a "wetback," and treated him as a slave.[10]

When Ruiz was 17, he was charged with car theft and incarcerated in an adult Texas prison farm in which the brutality was even worse. Paroled, Ruiz committed armed robbery. Back in prison, he was involved in fights and cut his Achilles tendon to avoid the field labor. However, when placed in solitary, Ruiz started writing poetry and painting Chicano images. Transferred to a new unit, Ruiz met Fred Cruz who helped him understand the connection between prison brutality and the outside world's opposition to minority demands for their civil rights. Due to Cruz's influence, Ruiz turned his anger to legal matters.

Lawrence Pope said, "David and I were different, but we both hated the prisoners who were building tenders; David was hotheaded and would get into fights with them."

Lawrence referred to this special group of inmates as members of a state-sanctioned gang, of all three races, who employed violence, along with a vicious sex trade. He added that building tenders, who could receive early release through "good time," developed an atmosphere that filled the farm units with so much tension that no prisoner felt safe.[11]

During a second interview, Lawrence told me that he was frustrated because the Sullivans' efforts at CURE to end the building tender system were thwarted. He explained that the Sullivans had lobbied for Texas Senate Bill 338, stating that no prisoner could have power over another inmate. While this legislation was passed in 1973, TDC officials began calling the building tenders "support service inmates" who saved the cost of additional guard salaries. At that time, the overall guard ratio to prisoners across America was 1:5, while in Texas it was 1:12, making a single Texas guard responsible for as many as four cellblocks, each of them containing three tiers.[12]

Lawrence made it clear that he viewed the Texas prison system as a vast waste of taxpayers' money, as well as a moral disaster. He found it ironic that men could get drugs in prison and he decried the lack of rehabilitation for the large number of addicted inmates. Preparing their lawsuit, Ruiz and the other seven litigants focused on the historic inhumane conditions in TDC, including the overcrowding that made predatory behavior easier and supervision of inmates more difficult. These plaintiffs brought the unconstitutional conditions to light and they were early voices warning about the rise of mass incarceration. Along with others who have acted in nonviolent social movements, these men said: "Basta!" "Enough!"

Then, the question facing these writ-writers became: "How will the Fifth Circuit Court rule in *Ruiz v. Estelle*?"

Notes

1. Interview with Charles Sullivan of CURE, March 1981
2. Molanphy, Helen Clarke, *Idea of Punishment: Texas Prison System as a Case Study*
3. Ibid.
4. Interview with Charles Sullivan of CURE, March 1981
5. Black Muslims did not have religious freedom at TDC. To practice Islam, Muslims had to transfer to the tightly run Ellis unit and their services had to be conducted by a Muslim inmate, not a minister from the free community. The Ellis Unit made no provision for their pork-free diet.
6. Molanphy, Helen Clarke, *Idea of Punishment: Texas Prison System as a Case Study*
7. Interview with Charles Sullivan of CURE, March 1981
8. Interview with Lawrence Pope, March 1981
9. Molanphy, Helen Clarke, *Idea of Punishment: Texas Prison System as a Case Study*
10. Interview with Lawrence Pope, March 1981
11. Lawrence Pope suggested I watch a film called *Brubaker*, starring Robert Redford. The film gives a visual picture of building tenders by telling the story of real-life Tom Murton, a reforming warden in 1950s Arkansas who investigated this kind of system in his state.
12. Interview with Lawrence Pope, March 1981

3
Ruiz v. Estelle

In 1972, the same year that Fred Cruz was paroled, Texas Department of Corrections (TDC) inmate David Ruiz submitted a 12-page petition addressed to the Fifth Circuit Court. Director Jim Estelle, the successor to Dr. George Beto, was adamant that this petition never leave the prison grounds, but Ruiz's attorney, Francis Jalet-Cruz, was a good strategist and she made sure that the documents reached the court. In April of 1974, Judge William Wayne Justice, who reporter Molly Ivins said brought the constitution to Texas, accepted the Ruiz lawsuit.[1]

Judge Justice consolidated six additional Texas prisoner petitions with *Ruiz v. Estelle* in order to develop a class action lawsuit against TDC that several groups, including the American Civil Liberties Union, backed. In 1978, the judge ordered the US Justice Department to intervene in *Ruiz v. Estelle* as an amicus curiae on the side of the prisoners whose lawsuit described violations in housing and living conditions; security and supervision; classification; health care; discipline; protection from violence; correspondence and visitation; educational and vocational work; staff behavior; and access to the courts.[2]

For the next two years, the Federal Bureau of Investigation (FBI) interviewed hundreds of staff members and inmates and the US Justice Department compiled a list of 4,000 incidents of alleged mistreatment. The court hired experts in the fields of medical treatment, security, and industrial safety to inspect the TDC units and this led to over a thousand exhibits being placed in evidence before Judge Justice. When the trial opened in Houston, Lawrence Pope was among the first to take the witness stand.[3]

After hearing from 349 witnesses, one hundred of them TDC inmates, Judge Justice began writing his recommendations for reform of the prison system, an institution he described as "pernicious" and built on "pain and degradation." In December of 1980, the judge ruled in favor of the plaintiffs and declared that TDC's practices were unconstitutional based on the Eighth Amendment's prohibition of cruel and unusual punishment and the Fourteenth Amendment's protection of due process and equal protection under the law. The judge's subsequent order, encompassing a broad area, gave TDC three years in which to meet the specific minimum standards the court set.

In this way, Texas joined prison systems in Alabama, Arkansas, Florida, Louisiana, Mississippi, and Rhode Island, all cited for violations of the Eighth and Fourteenth Amendments and then placed under court supervision. Other calls for reform in Texas dated back to the 1920s, but Judge Justice's orders were the most comprehensive. In his summary, he declared that TDC had

DOI: 10.4324/9781003280279-4

retained the worst inhumane elements described in the 1924 Texas Joint Committee on Prison Reform Report.[4]

Judge Justice's opinion was sweeping because the issues facing TDC had been previously covered by federal and state courts. Under federalism, decisions on criminal justice issues in one state are not judicially binding in other states, but Judge Justice wrote a comprehensive condemnation of the Texas prison system in hopes that his decision would survive any appeal and that the transparency shown in the courtroom would influence other states.

Overcrowding was the main complaint of TDC prisoners; Jose Gonzalez, who spent two years at the Coffield Unit, was one of several inmates testifying about the hardships that overcrowding caused. When we met in Charles Sullivan's office, Jose said that TDC Director Jim Estelle stated in court that triple-celling was unconstitutional on the grounds of the Eighth Amendment; with thousands of inmates sleeping on the floor, Estelle blamed the citizens of Texas for not providing enough money to build more prisons.

Jose scoffed, and said, "I was housed in a five feet by ten feet cell with two other prisoners. When the federal observers visited, the third mattress was hidden. Even with two men, the area available was about the size of a bedroom door."

At that time, lengthy sentencing policies, resulting from the War on Drugs and the War on Crime, had helped produce overcrowding in most US prisons and all but eliminated any programs addressing rehabilitation, with inmates spending idle days in their cells. Though older Texas prisoners had worked six days a week on the farm, Jose Gonzalez worked three days in the cotton fields due to the growth in the number of available inmate workers. Jose leaned back in his chair, and said, "Except for one morning of schooling and an hour of gym that same day, I spent the rest of the week in my cell."[5]

An appeals court agreed with Judge Justice that three to a cell was inhumane. However, this court did not back his recommendation for single-celling and, instead, held that two persons to a cell met constitutional standards. In ruling this way, they ignored testimony from penologists who asserted that double-celling made predatory activities easier and supervision more difficult in an arena where brutality, extortion, and rape were routine.[6]

In its 1973 report, the American Correctional Association (ACA) had also recommended single-cell usage, arguing that this arrangement provided maximum security, along with flexibility in classification of prisoners. The Association maintained that single celling helped to prevent rapes and fighting while providing protection to guards by letting them deal with one inmate at a time. The authors of the report harked back to the early Eastern State penitentiary in Pennsylvania and the one in Auburn, New York, both of which contained single cells fitted with quality sanitary equipment, only seen today in some European prisons.[7]

To solve overcrowding in TDC and reduce brutality, Judge Justice also recommended building smaller prison facilities, holding no more than 500 prisoners and located close to major cities. These urban prisoners, the majority at TDC, would be allowed more frequent visitations with family members, a reform supported by criminologists who asserted that access to family helps the incarcerated mend their ways. While Republican Governor William Clements supported Judge Justice's idea of moving facilities to populated areas, he limited the court's proposal to housing only nonviolent offenders in these metropolitan units. Governor Clements felt that these inmates could work during the day, return to minimum security at night, and repay their victims through their employment. If these metropolitan centers had actually been built, it would have marked a radical departure from the system of housing large numbers of inmates at the TDC rural farms.

Judge Justice suggested increased use of work release, widely used in Scandinavian countries, in order to lessen the number of prisoners in crowded day rooms and to allow certain cooperative prisoners time out of their cells. Next, the judge recommended expanding the "good time" practices and making it possible for more inmates to seek parole. Lawrence Pope told me that Director Jim Estelle backed the judge's recommendation to increase the availability of parole, testifying that one third or more of TDC's inmates could be released immediately with no harm to the public. Lawrence added that Estelle's predecessor, Dr. George Beto, had agreed, but proposals for increased parole opportunities met with opposition from citizen groups.

Judge Justice also addressed the absence of intelligent classification at TDC, resulting in nonviolent offenders being mixed with long-term inmates; he pointed out that this system contributed to inadequate security and did not help those inmates who he believed redeemable.[8]

The judge went on to excoriate TDC officials for not ending the inmate building tender supervision system as Texas Senate Bill 338, passed in 1973, had mandated. While prison officials pointed to the building tender system as a means of providing work for inmates with long sentences, the plaintiffs in *Ruiz v. Estelle* contended that the building tenders were used as an unruly police force, attacking inmates for minor offenses. Building tenders, who ran the drug activities and acted as pimps for widespread homosexual arrangements, were permitted to carry weapons and treat other inmates in a cruel fashion.[9]

Lawrence Pope testified that he had been raped by a building tender while he was in solitary confinement, reinforcing TDC's reputation as an institution in which sexual violence was common. Other testimony in the *Ruiz* case indicated that most building tenders selected "punks" who cleaned their cells, did their laundry, and cooked for them on hot plates. Often chosen because of their strong-arm tactics, the building tenders received special privileges from wardens for keeping order; TDC was purchasing cooperation by having these unruly inmates work for the authorities, not against them.

The court addressed the issue of the low ratio of guards to prisoners, leading to lack of security and causing additional stress for officers. The abusive conduct of the guards towards inmates appeared even more relevant as guard brutality was a frequent topic throughout the legal proceedings. A trustee-status inmate at the Ellis Unit said, "I've observed beatings at the 'bottoms' in Ellis where inmates suffered injuries so bad they had to be hospitalized. Even Director Beto called Ellis the end of the line."[10]

Judge Justice's memorandum decried the frequency of inmates' statements about guard violence. The testimony of attorney Frances Jalet-Cruz provided documentation of the abuse: prisoners were made to stand on rails, hung from bars in straitjackets, or forced to shell peanuts for several days; beatings with baseball bats, brass knuckles, and blackjacks were common.[11]

While maintaining discipline is a high priority in all prison systems, testimony taken during the *Ruiz v. Estelle* case revealed that TDC officials and inmates differed in their views on the conduct of disciplinary procedures. The officials felt that their approach was reasonable for keeping order among the numerous inmates who had committed violent crimes, while inmates testified that TDC's disciplinary procedures were oppressive. They maintained that officers possessed a great deal of discretion and that inmates, charged with violations of prison rules, were not given notice of the specific complaints, nor allowed to bring witnesses to defend themselves.

Judge Justice agreed with the plaintiffs, recognizing that many inmates had no understanding of the complicated prison rules because they read at the fifth-grade level, or were not English language speakers. The court also pointed out that many offenses did not appear in the Rulebook and that ignorance of the rules did not matter in these disciplinary cases. Judge Justice urged TDC to be in compliance with a Nebraska court case, *Wolff v. McDonnell* (1974), that critiqued similar arbitrary practices and declared that charges had to be proven before an inmate could be punished.[12]

Judge Justice criticized TDC for using solitary confinement to obstruct writ-writers. He based his admonitions on testimony from inmates who complained that they were strip-searched upon entering and leaving the writ room and that they were often moved from their cells to solitary, their legal papers put in disarray. Clients' attorneys had to obtain a court order to see files; when the inmates did see their lawyers, a guard was always present, negating privacy and confidentiality. Writ-writers, successful in taking their action to court, were harassed by guards or by other inmates encouraged by the administrators, the very reason that Judge Justice had mandated that Lawrence Pope be sent to an Oklahoma prison for protection.[13]

After Judge Justice reviewed the circumstances of solitary confinement at TDC, he expressed disgust that inmates were subjected to unsanitary conditions, lack of adequate food, poor ventilation, and harsh temperatures in winter and summer. The judge referred to criticism by the 1974 Joint Committee on Prison Reform about Texas' use of solitary confinement that specified the following:

> The inmates in segregation experience additional deprivations peculiar to that status. They are given few of the basic necessities ... Filth is allowed to accumulate. Although the solitary cells can get too hot in the summer, too cold in the winters, some inmates are placed in solitary even without any clothing. Meals in solitary usually consist of two bland vegetables although even these are sometimes stolen by building tenders.[14]

Judge Justice cited the harsh solitary confinement conditions for causing numerous self-cuttings, as well as mental breakdowns that accounted for about half of prison suicides. The court expressed concern that solitaries often flooded their cells or threw feces at guards and that those who had spent recurrent times in solitary showed physical damage for life.

The next issue that Judge Justice addressed was the inadequate medical care at TDC. Testimony to the court revealed that much of what passed for care was carried out by trustee prisoners who had little or no medical training; called medical assistants, they distributed medicine, administered tests, and processed laboratory results without any supervision. No regular dental care was provided and even dental emergencies were treated by amateurs.[15]

Judge Justice noted that adequate medical treatment at TDC was sacrificed due to, what he called, an exaggerated concern about security; he cited the great amount of red tape attached to processing sick calls, especially for those in solitary. In addition, the judge pointed out that inmate health problems were not considered when assignments for work duties were made; security, economy, and harshness were the hallmarks for health care in TDC.[16]

This same approach is evident today in American prisons coping with COVID-19. For example, during the pandemic, inmates had to work in the fields or other workplaces without any social distancing; meanwhile, prisoner advocates maintained that only essential work should be required until the coronavirus pandemic was under control. In addition, in many prison systems, inmates did not have hand soap or masks and those suffering from COVID-19 did not receive adequate care.

In a victory for the plaintiffs in *Ruiz v. Estelle*, the Fifth Circuit Court required TDC to establish a 213-bed hospital for inmates, staffed by the University of Texas at Galveston medical school. At the time, several state prison systems were employing a similar practice, but others had begun turning the medical needs of prisoners over to private contractors, inadvertently giving birth to the corporatization of corrections in which many private firms presently dominate the provision of prison medical care.

In a later meeting with Lawrence Pope in Austin, where he was lobbying state officials and testifying before legislative committees, he appeared discouraged by TDC officials' opposition to many of Judge Justice's recommendations on issues, such as overcrowding. Lawrence's round, lined face grew red as he mourned the fact that Republican Governor Bill Clements wanted the Fifth Circuit Court's prison administrator, Vincent Nathan, removed because the governor felt that prison authorities, not outsiders, were the only ones designated to run their institutions.

Pope called out, "Keep everything secret!"

With a frown on his lined brow, Pope remarked that Democrat Attorney-General Mark White had accused Judge Justice of encouraging prisoners to disobey the rules that he said resulted in an uprising at one of the farm units. Lawrence pointed out that Judge Justice was the perfect target for politicians looking to blame someone for the increased taxes needed to build more prisons. He added that no one had indicated that the rioting in the farm unit might be due to TDC authorities' failure to comply with the court's orders.

Lawrence said, "The truth is TDC is determined to set their own policies without outside input, even though a federal court has decided that the Constitution does not stop at the prison's walls."

While Lawrence Pope expressed his concern that Texas could have a rebellion on the scale of the 1980 New Mexico penitentiary riot in Santa Fe, he was pleased that Judge Justice's conclusions in *Ruiz v. Estelle* had shattered the myth that Texas had a modern rehabilitative penal system. He pointed out that, during the *Ruiz v. Estelle* legal proceedings, William Nagel, an expert witness for the plaintiffs, and the author of *New Red Barn: A Critical Look at the American Prison System*, decried the TDC system as antiquated and in the hands of authorities who acted in a high-handed fashion.[17]

Notes

1. Molanphy, Helen Clarke, *Idea of Punishment: Texas Prison System as a Case Study*
2. Ibid.
3. At the same time that the court proceedings began, African-American and Latino prisoners collaborated in a nonviolent sit-down aimed at supporting their fellow inmates expected to testify before Judge Justice.
4. Molanphy, Helen Clarke, *Idea of Punishment: Texas Prison System as a Case Study*
5. Interview with Jose Gonzalez, April 1981. Jose added that he was treated with dignity in the classroom by teachers who were concerned with helping the men, while the guards were only concerned with rules and regulations.
6. Molanphy, Helen Clarke, *Idea of Punishment: Texas Prison System as a Case Study*
7. Ibid.
8. Ibid.
9. Ibid.
10. Ibid.
11. Ibid.
12. Ibid.
13. Ibid.
14. Ibid.
15. Ibid.
16. Ibid.
17. Interview with Lawrence Pope, October 1981

4
Texas Prison Administrators

Texas Department of Corrections (TDC), renamed the Texas Department of Criminal Justice (TDCJ) in the 1990s, maintained its Huntsville headquarters, called the Walls, in which concrete turrets allow armed guards to watch for trouble. Granite buildings with barred windows are surrounded by a high electric barbed-wire fence. In 1981, I approached the Walls gate and informed the guard that I was expected for an interview with Dr. George Beto, the former director who was now a professor at Sam Houston State College, located near the prison headquarters.

The theory of punishment, be it retribution, deterrence, or rehabilitation, that is popular with prison administrators has a large influence on the direction that correctional facilities adopt. Yet, prison administrators are also subject to external factors, such as democratization, increased communication, mass education, and today's high use of social media, all of which can bring change. It appears that, approximately every 30 years, there are calls for rehabilitation to replace retribution and vice-versa.

During the Lee Simmons years, the Texas prison farms were viewed as simply a way station for criminals, whose offenses meant they should suffer; the O. B. Ellis administration viewed its mission as providing cleanliness and control. Director George Beto, influenced by the 1960s and 1970s movement demanding justice and opportunity for the marginalized, proposed rehabilitative efforts. Both George Beto and his successor, Jim Estelle, were directors at a time when the American Correctional Association was restating the idea that rehabilitation should replace retribution. Prisons were renamed "correctional training centers," and prisoners "residents." Guards became known as "correctional officers" and were encouraged to be friendly with the inmates, while expensive psychological and educational programs were put in place in many state prisons.

Rehabilitation has various meanings, depending on who is using it. The term can mean "hard work and discipline" to prison officials, such as O. B. Ellis, or it can mean "behavior modification" to others. Generally, rehabilitation implies that mere warehousing of prisoners should be avoided. In order for this model to take hold, prison administrators have to believe in the possibility of change in human behavior and they must gain support from members of society. In addition, a shift in the balance of power between prison administrators and legislators, the latter often bound to public opinion, needs to take place if rehabilitation is to have a chance of succeeding.

Several obstacles confront those who advocate rehabilitation. For example, prison administrators often prefer what is termed "custodial convenience" because new programs require work that understaffed, poorly financed institutions find hard to provide. Legislative agencies often consider prison reforms, but do not pass meaningful legislation, or allocate the necessary funds. In addition, the underlying fundamentalist notion that sin has been committed and that atonement has to occur is often at play. This retributive idea of punishment is mixed with the deterrent notion of punishment, for it assumes that, if the punishment in prison is harsh enough, the sinner will repent. The high rates of recidivism in America imply that years of depending on retribution and deterrence have backfired.

Reflecting on all of this on that fall day in 1981, I followed the guard into the Walls where Professor George Beto still had an office.

Dr. Beto had served as an ordained Lutheran minister and as president of Austin's Concordia Lutheran College until 1961 when he replaced director O. B. Ellis. While Dr. Beto did not have any formal experience in prisons, he had been a long-time member of parole boards. Given the past history of TDC administration under men, such as Warden Lee Simmons, some guards must have worried that a clergyman/educator would be too soft on the inmates. However, in his 10 years as director, Dr. Beto was hailed by the prison board for maintaining O. B. Ellis's control model and he was praised by politicians because he made improvements, while managing the prison system on a low budget.

Before our interview, I found a quote by Dr. Beto at the state library in Huntsville that revealed his approach to his occupation.

> We are required by law simply to feed you, house you and clothe you. While you are with us, however, we shall endeavor to furnish you experiences which will reduce the likelihood of your returning to prison. We are opposed to brutality aside from its intrinsic evil; we are persuaded that violence simply begets violence. On the other hand, we do not propose to hand the institution over to inmates.[1]

After the guard placed my purse in a safe for security purposes, he led me down a hallway to Dr. Beto's office. As I entered, the former director, an impressive figure at six feet four inches, stood and motioned me to sit down. Beto's brown Stetson hat sat on his desk and his keen eyes searched mine as he listened to a short description of my dissertation project. When I finished, George Beto began praising the prison system for its orderliness, cleanliness, and economic sustainability. He appeared proud that, despite his economy, prisoners could obtain GED's in the Windham School district that he had founded. Besides providing this schooling to decrease the vast amount of illiteracy among the inmates, Dr. Beto pointed to his establishment of the Institute of Contemporary Corrections at Sam Houston State College that catered to academic researchers.[2]

To George Beto, the school dropout rate of 90% among the inmates was appalling because it indicated that the persons in his charge came from permissive backgrounds and needed an injection of discipline that prison could provide. The former director maintained that the boredom and routine of prison life were relieved by both study and work. Regarding the latter, Beto said that the Texas system possessed agricultural technology, including the largest livestock program in any penal institution, and that the institution offered a number of industrial jobs, supplying goods to qualified tax-supported agencies. Under his leadership, the institution had become a self-sustaining system that paid for the initial investment and far surpassed programs in other states. During George Beto's ten-year tenure, the amount of money earned from prison-made goods rose from $598,000 to $6,000,000, saving taxpayers a great deal of money.

Records at the Sam Houston State library revealed that Beto handled his first prison "buck" by sending four wardens out on horseback, armed with wet rope and rubber hose and under orders to put the hoe squad back to work. Six years into his tenure, 160 inmates at the Ellis Unit, rioting over too much work and not enough food, fought with prison guards for several hours. They were quelled by tear gas, water hoses, and baton-wielding guards who placed them in solitary confinement. This situation occurred despite Dr. Beto's stated intent to avoid prison strikes through proper communication between the inmates and the administration.

When I broached the subject of "bucks," with Dr. Beto, he told me he was not sure he would handle these situations the same way, but he added that, without his action, there would have been strikes throughout the system. Beto defended the work ethic and lock-step discipline and he said that one of his chief functions was to demonstrate authority and keep order. In this, he was not unlike most prison directors who seek a control-oriented approach to managing their institutions, with treatment as the secondary purpose of incarceration. On a daily basis, prison directors are faced with gang activity; unruly inmates; assaults and killings of guards; poor equipment; prison riots; mentally unstable inmates; funding gaps; legal suits, the use of new technology; and difficulty in retaining staff.

After a pause in the interview, Dr. Beto stated that prisons were a poor way to handle human beings and he added that sentences were too long. He pointed out that sex deprivation was the most stringent aspect of prison punishment and the least discussed. While 50% of the population in the Texas prisons was under 25 years, Dr. Beto said that he was opposed to connubial visits, offered by the state of Mississippi, because this privilege would appear unfair to those who were not married.

The former director acknowledged that many of the Texas prisoners came from dysfunctional families and had witnessed much crime in their communities. Dr. Beto emphasized that his idea of rehabilitation depended on physical, spiritual, and educational experiences, not the use of psychological methods, utilized in California prisons at that time. In court testimony, one part-time psychologist testified that the state prison system's mental health services were inadequate and merely crisis-oriented with heavy dependence on psychiatric drugs.[3]

Just before Dr. Beto resigned as director in 1972, he made news headlines with his statement that prisons would soon be obsolete. However, his work, from 1962 to 1972, establishing a self-sustaining prison system, would be difficult to dismantle. During Beto's term of office, the Texas prison system was tagged as so superior that various states began to copy it; even police reporter Harry McCormick praised Beto's leadership. Yet, Dr. Beto had been sued by inmates and by one defense attorney and, if he had not resigned, David Ruiz would have entitled his lawsuit, "Ruiz v. Beto."

At first, Dr. Beto turned silent when I brought up the *Ruiz v. Estelle* case. Looking at me with strained eyes, he said that he should not comment due to the ongoing litigation. Then, after a pause, he added that he feared Judge Justice's unfair evaluation of the state correctional system would chip away at discipline and put the prisoners in charge. George Beto ended our interview by saying that prison administrators lived in a tension between being accused of coddling prisoners or being charged with brutality.

On my next trip to Huntsville headquarters, I sat in a similar office, facing Director Jim Estelle, Dr. Beto's successor. Estelle, as the son of a California prison guard, had seen the inside of prisons throughout his youth. Following in his father's footsteps, Estelle became a captain in the California system and a warden at a Wyoming state prison.[4]

In 1972, Estelle earned the position of Texas prison director after criticizing the laxity in the California correctional system. At that time, he announced that his personal philosophy and the philosophy of the Texas community were similar: prisons should be self-sustaining, secure, and clean. Estelle was named 10,000 times by writ-writing inmates, seeking either a release from prison or an improvement in their conditions of confinement. Most suits were trivial and easily dismissed, but some led to the development of a substantial body of law.[5]

A tall, thin man with sandy-colored hair, Jim Estelle was tight-lipped and appeared nervous during our interview. He expressed concern about the critical nature of my dissertation, even though I was a lowly graduate student, not a well-known journalist about to explode a story on prison conditions. During our interview, Estelle made the point that strict discipline and tight security provided efficiency and had resulted in very few escapes or homicides over the past 10 years, a contrast to the California prison system. Referring to Judge Justice, he said that his negative comments about some of the prison wardens had scarred one of the finest staff in the world. Following our interview, Jim Estelle did not permit me access to populated parts of the prison. Instead, a correctional officer showed me some empty cells used to isolate, what he called, "troublemakers."[6]

In some states in which prison suits were heard in court, the administrators accepted the burden of the evidence and acknowledged the charges. For example, in Alabama, the state correctional officials, frustrated by their low budgets, unofficially welcomed a court decision against their prison system. Knowing how Texas operated, Lawrence Pope said he was not surprised when Director Estelle denied all of the allegations brought by the plaintiffs. Lawrence added that Estelle, soon to retire by urging of the prison board, had declared that Judge Justice had gone too far in his recommendations, making the citizens of Texas pay for the mayhem.

Threatened by court fines, in April of 1982, Texas prison officials announced that they would abide by the Fifth Circuit Court's order to eliminate building tenders, but they did not indicate any need for a greater increase in manpower. This failure to provide adequate staffing allowed gang leaders to recruit more members, filling the vacuum caused by the termination of the building tender system. Soon groups, such as the Texas Syndicate, the Aryan Brotherhood, the Mexican Mafia, and the Mandingo Warriors were at war with each other. Even though the prison system was caught in an eruption of violence, authorities made no move to increase the number of guards.[7]

While Jim Estelle acknowledged the overcrowded conditions, he and other Texas authorities fought back against Judge Justice's plan to solve the problem by building smaller prisons in more populated areas. Maintaining that the Texas system's unique agricultural emphasis did not fit into the court's recommendations, officials proposed alleviating overcrowding by building several new farm units. Officials also maintained that building more facilities was the best response to fixing other problems cited in *Ruiz v. Estelle*. The latter has been the most frequent American correctional response, with inmate units filling up as fast as they are built.

Had Lawrence Pope lived beyond 1989, he would have been appalled by the size of the Texas prison complex. Between 1972, when *Ruiz* was written, and 1999 when Judge Justice gave his last rendering, the inmate population increased by 706%, and 75 more prison units were erected in Texas.[8]

Texas was not alone in the push towards mass incarceration. Colorado gained four times as many inmates; Missouri, Ohio, and Illinois tripled their prison population; and Florida, Mississippi, and Georgia doubled it. North, in the state of New York, the results of the harsh Rockefeller drug laws continued to be felt, so that by 1985 that state's inmate population was triple what it was at the time of the Attica uprising in 1971. Similarly, in California, between 1983 and 1991, the prison population soared from 35,000 inmates to 100,000. In 1981, at the start of the Reagan administration, there were 370,000 federal inmates; in 1989, after President Reagan's second term, the number of federal prisoners had grown to 713,000.

New Mexico, a Texas neighbor, also suffered from overcrowding and brutality and the state's prison administrators were just as reluctant as their counterparts in Texas to cooperate with court-ordered reforms. At the New Mexico maximum-security penitentiary in Santa Fe, authorities had devised a snitching system after a prison work strike. In this surveillance program, inmates who came forward with information about other prisoners' activities were rewarded with improved classification, better housing, earlier parole, and even drugs and cash. To make matters worse, if prisoners refused to be snitches, wardens put them in "snitch jackets," endangering their lives.

Hating this system, Dwight Duran, a repeat felon, decided to become a jailhouse lawyer when his prison friend was beaten by guards and left naked to die after a heroin overdose. A federal court called for vast reforms, including ending the snitching practice. Despite the appointment of court monitor Vincent Nathan, the same person in charge of the implementation of the Texas reforms, penitentiary authorities continued to tolerate the corruption and brutality that eventually resulted in the massive Santa Fe penitentiary riot of 1980. In 1998, a federal judge ended the court's oversight of the penitentiary, but the suit lingered on, similar to events in Texas.[9]

Democrat Governor of New Mexico, Michelle Lujan Grisham, has recently agreed to settle the decades-old *Duran* suit. Overcrowding was addressed with the state confirming that only one inmate would inhabit the small cells at the penitentiary and community rooms would not be employed as dormitories. In addition, authorities agreed to move inmates from overcrowded facilities to better quarters, ensuring that the total prison population would not exceed 120% of capacity. This agreement took almost 40 years to occur; Texas settled *Ruiz v. Estelle* in approximately thirty years after David Ruiz first sent his petition to the Fifth Circuit Court.[10]

Following these major inmate lawsuits, formal attempts at rehabilitation and improved living conditions were ended by prison administrators for a variety of reasons. With the advent of the Reagan administration, the wealthy received large tax cuts and government budgets, including state grants, was reduced for social services. Prison administrators felt forced into a more punitive model with reduced quality of food and other daily needs, while certain privileges, such as family visits or access to the outside world, were placed on hold.

Another reason for the withdrawal from the rehabilitative model was the fact that no significant decline in recidivism rates occurred. These high rates infuriated critics on the right, while those on the left opposed the practice of indeterminate sentencing that they felt gave too much authority to prison administrators. This distaste for rehabilitation led to further warehousing of inmates; staff were locked in control rooms, no longer walking outside in the yard with inmates; prison security depended on concrete and steel.

Director Jim Estelle, burnt out by his experience of rehabilitation programs in California, strengthened the Texas control model. He left his mark with the Estelle unit, erected as a bunker below ground in which solitary cells were lined up next to each other. The Estelle unit was not alone, as Super-Maxes grew in number during this renewed punitive period. Today, facilities, such as Greene State Correctional Institution in southeastern Pennsylvania, are so hidden that locals don't even know they are there.

As a nation enamored of war and technology, these cultural aspects inform the American prison system. At annual sales conventions, correctional administrators can purchase various technological tools: biometric readings that indicate who can make it in the free world; armored clothing for guards; chips that are injected by a syringe into prisoners or parolees for monitoring purposes; robots that roll around on tank treads to areas difficult for guards to see; and new, more deadly stun guns, lightweight batons, and acoustic grenades that can deafen an inmate. As the warehousing becomes more fortress-like and secretive, transparency, a vital ingredient for humane treatment, disappears.

Notes

1. Molanphy, Helen Clarke, *Idea of Punishment: Texas Prison System as a Case Study*
2. Interview with Dr. George Beto, October 1981
3. Molanphy, Helen Clarke, *Idea of Punishment: Texas Prison System as a Case Study*
4. Interview with Director Jim Estelle, January 1982
5. Molanphy, Helen Clarke, *Idea of Punishment: Texas Prison System as a Case Study*
6. Interview with Lawrence Pope, February 1982
7. Ibid.
8. Ibid.
9. During New Mexico State Penitentiary Director Joe Brown's lecture in my classroom at the Santa Fe community college, he admitted that conditions did not improve after the riot. Reform attempts were limited and life in New Mexico prisons continued to be brutal. This occurred despite the appointment of court overseer Vincent Nathan, the same person who had been Judge William Wayne Justice's appointee for the implementation of the Texas reforms emerging from *Ruiz v. Estelle*.
10. KSFR radio station in Santa Fe, New Mexico, May 2021

5
Texas Today

Following Jim Estelle's forced retirement, his successor, Raymond Procunier, a former California administrator who had been sued by that state's prisoners for restricting legal activities, tried to restore order and squash gang violence in Texas. Procunier introduced metal detectors and high-tech listening devices, along with Special Operations teams, to counteract the violence at Texas Department of Corrections (TDC). Because of criticism from staff, government officials, and inmates, Procunier resigned after one year on the job; at that time, he announced that directing the Texas prison system was his hardest job in his 35-year career.[1]

Procunier's successor, Colonel Lane McCotter, used a combination of Director OB Ellis's control model and Director George Beto's habit of walking around the prison units unannounced. Under a court order to treat the inmates humanely, meaning no more beatings, McCotter increased solitary confinement that he called, "administrative segregation," despite the federal district court's criticism of this practice. This enhanced solitary policy troubled Lawrence Pope who was especially upset by the creation of "super segregation" cell blocks at the Eastham unit and in several of the new units that Texas built. The latter was modeled after the federal high-security total isolation prison at Marion, Illinois, the replacement for Alcatraz in San Francisco. The TDCJ, known for its self-sufficient forced-labor model, shifted to confinement and separation. Frequent lockdowns, due to prisoner fights, also became a regular part of the system's regiment.

Attorney Frances Jalet-Cruz had insured that *Ruiz v. Estelle* found its way to Judge Justice's court in the 1970s. Now in the 1990s, another dedicated attorney, Donna Brorby, worked to keep the case alive, despite changes in federal law during the Clinton administration that severely limited prisoner lawsuits, as well as judicial oversight of penal institutions. This federal legislation, initiated on the grounds that too many trivial lawsuits were emerging from America's prisons, substantially reduced the number of all prisoner lawsuits.

Hopeful that the federal government, acting on these new limitations, would end *Ruiz v. Estelle,* TDCJ authorities came back to court and requested release from the Fifth Circuit Court's judicial supervision. Responding to this TDCJ motion, 79-year-old Judge William Wayne Justice decided to take testimony from both administrators and plaintiffs before considering whether to end court supervision.

In his 274-page ruling of March 1999, the judge acknowledged that the Texas prisons were operating in a professional fashion, but he wrote that systemic constitutional violations continued, including the lack of physical safety due to overcrowding, poor supervision, and the power of prison gangs. Overcrowding negatively affected educational programs, prison resources, staff, inmate to guard ratios, and health services. Within this milieu, correctional officers engaged in violence that was overlooked by administrators and they placed troublemakers and the mentally ill in long-term administrative segregation; the judge was most disturbed by reports that self-mutilation and constant shrieking occurred on a daily basis in these solitary cells.

In his summary, the judge repeated his disappointment that his recommendations on how to handle the overcrowding had been opposed by TDCJ officials and ignored by Texas governors. In 1987, Republican Governor William Clements pushed prison expansion, using a bond issue that did not require voter approval, an expensive move in a state dedicated to fiscal conservatism. Clements' successor, Democrat Ann Richards, followed suit, approving massive building projects. When Judge Justice's last ruling reached the desk of Republican Governor George W. Bush in 2000, the future president answered the court's criticisms by authorizing the building of more Texas prison units, funded again by issuing a bond.[2]

Judge Justice also expressed concern about the power of private prison corporations. At one point in the early days of the *Ruiz v. Estelle* suit, the judge, frustrated over the amount of violence at TDC, had threatened to fine the administrators $800,000 if they did not remedy the situation. As an example of unintended consequences, his threat motivated the Texas legislature to support emerging private companies who made deals with county sheriffs to build prison units in small Texas towns where they were welcomed as a way to provide much needed employment.[3]

When Texas governors began expanding the state-run prison-building program in the 1980s and 1990s, the owners of these companies began offering their privately-run empty beds to overcrowded prison systems throughout the nation. "Rent a cell" became a common phenomenon and made private prison owners more powerful as they used some of their profits to lobby officials to oppose any policies that would reduce the prison population.

Despite these problems, in 2002, 30 years after the advent of *Ruiz v. Estelle,* Judge Justice released TDCJ from federal court oversight. Meanwhile, it became known through the prison pipeline that David Ruiz was being kept in solitary confinement; despite being very ill, he was denied medical parole or even admission to a hospital until he was on his death bed in 2005. Few knew that Judge William Wayne Justice attended Ruiz' funeral service in a San Antonio church.

As a jailhouse lawyer, David Ruiz had tried to pull back the curtain on the inhumanity in the Texas prison system and he had acted in the tradition of Houston reporter Harry McCormick and reform-minded Texas legislators who, over many years, had battled a massive bureaucracy that enjoyed secrecy and seclusion. Judge Justice, never publicly commenting on the state of affairs at TDCJ, continued to preside over cases in Austin until his death in 2009 at age 89. His handling of the *Ruiz v. Estelle* lawsuit brought public opprobrium to his front door; builders would not work on repairs on his home and his wife was denied service at the local beauty parlor. Yet, the judge always maintained that his rulings in the *Ruiz* case had been correct, despite the limited outcomes.

Texas now housed more prisoners in privately-run facilities than any other state and federal court oversight of these institutions was not permitted. In addition, the state legislature, not the courts, was in charge of publicly run TDCJ facilities and Texas politicians did little to check the growth in the prison population. Hardliners used the *Ruiz v. Estelle* case to create a prison bureaucracy that reinforced the Texas control model while keeping costs as low as possible and outside oversight at a minimum.

Recently, through Charles Sullivan of Citizens United for Rehabilitation of Errants, I gained an interview with a former Texas inmate, who, despite the brutal atmosphere of the unit in which he was first placed, changed his life. Guided by a volunteer professor, Ed participated in formal debates with other prisoners, an involvement that led to his completing his Associate's degree through a local university.

Ed served 10 years in the violent unit in which 90% of the inmates were members of gangs who maintained a great deal of control. As an example, Ed said new inmates faced a challenge by gang members to fight with them, or be used as slave workers. When I asked how he had responded, Ed laughed and assured me that he had engaged in the fight in order to avoid worse punishment. Eventually, Ed was moved to a different unit that provided far more safety, attesting to the fact that units in prison systems vary widely.[4]

According to Ed, sexual assaults were numerous, with five of the ten most sexually violent prisons in the country located in Texas. Prison rape is a national problem; thousands of allegations of sexual victimization were reported in 2015 and many of these crimes were attributed to prison staff members whose abuse was ignored by administrators. This travesty continues, despite the passage of the Prison Rape Elimination Act during President George W. Bush's administration.[5]

Ed reminded me that, at one point, Texas prisoners were forced to live in open-air tents in the heat. Today, lack of air-conditioning in the hot summers and inadequate heat in the winters are the most frequent complaints of both Texas prisoners and their guards. Ed said he witnessed prison guards, wearing heavy Kevlar vests, become ill from the heat inside the cellblocks. He added that 17 prisoner lawsuits have been directed against TDCJ in which plaintiffs argue that working in the open fields or sitting in windowless cells in over 100-degree temperatures contributes to increased violence, illnesses, and even deaths. Ed expressed anger that TDCJ claimed that extending universal air-conditioning would cost too much money and he blamed the "lock them up and throw away the key" mentality of much of the public for this needless suffering.

Ed reported that, in the summer of 2018, prisoners at the Wallace Pack Unit in Navasota were promised relief from heat by Houston Judge Keith Ellison. The judge ordered TDCJ to install air-conditioning systems for these older ill inmates who had sued the state, citing 23 heat-related deaths and 200 heat-related illnesses over the last 10 years. When prison administrators did not comply with his order to air-condition the Wallace-Pack Unit, Ed said Judge Ellison threatened to incarcerate these officials in hot cells.

TDCJ authorities concerned that the court would address conditions at other units, offered an intermediate plan that would provide prisoners in all units with access to air-conditioned respite areas, cold showers, personal fans, and extra ice water. However, Ed indicated that inmates were being ignored when they requested respite or ice water and he acknowledged that their demands did put an extra burden on the understaffed system. As a result of the staff shortage, authorities found ways to discourage inmate requests through internal checks on their rectums, threats of cell shakedowns, or loss of access to the commissary. Ed described an inmate who, after asking for respite, was forced to stand in the heat while waiting to enter the prison law library, even though the respite area was only 20 feet away. Besides being denied relief, this inmate was threatened with being beaten and placed in a lockup.

Instead of gradually using funds to add air-conditioning, TDCJ spent $7 million to fight the Wallace Pack lawsuit, saying it would cost them $20 million to install the air-conditioning. In the end, they spent $4 million for the units. Because most of the new prison buildings were erected with the option to add air-conditioning, Ed said that TDCJ could start installing more cooling systems to end the suffering of both inmates and their guards.

I asked Ed, who seemed to be adjusting well to the free world if he thought that other conditions had improved in TDCJ since the various prison suits of the late twentieth century were settled. Ed responded that fewer instances of overt violence by guards exist, but he said administrators had substituted wider use of solitary.

Since his release, Ed has become affiliated with a nonprofit research group that claims TDCJ holds more persons in solitary, and for longer periods than any other state correctional institution. The *Texas Observer* has asserted that over 4,400 inmates out of 145,000 are in TDCJ solitary units, called "restrictive housing." One Texas inmate was held for 26 years in a solitary cell of 6x10 foot space that he occupied for 22 hours a day. While most prisoners have been kept in this status for about six years, 100 or more inmates have been in solitary confinement for 20 to 30 years.[6]

Among Ed's other serious criticisms of TDCJ were that no rhyme or reason exists within its classification system and that the grievance process is "laughable." Ed said complaints of unconstitutional conditions go unheeded by authorities because no outside oversight of conditions in the prison units exists. For example, he cited a recent scandal involving correctional officers who, told by their supervisor that they must have a certain quota of offenses by inmates, planted a screwdriver in an inmate's cell.

Hearing Ed says that the General Educational Development (GED) program was often taught by unqualified guards, reminded me of Dr. George Beto who built a basic educational system run by licensed teachers. Ed attributed much of the violence and rioting at TDCJ to chronic idleness and lack of programs, such as job training that could be translated to the free world. He pointed out that the Texas legislature slashed prison educational programs in 2011 as a response to the Great Recession.

In 2012, the legislature also began cutting TDCJ staff, resulting in a one-third loss of personnel by 2014, with only 65% of guard positions filled. A major reason for this relates to the fact that, between 1990 and 2000, Texas built 75 new prisons, housing 100,000 inmates, all located in remote small towns in order to give jobs to local residents and to have lower real estate costs. Due to an upswing in the gas and oil industries, offering higher salaries, it had become difficult for TDCJ to hire sufficient staff for the rural system.

Ed emphasized that mass incarceration was the biggest problem in TDCJ, preventing real reform. In this, Ed was in agreement with many critics who maintain that reform can only be carried out if the high numbers of inmates are drastically reduced. US prisons now hold six times the number of persons than our European counterparts, at a cost of $80 billion a year. Critics point out that some of those funds could bring major improvements to troubled communities and prevent crime in the first place. Instead, our penal system is asked to address problems that run deep in our society, such as broad economic inequality, racism, and sexism.

Ed added that COVID-19, besides being a health risk to inmates and guards, also caused additional stress in the prison units because the inmates who become ill cannot report for their work duties, many of which are essential to the running of the institutions. It is no surprise that places in which people sleep, eat, and recreate in close proximity see infectious disease spread quickly. During the coronavirus pandemic, nursing homes, military bases, prisons, and jails witnessed a very high rate of illness and death. Accurate statistics on prison illness and death, caused by the pandemic, are unknown because some states do not include these numbers in their reports. However, several journalists, as well as academics, have been investigating the effects of COVID-19 on inmates.[7]

Given the extent of COVID-19 and the delayed reaction to it by the federal government, plus the national lack of adequate equipment, TDCJ appeared to be trying to protect both inmates and staff in the immediate days of the pandemic. However, when Federal Judge Keith Ellison of Houston, Texas, who had ordered air-conditioning for elderly inmates at the Wallace Pack unit, became aware of the negative impact of COVID-19 at this same geriatric center, he ordered masks for staff and inmates, widespread testing, and provision of hand sanitizers. The latter was not permitted by TDCJ because of the possibility that they could be used to start a fire.[8]

The pandemic also meant that inmates were given bagged meals made up of peanut butter sandwiches and rotten meat that showed signs of roaches and rats. For some in the free world, spoiled and contaminated food in prisons may seem inconsequential and another way that people are punished. However, bad food contributes to illness and even to chronic conditions that cause physical suffering, costly to the inmates and to the public. In a society awakening to the need for healthy food to prevent illness, the lack of nutritious food in prisons deserves attention.

Texas is not alone in regard to the food problem. Impact Justice, a nonprofit organization, issued a report entitled, "Eating Behind Bars: Ending the Hidden Punishment of Food in Prison." After surveying thousands of inmates, Impact Justice found that three out of four prisoners reported being served spoiled or rotting food and nine out of ten said they did not receive sufficient food. The Office of the Inspector General backs up these statistics.[9]

As we ended our conversation, Ed indicated that the prison labor system, managed by Texas Correctional Industries, was valued at nearly $90 million in 2014. Texas, along with Georgia, Arkansas, and Alabama, does not pay inmates for their labor because officials argue that their free work offsets costs of room and board and equips inmates with skills useful after release. Dr. George Beto, as the entrepreneur he was, would be pleased that the Texas prison system continues to be run economically. On the other hand, Dr. Beto, as a former educator and a Christian minister, might be disappointed with the overall state of affairs at TDCJ.

Even so, Texas has made some changes in its prisons. The state passed laws that encouraged alternatives to prison for some nonviolent offenses, expanded drug courts, and aimed at reducing recidivism, an approach that allowed lawmakers in Texas to close several prisons and end plans to build 17,000 more prison beds, saving taxpayers $2 billion. One of the units is utilizing restorative justice principles, a subject for the last essay in this book.

We leave Texas and its control model that has influenced many other states to continue with essays that describe the overall demographics of American prisons.

Notes

1. Phone calls to Lawrence Pope, 1982–1988
2. Molanphy, Helen Clarke, *Idea of Punishment: Texas Prison System as a Case Study*
3. Ibid.
4. Phone conversation with former inmate Ed, October 2020
5. As governor of Texas, George Bush took a hardline on the treatment of prisoners and he tightened parole regulations.
6. "Solitary Confinement in the Texas prisons," http://www.TexasObserver.org
7. CURE Newsletter, Spring 2020
8. Madison Pauly, "Hell's Kitchen." *Mother Jones*, March/April 2019
9. "170 Texas Prisoners Tested Have the Coronavirus," https://ktxs.com (radio broadcast, April 11, 2020)

PART II
DEMOGRAPHICS OF AMERICAN PRISONS

6
The Unschooled

In the early days of the American penitentiary, education consisted of Bible reading; later, some trades were introduced. In the 1930s, amid a general call for prison reform, social scientist Austin McCormick developed a correctional educational model for the federal Bureau of Prisons (BOP) in which basic education was compulsory and trained instructors were hired.

In contrast, in Texas, prison chaplains acted as the teachers and attendance was voluntary; in 1924 the state's committee on reform only urged schooling for promising white males. Later, when the Texas legislature mandated the development of basic schooling, the prison board hired a supervisor, but teachers were chosen from among the inmates themselves. While Texas officials claimed that 52% of the prison population was enrolled in school, a 1937 federal report, "The Prison Labor Problem in Texas," stated that the Texas legislature did not appropriate sufficient funds for educational materials and teachers' salaries.

When Dr. George Beto, an educator himself, became director of the Texas prisons in 1962, he used his persuasive abilities to gain funds from the legislature to establish the Windham School District that granted GED degrees. At that time, the educational level at TDC consisted of the following statistics: 15–20% of inmates were illiterate; 90% were school dropouts; 90% were below ninth-grade achievement levels; 52% had IQ's below 100; and 10–15% were retarded.[1]

During our interview in 1981, Dr. Beto told me that, as the son of German immigrants, he had an immigrant child's faith in the value of education. By the time he resigned in 1972, one-fourth of the Texas prison population was in attendance at the Windham School District and some inmates were receiving limited training for various blue-collar jobs.

At a prison board meeting in 1963, Beto cited his plan for education.

> Our educational program should have two objectives. First, compulsory formal schooling for illiterates; second, directed study correlated with work assignments. For instance, a boy working in the welding shop should be taught how to read blueprints and some physical characteristics of metals.[2]

With options for legitimate employment in a country enamored of automation and globalization growing fewer, many unschooled American inmates have become recipients of a high school diploma, despite this process being historically slow. Several problems related to educational opportunity for prisoners exist, among them the difficulty of attracting staff to this dangerous,

DOI: 10.4324/9781003280279-8

often anti-intellectual, environment. Other factors limiting prison schooling are the amount of time that many inmates spend at mandatory work, along with an atmosphere in which there is a lack of incentives and in which educational opportunities can be used as a reward, or as a punishment.

Another problem is the scarcity of sufficient data on the educational and skill levels of those incarcerated. However, based on statistics from the Department of Justice, it appears that 86% of free world persons have high school diplomas or GED certification. While 70% of prisoners have the same credentials, many of them cannot compose a letter to a company or do basic math, indicating that more education for inmates would be very useful.

During Dr. Beto's years administering the Texas system, little effort was made to offer college courses to prisoners. Even so, George Beto may have been familiar with an innovative college program that significantly lowered the recidivism rate of those involved. In the 1920s, Howard Belding Gill, a Harvard graduate, developed an educational system at the Norfolk State Prison Colony in Massachusetts in the belief that educational level was a strong predictor of recidivism.

Norfolk inmates, wearing normal clothing, took academic courses taught by professors from Harvard, Boston University, and Emerson College, and engaged in a debate society in which they faced off with Harvard students and often won. They also participated with staff in cooperative self-government. As an innovator, Howard Gill kept prisoners in contact with the outside world by offering a well-stocked library, a newspaper, a radio show, and a jazz orchestra, along with a released time program. While Howard Gill's program was an anomaly, decades later, the federal government began offering Pell grants to cover college tuition for prisoners in all states.

When a movement to severely punish offenders arose in the 1990s, President Bill Clinton, representing the moderate wing of the Democrat party, signed into law the Violent Crime Control and Law Enforcement Act of 1994. This legislation, a reaction to Republican electoral success through the party's calls for law and order, included a federal "three strikes" mandatory life sentence for repeat offenders; funds to hire 100,000 new police officers; and an expansion of death-penalty offenses. The 1994 law also stripped away all Pell Grant funding of college courses, despite the testimony of many criminologists who pointed to education as an effective tool to lower recidivism rates, as high as 70% in some parts of our nation.

At the time, President Clinton's Attorney General, Janet Reno, along with many other attorneys, as well as a good number of correctional officials, opposed the ban on Pell grants. However, their opinions were ignored and thousands of colleges ended their educational programs, with only eight institutions continuing on. In 2015, the Obama administration restored some of the Pell grants, instructing the US Department of Education to fund the Second Chance Pell pilot program, a move that encouraged 67 colleges and universities to offer 10,000 inmates educational grants, amounting to as much as $6,000 a year per student. The Trump administration backed this program, declaring that it prepares released inmates for the workforce; Pell grants remain on the Congressional budget agenda and the Biden administration is encouraging passage of increased aid.

Since 1997, my undergraduate alma mater, Marymount Manhattan College, has run the New York Bedford Hills College Program, along with the Tacoma College Program, in order to give female inmates the opportunity to earn an Associate of Arts degree or a Bachelors degree in sociology or political science. This program was the first project in New York State to offer an uninterrupted pathway to a degree for women who were transferred for good behavior from maximum-security to medium-security facilities. Since the founding of the program, Marymount Manhattan has granted women 235 degrees.[3]

In 2020, television award winners Ken Burns and Lynn Novick produced a two-part Public Broadcasting Service (PBS) special called, "College Behind Bars," that highlighted New York Bard College's program offering associate and bachelor degrees to gifted men and women, many of them incarcerated for violent offenses committed when they were young. These inmates live in two worlds, one of intense study, equal to the same difficult academic work that free Bard students engage in, and the other, regulation by guards who sometimes demean what these inmates have accomplished.

Meanwhile, critics among the public oppose prisoners receiving free college education.

The narrator in "College Behind Bars" discusses the controversy surrounding free college education for inmates, offering the argument that the program, paid for by Bard College, provides education to persons who can make significant contributions to society after their release. In addition, a New York State corrections administrator interviewed in the film suggests that the public does not understand that the loss of liberty and privacy is punishment in itself; he adds that administrators prefer that inmates study, rather than give staff trouble.

One prison administrator admitted to me that he does not broadcast inmate training and educational programs for fear that sectors of the public might view these as examples of coddling criminals. In our interview, he added that the demand for college courses is greater than the supply and that this lack necessitates a slow progression for qualified inmates.

The conservative think-tank, Research and Development (RAND) Corporation, has estimated that inmates who take college classes have a 43% lower likelihood of recidivism and a 13% higher chance of obtaining work after being released from prison. According to the Pew Charitable Trust, a 10% reduction in recidivism saves approximately $635 million per year in incarceration costs. Given these statistics, Arthur Rizer, a former prosecutor, employed by a center-right think tank in Washington DC, has stated that providing postsecondary education to prisoners makes society safer.[4]

Besides those who advocate college studies in prison in order to lower recidivism and to ensure public safety, other supporters, such as Kevin Ring of Families against Mandatory Minimums (FAMM), believe that college education offers inmates a sense of self-worth and dignity. While these testimonies are impressive, FAMM also suggests that inmates who are able to participate in these college programs may have been less damaged in their earlier lives and enjoyed better schooling.[5]

The various college educational opportunities around our country are good news to a limited number of prisoners.

Meanwhile, all literate inmates have been affected by cuts in prison library budgets after the Great Recession of 2008. In addition, some prison officials limit access to owning books; correctional facilities in Pennsylvania, Washington State, and New York tried to stop the practice of inmates receiving secondhand books, but advocacy groups prevented this. Several Ohio prisons have banned book donations and the state's prisoners must order books through private contractor JPay, a company that charges a fee.[6]

When West Virginia inmates receive free electronic tablets to read books or send emails to their families, they are charged three cents a minute by Global Tel Link, even though the books all come from Project Gutenberg, a free online library housing 60,000 texts. In addition, the West Virginia prison system receives a 5% commission on the revenue from the tablets, a situation reduplicated in many other correctional facilities.[7]

Prisoners are also restricted in their choice of reading materials because administrators censor which books come into their facilities. New Jersey bans Michelle Alexander's book, *The New Jim Crow: Mass Incarceration in the Age of Colorblindness*, that focuses on the racist elements of our punishment system. The state of Texas bans 15,000 books, including works by Alice Walker, John

Grisham, Tony Morrison, and former Republican Senator Bob Dole, while books by Adolph Hitler and white supremacist David Duke are permitted. When Tony Morrison was informed that one of her books was banned because it might make Texas prisoners riot, she laughingly remarked that she had no idea her book had such power.[8]

Censorship has affected the University of Illinois's Education Justice Project (EJP) in which volunteers offer classes, ranging from anti-violence work to improving writing and job interview skills, for inmates at the Danville Correctional Center. A faculty member at the University of Illinois, concerned by censorship at the Danville prison, addressed the Illinois state legislature and emphasized that EJP complies with the pre-approval process at the prison, even though this process changes frequently and is only communicated orally by prison staff. The professor informed the legislative committee that sixteen of the 28 books that EJP recently submitted, including *Uncle Tom's Cabin* by Harriet Beecher Stowe and *The Souls of Black Folks* by W.E.B. Dubois, were denied.

In addition, this faculty member said prison staff seized approved assignments, tore out pre-approved materials from the texts, and suspended EJP for a week. When over 200 books in the library collection, concerning social struggle among African Americans, were removed, the warden maintained that the books on race were divisive. As a result of these new restrictions, Illinois university administrators dropped their plan to implement a four-year degree program at Danville prison.[9]

Despite the limitations of living in prison, some inmates have engaged in self-education and writing. Prizefighter Ruben "Hurricane" Carter spent his imprisonment years writing *Hurricane: The Life of Ruben Carter*, a book that ultimately reached four Canadians who became Carter's support system and helped free him from a wrongful murder conviction.

Shaka Senghor is a former inmate who also began writing in prison. His memoir entitled, *Writing My Wrongs: Life, Death, and Redemption in an American Prison*, emphasizes the power of learning and traces Shaka's road from his middle-class life, hoping to become a doctor, to that of a drug dealer and, finally, a murderer.[10]

In his book, Shaka reveals the violence and chaos he witnessed during his 19 years in a Michigan prison, but he says that, while incarcerated for second-degree murder, he was mentored by older prisoners who were his best teachers. Even so, he admits he was disruptive and, as a result, spent seven years in solitary confinement; isolated, Shaka began acknowledging the effects of his divorced mother's abuse, as well as the reasons for his pursuit of a criminal life. After receiving a letter of forgiveness from the godmother of his murder victim, this act of love from a basic stranger, plus his own journaling about his life and his errors, provided a path to his renewal.

In Shaka's memoir, he expresses his admiration for poet Dante Alighieri, author of the *Divine Comedy*, an epic poem dealing with punishment and reform. Shaka Senghor has dedicated his life to three goals suggested by Dante: atonement, forgiveness, and redemption. In line with Dante's path towards redemption, Shaka established a literacy program for juveniles and gained fellowships at Massachusetts Institute of Technology (MIT) and the Kellogg Foundation, as well as directorships of the Atonement Project and #Cut 50.[11]

While Shaka's own experience is unique, he believes that most inmates are redeemable provided prisons become more humane and introduce rehabilitative programs, including access to education.

In another heartening story, revealing the power of education and communication, former inmate Jarell Daniels, who spent seven years in prison for wounding an attacker in self-defense, participated in a Columbia University educational program. Lasting eight weeks, the seminar involved assistant district attorneys who engaged with newly released New York City inmates to promote understanding between the two groups. In his TED Talk, Daniels tells the viewer that, like Shaka Senghor, his best teachers in the correctional facility were the long-term inmates who encouraged him to take a new path, despite his background of family abuse and a crime-infested neighborhood. Also similar to Shaka Senghor, Jarell Daniels is dedicating his time to helping young people stay in school, one of the most effective ways to avoid prison.[12]

Notes

1. Molanphy, Helen Clarke, *Idea of Punishment: Texas Prison System as a Case Study*
2. Ibid.
3. Phone interview with Marymount Manhattan Academic Dean
4. "Can Yoga in Prison Help Reduce Recidivism Rate?" https://www.theglobepost.com/2019/12/11
5. Ibid.
6. Investigative journalists discovered that the director of the Ohio Department of Corrections was the former general manager of JPay.
7. "West Virginia Inmates Will Be Charged by the Minute to Read E-books on Tablets," https://www.reason.com/2019/11/22
8. Molanphy, Helen Clarke, *Idea of Punishment: Texas Prison System as a Case Study*
9. "Illinois Prison Removes More Than 200 Books from Prison Library," https://www.freedom-to-learn.net/blog/illinois-newsroom-illinois-prison-removes-more-than-200-books-from-prison-library
10. Shak Senghor, "Why Your Worst Deeds Don't Define You," TED Talk, June 23, 2014
11. #Cut 50, which aims at reducing the present prison population to half what it is today by 2025, was founded by activist Van Jones, a member of the Obama administration in its early years and a television news correspondent.
12. Jarell Daniels, "What Prosecutors and Inmates Can Learn From Each Other," TED Talk, May 24, 2019

7
The Young and the Old

In 2004, I interviewed Anna, a psychiatrist at the New Mexico Penitentiary, located in Santa Fe. Anna told me that she had considered becoming a child psychiatrist because so many of the New Mexican inmates had endured extreme abuse as youths in conditions unimaginable to the public. The violence these persons suffered in their early years was repeated against others in their adult years.[1]

Other psychiatrists and counselors have been speaking out about the impact of abuse on children and they have indicated that the neurological parts of young people's brains, involved in planning, impulse control, and learning from mistakes, are still developing. Youth are also more susceptible to coercion and more likely to take risks. To what extent these factors should influence criminal penalties is controversial, with some authorities giving them more weight than others.

The US Supreme Court has taken into consideration the immaturity of youthful offenders in three important cases. In *Roper v. Simmons* (2005), the court held that children could not be sentenced to the death penalty and the court in *Graham v. Florida* (2010) decided that juvenile life without parole was unconstitutional in nonhomicide cases. The court went further in *Miller v. Alabama* (2012) when it decided that mandatory sentences of life without parole for youth under the age of 18 were unconstitutional. However, these court mandates were often not applied retroactively.

The *Miller* case is a tribute to attorney Bryan Stevenson's nonprofit organization, Equal Justice Initiative (EJI), that has been instrumental in bringing attention to the many thousands of juveniles who were given life without parole sentences. Stevenson, who Archbishop Desmond Tutu of South Africa has called "America's Nelson Mandela," says that more work needs to be done in persuading jurisdictions to consider alternative sentences for youth because residency in juvenile centers can cause more delinquency.

Youth in detention often wind up in solitary confinement, a situation that various international groups, such as the United Nations, have condemned. Many youthful offenders spend more than 22 hours in solitary with only a Bible. Added to this, in some detention centers, youth who report symptoms of mental illness are punished by being strapped to their beds in leather restraints for four hours at a time. Incarcerated youth have double to four times the amount of suicides than do nonincarcerated youth in their home communities. As their rational capacity deteriorates, these youth may turn bitter and be unfit to be in society.

In 2010, Kalief Browder, a 16-year-old African-American youth, was arrested in New York City for allegedly stealing a backpack. Kalief claimed that he was innocent and he refused plea bargains from an insistent prosecutor. With no prior criminal record, Browder spent three years awaiting trial in the solitary confinement section of New York City's Rikers Island Jail, largely due to the shortage of public defense attorneys, as well as to the recalcitrant attitude of the prosecutor in charge of his case. Browder was severely beaten by guards, episodes that were captured on video and included in journalist Bill Moyer's 2017 documentary film, "Rikers: An American Jail." Even though charges against Kalief were eventually dismissed and his suit against the jail brought him a financial settlement, he was traumatized by the brutality he suffered and took his own life.[2]

In his film, Bill Moyers, winner of 30 Emmy awards, included stories of a dozen inmates at Rikers who he described as living in a madhouse. At the time, 7,500 inmates, 78% of them awaiting trial, were incarcerated in this hell hole of a modern penal colony in the East River that has no transparency because of its location on an island and because of the insular attitude of its officials. Parents can spend eight hours, waiting to visit their sons and daughters and then be able to stay for only a few minutes, a situation that adds to the isolation and guarantees that what is going on behind closed doors does not reach the public.

Federal investigators heard numerous stories of brutality towards youth at Rikers, including beatings with broomsticks, batons, boots, and closed fists. According to their reports, 44% of adolescent boys at Rikers claimed being abused, suffering injuries considered alarming; those who complained to officials were met with retaliation.

New York State Court of Appeals Judge Jonathan Lippman, moved by the investigations and the horrors shown in Bill Moyers' film, formed a commission focused on reform at Rikers. His panel recommended the closure of the Manhattan jail and the establishment of smaller jails in each of New York City's five boroughs. To date, there has been some reduction in the number of persons held at Rikers Island Jail.[3]

Rikers Island Jail is by no means the only place where juveniles have been abused. Only recently, the Annie E. Casey Foundation reported that juvenile facilities in most states violate young people, many of them suffering from mental illnesses. The Casey Foundation also found that black youth are five times more likely to be confined than their white peers and that Latino and Native-American youth are twice as likely. Despite representing 15% of children in our country, African-American children make up a third of those arrested, two-fifths of those detained, and half of all children whose cases are referred to social services, mainly because they have a parent charged with a crime.

The Casey Foundation has reported that many youths have parents in prison, with 25% of African-American children in this category. In 1980, 350,000 children had parents in prison but, today, 2.7 million children, 1 in 28, have a parent behind bars. Five million children, 7% of the total number in our country, have had a parent incarcerated at some point in their lives. Half of the American prison population has minor children and many of these children endure higher than average rates of drug and alcohol use, asthma, migraines, high cholesterol, and HIV/AIDS.[4]

The Texas Youth Council (TYC) has been plagued with scandals concerning sexual and physical abuse of young offenders. In 2008, the American Civil Liberties Union filed a class action lawsuit, *K.C. v. Nedelfoff,* against the TYC on behalf of five girls at the Brownwood State School. These females were often placed in solitary confinement and, when they were released from solitary or finished a work assignment, they were subjected to invasive strip searches. If the girls resisted, guards used physical force, pepper spray, handcuffs, and leather straps to force their compliance. American Civil Liberties Union (ACLU) argued that this treatment violated the

US Bill of Rights, as well as the International Rights of the Child promulgated by the United Nations International Covenant on Civil and Political Rights.

New Mexico plaintiffs in a 2007 case, *ACLU of New Mexico v. The New Mexico Children, Youth and Families Department et al.*, asserted that the state denied youth adequate mental, medical, and educational services and that they were emotionally abused by staff and other youth. The ACLU pointed out that no independent grievance system was in place to protect juveniles.[5]

A study at Sam Houston State in Huntsville, Texas, found that 43% of those admitted to juvenile detention centers are members of gangs who come from dysfunctional homes and communities. The number of juvenile gang members in the United States is over one million which means that 2% of youth are gang members, with membership highest at age 14. The Sam Houston State study also discovered high turnover rates in gang membership, with approximately 36% leaving every year; gang leaders recruit new members, replacing those who become disenchanted with promises of girls, cars, and money. Because both youth who leave gangs and those who remain have many negative life outcomes, the author of the study emphasized how important it is for society to attend to this crisis among so many youth in our country.[6]

Jesuit priest Greg Boyle of the Dolores Mission in Los Angeles founded a three decades old nonprofit, called Home Boys Industries. From its beginnings, this organization has offered local gang members a way out of their crime-ridden lifestyle through job training and eventual employment in its numerous industries. In an interview on the Public Broadcasting Service (PBS) Amanpour & Company public affairs program, Father Boyle acknowledged the beneficial effect of providing jobs, but he stressed that Home Boys Industries' main purpose is offering a safe environment in which healing can take place and former gang members will want to become responsible members of society. Boyle claims that counseling and case management play a major role in the stories of redemption of these young men, all badly abused in their childhood.[7]

Hearing Father Boyle describe one youngster's horrific background of physical and mental cruelty, resulting in his running away from home at age nine, I was reminded of my conversation with Anna, the psychiatrist at the Santa Fe penitentiary, about the large number of prisoners who, as youth, suffered an inordinate amount of violence in their family homes.

Forty-five gangs operate in the Los Angeles area and, due to the work of Home Boys Industries, the number of deaths among these gangs has decreased substantially. Father Boyle, who was originally motivated to establish the nonprofit by the lack of healthy relationships and the vast suffering that he witnessed in his community, has added Home Girls Industries to the organization. In addition, his nonprofit mentors other groups in our country and abroad in order to help these entities develop similar models of compassion that Father Boyle refers to as "gentleness."

While the 1967 Supreme Court case, *In Re Gault*, guaranteed constitutional protections to youthful offenders, Father Boyle decried the fact that a more punitive approach to juvenile offenders took precedence. The "school to prison pipeline" was born and offenses that once resulted in expulsion from school for a short time brought lengthy sentences at juvenile detention facilities; in addition, prosecutors began ordering more youth into adult prisons. Several states have no limit on the age a minor can be sentenced as an adult and juveniles can be given life sentences without parole in many places.

Even though youthful arrest rates have declined considerably since the mid-1990s, mainly due to a general reduction in crime, existing detention centers are overcrowded because states, under financial pressure, have been closing some of these facilities. However, these closures may be beneficial in the long run because the juvenile detention system has a bad record of keeping youth out of future incarceration; many juvenile detention centers have a very high recidivism rate, sometimes as much as 85%.

Forty years after this punitive approach was intensified, reform of the juvenile justice system is on the agenda again, characterized by an acknowledgement of the underlying causes of juvenile offenses and of the consequences of so many young people facing imprisonment. Trying to offset this situation, Missouri has developed an alternative model; smaller facilities, with staff trained to connect with youth, serve a large proportion of inner-city youth, affected with mental, educational, and physical limitations. This state's experiment has proved so successful that the Missouri Youth Services Institute helps other states across the country revamp their juvenile justice systems.[8]

Other states are experimenting with what are called "evidence-based" programs in which the young person is assigned a caseworker who is on call 24 hours a day, allowing the youths to remain in their homes with their families. The Campaign for Youth Justice recommends more community-based initiatives, such as evening centers providing community service opportunities.[9]

The literary community has joined the effort to shine a light on correctional conditions for juveniles. For example, Colson Whitehead's recent Pulitzer award-winning novel, *Nickel Boys*, is based on a 1940s true event at a Florida inhumane juvenile detention center in which an African-American teenager, wrongfully convicted of a crime, was incarcerated. The theft of the detention center's food and resources by members of the administration revealed that others, besides the juvenile offenders, were criminals. The sadism of the administrators toward the boys, both black and white, reflects eighteenth-century Italian philosopher Cesare Beccaria's belief that certain people enjoy torturing others and also mirrors the brutality of pre-Civil War white southern plantation owners towards black slaves.

Efforts towards a more humanitarian approach to young people provide hope, but much more attention needs to be paid to conditions in juvenile detention centers.

At the other end of the age spectrum, older prisoners, those over 55 years, make up 10% of the American prison population and have their own special needs.

While teaching at Adams State University in Alamosa, Colorado from 2000 to 2004, I interviewed a counselor at a correctional center located in Canon City, in which most of the older men were incarcerated for long periods of time due to serious offenses committed in their youth or because they had received lengthy sentences in their mid-years. The counselor said that nationwide the number of prisoners, 55 years and older, had increased 400% since the 1980s and, if the trend continued, a third of all prisoners would be aged in 10 years. Many of this demographic group suffer from chronic conditions, such as cancer, heart disease, high blood pressure, and diabetes; their care, amounting to billions a year, would also increase.[10]

Many in the medical field believe that compassionate release of dying inmates is a constitutionally protected right, but the Colorado counselor spoke about the complex process to qualify for compassionate release, with prisoners' medical conditions and their age and time served determining eligibility.

Over the years since that interview, little has changed; inmates who have committed serious crimes are generally excluded from compassionate release and most states allow victims, police, and legal professionals to have a large say in prerelease decisions. Today, the number of prisoners who require end-of-life care is growing. In the free world, a diagnosis of terminal illness often results in family members gathering to decide end-of-life options for their loved one, but prisons are not well equipped to provide dignity as death approaches.

Yet, nearing a crisis point, made worse by the pandemic, the situation for aging prisoners has produced calls to parole people of a certain age, if they seem unlikely to commit crimes. Many of these older inmates have provided a public service by helping younger inmates adapt to prison and turn their lives around. Prisoner advocates also contend that the policy of denying parole because of earlier violent acts is antiquated because research at Stanford University has shown that older inmates are unlikely to repeat their crimes.

In our conversation at the Canon City facility, the Colorado counselor referred to potential problems when elderly inmates are released. He said that those who wish to parole elderly inmates for economic reasons need to recognize that these returning citizens, many with chronic conditions, will require health care, much of it through federally funded Medicaid and Medicare. The counselor emphasized that releasing older inmates raises the question of whether our society will provide them with costly community assistance.

An advocate from the nonprofit, Restore Justice, gave an interview for the "Democracy Now" program in July of 2020 regarding the treatment of elderly prisoners during the pandemic. He emphasized that, because the majority of older inmates have underlying conditions, they are very susceptible to other diseases, easily transmissible behind closed doors.

This man gave one example in which 120 inmates, suffering from COVID-19, were mysteriously moved from the Chico, California prison to San Quentin prison in Marin County, a facility that had not experienced occurrences of the deadly virus among its numerous elderly inmates. In comparison, 16 of the 19 coronavirus deaths in California prisons had occurred at Chico. Due to this untimely transfer, 400 members of the prison population at San Quentin acquired COVID-19 within a week and a half of the arrival of the newcomers; many of these victims were then locked up in administrative segregation, while others were lying in the gym and in hallways with no medical care or access to bathroom facilities.

The Restore Justice representative said that a judge, reviewing pleas for release of San Quentin inmates, cried over this heartless move, a complete failure of administrative planning. The judge added that thousands of California staff members go in and out of state correctional institutions every eight hours, so no one should assume that COVID-19 could be contained inside prison walls in California, or in any other state.[11]

Other examples of public reluctance to release prisoners due to the pandemic have revealed widespread attachment to retribution, along with the absence of enlightened self-interest. In the next two essays that cover the conditions for female and minority inmates, this tendency to rely on retribution, rather than common sense, is once again manifested.

Notes

1. Interview with psychiatrist Anna Stevens, Colorado, August 2004
2. As a result of this case, President Barack Obama announced a plan to decrease the use of solitary confinement in federal prisons by banning solitary for juveniles and for adults who have committed low-level offenses.
3. "Inmate's Hanging Attempts Points to Supervision Lapses at City Jail," *New York Times*, December 5, 2019
4. "Maltreatment of Youth in Juvenile Correction Facilities," https://www.aecf.org/resources/
5. Prison Legal News, February 18, 2006
6. "Sam Houston Study Finds Gang Membership is Short-Lived," https://www.eurekalert.org/news-releases/723830#:~:text=HUNTSVILLE%2C%20TX%209%2F24%2F,at%20Sam%20Houston%20State%20University
7. PBS, Amanpour & Company
8. Marion Wright Edelman, "Juvenile Justice Reform: Making the 'Missouri Model' the American Model," https://www.childrensdefense.org/child-watch-columns/health/2010/juvenile-justice-reform-making-the-missouri-model-an-american-model/
9. The governor of California, Gavin Newsom, has announced that the state will be closing all of its juvenile detention centers, saying that these facilities are overcrowded, chaotic, and filled with violence.
10. Interview prison counselor, Canon City, Colorado, Spring 2003
11. Restore Justice interview on "Democracy Now" program, June 2021

8
The Female Inmate

One afternoon in 1983, sitting in a Dallas theater, I watched the curtain rise on a play that featured women about to be released from prison. Three actresses, lounging on cots, discussed how they might find a new life in the free world. After the curtain fell, two other women took the stage and sat facing the audience on folding chairs. A slight woman in a plain black woolen suit told the audience that she was Sister Genevieve O'Neil, a chaplain at the women's prison in Gatesville, Texas. Turning to the second woman, an attractive brunette in her thirties, Sister introduced her as Beth, an inmate at Gatesville prison.

When the question-and-answer period ended, I spoke with Sister Genevieve and the kindly woman related Beth's story. A mother of two children, a girl and a boy, Beth had been a successful elementary school teacher, but her marriage was another matter. Her sadistic husband would force her onto a bed and hold a gun to her head, playing Russian roulette for hours on end. On the suggestion of friends, Beth hired two men who charged her 200 dollars to murder her husband.

Sister paused, her eyebrow raised.

> Can you imagine? The two men are on death row. Beth plea-bargained, but the judge sympathetic to her case died. The second judge gave her a 25-year sentence.[1]

Beth was part of a large club; domestic violence occurs in 25% of American marriages and can be perpetrated by wives, as well as by husbands. However, 85% of the attacks are by men and the physical harm from the males is far worse than from the females. 50% of murdered women are killed by male partners, while 4% of men are murdered by female partners. In some states, such as Oklahoma, where more women are in prison than in any other state, mothers are held criminally liable if their children are abused by their male partners.

Studies of domestic abuse indicate that many women have been murdered when they try to end the relationship, while other women do not have the economic means to separate from their abusers. Domestic violence is a direct cause of homelessness for over half of women who leave violent situations.

When abused women who murder their husbands or boyfriends are tried in court, they are often at a disadvantage because too many prosecutors, judges, juries, and defense attorneys show a shocking amount of ignorance of domestic abuse. Judges may not allow evidence of violence

DOI: 10.4324/9781003280279-10

by the deceased male to be recorded and they may disallow arguments for self-defense or give improper instructions to the jury. Beth was not permitted to use self-defense or battered wife syndrome and she fit the profile of the small number of domestic violence victims who retaliate against their attackers, but, in doing so, receive longer sentences than other murderers.

On my visit to Beth after she was transferred from her cell in Gatesville prison to the Dallas County Jail to testify against the hired killers, she stood tiptoe speaking on a microphone through a glass window, surrounded by tough-looking females who appeared to be in charge of the jail dormitory.

Beth whispered through her microphone, "When fights break out, the guards look the other way."

However, Beth added that she felt safer in the Dallas jail and at Gatesville prison than she ever felt while living with her husband.

Once Beth returned to her cell in Gatesville, she painted four watercolors of lavender-toned flowers as a gift for me; each picture features a Chinese symbol: peace, love, tranquility, and beauty. Hanging in their grey steel frames, they make me hope that Beth has had a better life after she was paroled from prison and returned to her two children who had been cared for by her parents.

In a similar case in California, Brenda Clubine, whose husband's attacks had put her in an emergency room many times, took action when she was threatened once again with death. In defense, Clubine took a wine bottle and hit her abusive husband, a retired police officer, on his skull, killing him. She spent 26 years in a California prison and, while there, founded Convicted Women Against Abuse with other women having similar stories. As a result of their work, the California legislature deemed battered women's syndrome an admissible defense in 1992.[2]

Soon after my visit with Beth at the Dallas County Jail, chaplain Sister Genevieve sent me an invitation to join her at the women's prison in Gatesville for a Sunday liturgy. On that morning, accompanied by a guard, I entered the large metal gates of the prison, and, once inside, was directed to Sister's office by the head chaplain who, in Texas style, was dressed in cowboy attire. Sister Genevieve led me to the chapel where I watched fifteen sad-looking African-American women in their white cotton uniforms file in. When the short service ended, the women headed back to their dormitory, settling in for an idle day. Though it was a beautiful sunny afternoon, Sister Genevieve said that the women were not permitted to gather in the outdoor recreational area located outside their dormitory.[3]

She whispered, "The authorities maintain that this rule helps prevent homosexual contacts, but they're just being punitive."

Back in Sister Genevieve's office, our conversation turned to Beth. Like most other female prisoners, Beth's children were under age 18 and, also like them, she had borne the cost of attorney fees, court fees, telephone charges, visitation expenses, plus the upkeep of her children. Fortunately, Beth had some savings and her parents were helping her, a contrast to the many female prisoners who are forced to go on welfare when they return to the free world.

Sister Genevieve confided that Beth suffered from anxiety and depression because of her imprisonment and her separation from her children, a condition very common among female inmates. However, Sister stressed how fortunate Beth was compared to most other women at Gatesville because her children were safe with their grandparents and were protected from harassment about their mother because Beth's parents lived far from their grandchildren's town.

Sister indicated that Beth worried about her daughter and especially her teenage son who was a member of a demographic group highly likely to drop out of school when a parent is incarcerated. Beth wished she could see her children more often but, because they were living at her parents' home in Beaumont, Texas, a good distance from Gatesville prison, their visits were few, as is typical for many other women, incarcerated long distances from their homes.[4]

Years later, as a class in correctional philosophy watched a recent film, "The Sentence," memories of my time spent with Sister Genevieve and Beth came back. This documentary focuses on Cindy Shank, a Florida woman, who, like our Texas friend Beth and many others, left children behind when she went to prison. This intimate portrayal is the work of Rudy Valdez, a screenwriter who, after deciding that his sister Cindy should know what was happening in her children's lives, gave up his own work to film family events.

"The Sentence" opens by telling viewers that Michigan, the state where Cindy resided with a drug-dealing boyfriend, did not press charges against her when her boyfriend died in a violent exchange with other dealers. Yet, six years after his death, FBI agents appeared at Cindy's home and arrested her for conspiring with the boyfriend, a man who had threatened to kill Cindy if she left him. At the time of her arrest, Cindy was married and pregnant with her third child, and, when she was brought to trial, her three daughters were ages six, four, and five months. The federal prosecutor, who asked for a lengthy sentence, was disappointed when the judge gave Cindy fifteen years in prison, a mandatory minimum sentence. Based on charges that criminologists call "the girlfriend problem," Cindy was remanded to federal prisons in two different states, far away from her children.

Unlike children of many imprisoned women, Cindy's three daughters were fortunate to have a father, even though he later divorced Cindy and handed the care of his daughters to Cindy's elderly parents. At one point in Rudy Valdez's film, her eldest daughter remarked, "I remember Mommy being home." After speaking to Cindy on the phone, another daughter said, "I'm going to lay down on my bed and think about you."

At the end of an interview on YouTube, Cindy's brother, Rudy Valdez, says, "Her case wasn't special. I just want people to know that the people who are behind these bars are your mothers, your daughters, your sisters, your wives. They deserve fair sentencing, they deserve to be looked at, they deserve not to be forgotten."

Learning of this film that won an award at the annual Sundance film festival, Republican Senator Mike Lee of Utah insisted it be shown to Congress. Following this event, Senator Lee partnered with Democrat Senator Cory Booker of New Jersey to work on reform of sentencing practices in our nation. Due to the notoriety given her in" The Sentence," Cindy Shank was pardoned by President Obama after she served half of her sentence.

The Alice Project, a collaboration composed of the Sentencing Project, the National Black Women's Justice Institute, and Cornell University's Center on the Death Penalty Worldwide, has issued a report on sentencing practices towards thousands of American women. Of more than 6,600 women in the study, one of every 15 is serving a life sentence; one-third of these women are serving life without parole. The latter form of sentencing has grown by 43% since 2008 and the states of Florida, Pennsylvania, California, Michigan, Louisiana, and Mississippi lead the nation in its use. One of every 39 African-American women in prison is serving a life without parole sentence. Approximately four out of ten women on death row are people of color.[5]

On a subsequent visit with Sister Genevieve, when I asked for Beth, Sister said she was being considered for parole. We agreed that Beth had a good chance to leave the prison earlier as she was a middle-class educator and had served as the warden's secretary.

Then, Sister Genevieve surprised me by saying that she was resigning from her Texas chaplaincy position to accept a similar one in the state of Washington where a prison reform movement was in high gear. Sister Genevieve said, "Dr. Beto increased the number of prison chaplains in Texas. I wouldn't have had this job otherwise. He was known as the preacher/director with a Bible in one hand and a baseball bat in the other. He was a tough man, but I think he had the best of intentions and I'm grateful for my years in Texas."[6]

My conversations with Sister Genevieve allowed me to present a realistic picture of what life behind bars constitutes for American females when I taught this topic. Unfortunately, the conditions for imprisoned women have only deteriorated since the 1980s. During the last 40 years, the number of women in state prisons has increased by over 800%, with 200,000 American women in prison and over a million on probation and parole.

Many female prison inmates are caught up in the War on Drugs; "three strikes" laws, that call for life sentences after three felonies, have also had a large impact on women. In addition, fourteen times as many women sit in jails than in the 1970s, mainly because they are too poor to make bail, a consequence of the widening income gap in our country. Most jailed women have committed nonviolent low-level offenses, such as parole violation, shoplifting, and drug use.[7]

Female inmates face many problems, some of these resulting from their lives prior to incarceration. A high percentage of these women were sexually abused as children, have drug and alcohol problems, and report being diagnosed with some serious mental health condition. When incarcerated, females are mainly supervised by male guards who can view them when they are scantily dressed in their cells or naked in the open area showers. Many women, who were abused as children, now face abuse by their guards.

Female inmates do not receive as many services as men for their various disabilities and fewer prison diversion programs exist for women than for men who may have the option of boot camps for first-time offenses. Due to the lack of facilities, women who are sentenced for nonviolent crimes, such as drug use or property crimes, are housed with a small number of women who have committed violent crimes; the nonviolent have to live under the same high-security restrictions as the serious offenders.

Sister Genevieve felt special sympathy for the numerous women who give birth in prison and must say goodbye to their offspring. Until recently, all female prisoners were shackled while giving birth, but the federal First Step Act has eliminated this practice in the Bureau of Prisons and some states have done the same. In Minnesota, volunteers developed the Prison Doula Project in which professionally trained women prepare inmates for giving birth and then help them in the hospital delivery room. New mothers, who have 24 hours to bond with their babies before they are separated, have someone with them during their delivery besides a doctor and a corrections officer.[8]

Another advance for women giving birth in prison is a result of the work of recently deceased Catholic nun, Sister Elaine Roulet, who began as a volunteer teaching reading at the Bedford Hills women's prison in New York State. Sister Roulet went on to develop the Children's Center where new mothers can keep their babies until their first birthday. The Center, supported by actress Glenn Close, also sponsors children's visits to their incarcerated mothers.[9]

Regarding domestic abuse, some progress has been made; in 1994, Congress passed the Violence Against Women Act (VAWA), legislation that established the Office on Violence Against Women in the Department of Justice and authorized 1.6 billion dollars for investigation and prosecution of violent crimes against women, as well as the imposition of mandatory restitution and the provision of civil redress in cases that were not criminally prosecuted.[10]

Sister Genevieve O'Neil advocated training clergy, doctors, and police to recognize signs of domestic abuse and she believed that direct interventions in the cycle of domestic violence could also be effective. Sunny Schwartz, a corrections officer at San Bruno jail, south of San Francisco, supports the interventionist approach and she inaugurated a program called "Man Alive" to reduce domestic violence. Many of the male abuse offenders at the San Bruno jail were seriously harmed by family members in their youth, but through "Man Alive," they began to realize how they, in turn, had damaged their victims. By employing talk therapy and other healing methods, including meditation and yoga, this experimental interventionist system lowered the recidivism rate of domestic violence cases at San Bruno by 80%.

Sunny Schwartz regrets that more penal institutions have not adopted programs like "Man Alive," but she surmises that the financial cost of such a hands-on program is the problem. Schwartz says that society has to decide how to spend money, for prevention or for prison.[11]

Notes

1. Interview in 1984 with Chaplain Genevieve O' Neil, Dallas, Texas
2. "Domestic Abuse Victims Get Chance at Freedom," https://www.npr.org/2012/10/05/162169484/jailed-domestic-abuse-victims-get-chance-at-freedom
3. Visit to Gatesville Women's Prison – Fall 1985
4. A nonprofit group called, "Girls Embracing Mothers," has started bringing groups of youngsters for monthly visits with their mothers at Gatesville prison. Girls, among the five million youngsters who have a parent in prison, are able to be with their mothers for four-hour sessions. NBC Dallas-Fort Worth, May 12, 2017.
5. "1 in 7 People in Prison is Serving a Life Sentence," https://sentencingproject.salsalabs.org/lifesentences
6. Both Sister Genevieve and George Beto would have been disturbed that the Texas legislature, due to fiscal considerations, tried eliminating the prison chaplaincy program in 2011, ignoring the fact that chaplains have been the longest-running noncustodial persons employed. The legislation failed and chaplains continue to serve Texas inmates.
7. "African-American Women Represent the Largest Increase in Female Incarceration in Today's Prisons and Jails," https://www/Marshallproject.org
8. "The Separation," https://www.themarshallproject.org/2020/05/06/the-separation
9. A 2011 documentary, *The Mothers of Bedford*, covers the story of Sister Roulet's work.
10. At this writing, the US House of Representatives has authorized spending for this office, after several years of nonfunding, but the Senate has not signed on to the bill.
11. Sunny Schwartz wrote a book entitled *Dreams from the Monster Factory* (Scribner, 2009); her work has been featured by the International Institute of Restorative Practices.

9
Poor People of Color

Ava DuVernay's documentary film, *13th*, utilizes a narrator who explains how the exploitation of African Americans lies partly with the Thirteenth Amendment to our Constitution. While formally freeing African-American slaves, this amendment states that labor can be imposed "as punishment for crime whereof the party shall have been duly convicted." Currently, a grassroots movement advocating the elimination of this section of the Thirteenth Amendment has gained strength.

Using the Thirteenth Amendment, southern officials targeted former slaves who were unemployed and charged them with Black Code misdemeanor offenses, such as "walking without a purpose," "walking at night," or "hunting on Sundays." The point was to assuage white people's fear of newly freed slaves and to provide a cheap labor force in the economically depressed South, hurting from the Civil War.

By 1870, 95% of the Southern region's prisoners were African Americans, working as convict lessees in agriculture and industry. Their conditions were as harsh as under slavery and sometimes worse, because if a black worker died, the white bosses could obtain another black worker without any cost. Chain gangs, mainly composed of African-American prisoners, were also organized to repair roads and other infrastructure damaged in the Civil War. Rebuilding the private and public sectors of the South was the work of former slaves who had labored in the antebellum cotton and tobacco fields.

By gradually stripping African Americans of their citizenship rights and voting privileges, southern officials removed the possibility of the Black Codes being overturned. In 1871, when African-American inmates sought legal redress from their hardship, the Virginia Supreme Court pronounced incarcerated persons "slaves of the state."

Segregation of the two races was formalized at the end of the nineteenth century with the U S Supreme Court's decision, *Plessy v. Ferguson*, that condoned this practice. Meanwhile, lynchings of untold numbers of innocent black men became a large part of southern life, while several attempts in Congress to make lynching a felony never succeeded. In 1915, D.W. Griffith's "Birth of a Nation," a film praising the Ku Klux Klan and belittling Blacks, was shown at the White House to Democrat President Woodrow Wilson.

DuVernay's film offers the proposition that the African-American civil rights movement in the 1960s led to a backlash by politicians who initiated the War on Crime and the War on Drugs. The so-called "Solid South," loyal to local Democrats for their segregationist principles, had existed ever since the Civil War, but, in the 1960s, southerners became disenchanted with Democrats, especially after Texan Lyndon Johnson urged the passage of civil rights legislation. Associates of President Johnson's successor, Richard Nixon, designed the "Southern Strategy," in which they convinced southern voters to switch from the Democrat Party to the Republican Party in order to enforce law and order. The "Southern Strategy" was an opportunistic move that brought southern electoral landslides to the Republican party, as well as establishing a linkage between chronic crime and poor people of color.

Law and order rhetoric was compounded by the loss of jobs in the African-American community during the 1970s recession. In the 1980s, as middle-class whites and blacks left city neighborhoods for the suburbs, poor black people were isolated in urban ghettos in which few municipal services or legitimate opportunities for employment existed. This intersection of poverty and crime has led to recent calls to allocate more funds to create jobs, better schools, low-rent housing, and good medical facilities in impoverished communities of color.

Today, 44% of state prisoners in our country are incarcerated in southern prisons, even though these states hold only 34% of the nation's population. Texas holds the record for the most racially disproportionate prison population in the nation; although four of every ten Texans are either African-American or Hispanic, seven of every ten prison inmates in the state are from these two minority groups. Harking back to Fred Cruz and David Ruiz, jailhouse lawyers in Texas influenced by the Chicano movement, current statistics indicate that the number of Mexican Americans who are incarcerated has dramatically increased.

Racism is reflected nationwide.

While visiting Chicago to present a paper on prison reform at a correctional conference, I interviewed an Illinois parole officer who told me that poverty and high unemployment reign and that long-time African-American street gangs run the neighborhoods of the south side of Chicago. Murders occur at much higher frequency than in Los Angeles and New York, even though investigative reporters have revealed that the Chicago police department has manipulated crime statistics to make them appear lower.[1]

The parole officer indicated that impoverished African-American communities in Chicago have been prime targets in the War on Drugs, with a wide use of militarized police forces and frequent stops and frisks. He said that some arrestees had even been subjected to forced confessions obtained by police officers in a hidden warehouse. The officer added that nationwide one-third of all African-American male high school dropouts, between the ages of 20 and 39, are imprisoned, compared to approximately 13% in white demographic groups of the same ages and backgrounds.

The War on Drugs began when New York Republican Governor Nelson Rockefeller initiated the most severe drug laws in the United States. Under the Rockefeller laws, selling two ounces or more of heroin, cocaine, or marijuana brought sentences of fifteen years to life. While the penalties around marijuana in New York State were reduced by Rockefeller's successor, Democrat Governor Hugh Carey, much of the Rockefeller legal system remained in effect for years.[2]

President Richard Nixon joined Governor Rockefeller to announce the federal War on Drugs that included listing marijuana as a controlled substance, meriting felony charges.[3]

When Ronald Reagan was elected president in 1980, he signed the Anti-Drug Abuse Act that established federal mandatory minimum sentences for drug offenses, an action that pushed the War on Drugs into full gear. After the crack cocaine epidemic broke out in poor neighborhoods, adherents of Reagan's policies appeared vindicated and the War on Drugs became a permanent fixture.

Because numerous researchers have concluded that white people use illegal drugs in a higher proportion than blacks and browns, the question arises as to why African Americans and

Hispanics are more likely than Anglos to be incarcerated for the use and sale of drugs. A major reason is the widespread police crackdown on drug offenders in poor minority neighborhoods, while white suburban neighborhoods or those residing in penthouses do not receive the same attention. Another stark example of racial discrimination in the area of drug policy is the severe sentencing for crack cocaine, used by minorities, and the less onerous sentences for the use of powder cocaine by middle- and upper-class persons.[4]

Racism in our society follows African Americans and Hispanics into the prison system. Utilizing journalists' work on conditions at New York's Southport Correctional Facility, the Correctional Association of New York released a report citing brutality towards the Southport prisoners, 99% of the African Americans and Hispanics and 25% between the ages of 18 and 25. The Correctional Association noted pervasive violence and racism from the nearly all-white staff, including brutal beatings and extended stays in solitary confinement for talking back to staff.[5]

African-American Jerome Wright, an inmate in a class-action suit against New York's Elmira Correctional Facility for racist behavior and discrimination, is incarcerated at Southport. After testifying in court about conditions at Elmira, Wright was beaten by Southport staff members as retaliation for suing their colleagues. To add to the abuse, prison authorities charged him with attacking the guards and, when he was prosecuted in the local courts, he was given a six-year sentence in solitary confinement and often denied his one-hour out-of-cell recreation.

Wright believes he would have been treated even more brutally if he had not enjoyed visits from family members and from lawyers, assisting him with his Elmira lawsuit. Despite risking more retaliation, Wright testified to the Correctional Association about the brutal attacks by staff at Southport Correctional Facility in which hundreds of lawsuits have cost 10 million dollars in settlements. These expensive lawsuits have been reduplicated in prisons throughout our nation and often far outweigh the costs of improving conditions.

Jerome Wright ended his interview with the New York Correctional Association representatives by saying, "A friend of mine had his dreadlocks ripped out of his head."[6]

Governmental neglect of poor communities, negatively affected by huge changes in the economy and in the penal codes, adds to the problem of racism. As an example of the latter change, twenty states, among them Wisconsin, eliminated prison Good Conduct Time (GCT) after using it for more than a century. This effort to conform with demands for greater certainty of punishment negated encouragement of good behavior and inmate progress towards crime-free lives.

While there were thousands of prisoners in Wisconsin facilities in 1985, today there are four times as many, over 23,000, and the state has the highest ratio of prisoners to state residents in the upper mid-west. One Milwaukee zip code, 53206, has the highest rate of incarceration in America, along with a 22% unemployment rate and a 45% poverty rate. More than half of the African-American men in this community have been incarcerated in state prisons and others have served time in jail.[7]

These offenders affect their communities. Lack of economic prospects and high incarceration rates create community instability; the social fabric is changed by lower rates of marriage, higher rates of nonmarital childbearing, distrust of the police, and increased recidivism rates. When minority members commit crimes as a reaction to poverty, their incarceration puts them even lower on the economic ladder; finding it impossible to be employed in the new global economy, they renew their criminal activities. This vicious cycle of underclass incarceration occurs all over our nation.

It is also significant that many of those charged with felonies were often initially jailed on misdemeanor charges, rather than being fined as was the previous custom. Scholar Alexandra

Natapoff has addressed the impact of incarcerating so many people for misdemeanor offenses in her book, *Punishment Without Crime*. This author stresses how arrests for misdemeanors affect people in serious ways, causing loss of jobs and income, as well as housing access, student loans, and contact with their families. As misdemeanor charges set up persons for felony convictions, they can also fuel racist stereotypes that most poor African Americans and Hispanics are criminals.[8]

During the coronavirus crisis, some jurisdictions sought alternative ways to handle misdemeanor charges in order to avoid further spread of the disease among inmates and staff. States, such as California and Illinois, made progress, while many states in the Deep South, such as Louisiana, did not consider the consequences of COVID-19 in their misdemeanor policies. As a result, southern jails were overrun with the virus.

Economic inequality makes racial matters worse. The income and wealth gap in our country has grown wider, despite increased production, and presents the worst inequality in the industrialized world. 50% of households in 2019 accounted for 1% of the nation's total wealth, while the top 10% accounted for 76%. Compared to 1968, 60% more Americans of all races find themselves below the poverty line, with 43% more American children living below the minimum income level, considered necessary for basic family needs.

Nearly 81 million Americans struggle to find the funds for basic household expenses; 22 million lack enough food and 11 million are worried about their next house payment. Millions of Americans die each year from lack of access to health care and many of all races turn to drug-dealing for a living or to the use of drugs as a panacea, evident in the narcotics epidemic among recently unemployed blue-collar workers.

New Mexico, with its large Hispanic and Native American population, ranks at the top of states for its high poverty rate, inadequate educational system, and record numbers of domestic violence, rape, and incest cases. Today, violent crime in New Mexico is on the rise, as well as incarceration; this situation contrasts with other states who have seen a decrease in their inmate population due to a slowing in criminal offenses, as well as to the passage of sentencing reforms.

These statistics were gathered before the pandemic accelerated the income disparity, with 18 million Americans at one point receiving unemployment benefits. During the pandemic, it became even more evident that America has a huge inequality problem because the coronavirus affected large numbers of working-class African Americans, Hispanics, and Native Americans, substantially more than Anglos. Minority groups face poverty and lack adequate medical care, even in the best of times. Because of their lower economic status, they are forced to use public transportation to get to workplaces, such as meatpacking plants, alive with this virus. In addition, for financial reasons, minority members' housing arrangements often consist of numerous family members that make it impossible to isolate.

Addressing the issue of racism and classism in an interview on the "Democracy Now" newscast, African-American Dhoruba Bin Wahib, a former inmate, urged poor people to take charge of their communities in a responsible fashion, by calling for the decriminalization of narcotics and by ridding their neighborhoods of the scourge of drug usage. He expressed the hope that police officers would become proponents for the establishment of decent living conditions in poor communities and would not be so predisposed to view minority members as dangerous criminals. Bin Wahib's words could not have been timelier, given police use of unjustified force against African Americans in several of our states.[9]

Another aspect of inequality is the discrepancy in the treatment of "white-collar criminals" versus that of "street criminals," the latter paying a heavier price for their actions. White-collar crime is a term created by criminologist Edwin Sutherland in 1939 to describe crimes committed by persons of high social status in the course of their occupation. Examples include insider trading, labor racketeering, embezzlement, cybercrime, money laundering, identity theft, fraud, and forgery. Today, corporate crimes that harm health and safety, along with organized transnational crimes, are treated as white-collar crimes.

Differences in sentencing for white-collar offenders, compared to street offenders, exist; for example, white-collar criminals are fined, made to pay restitution, and given community service or probation, rarely prison, a situation that critics call a "slap on the wrist." After the Enron corporate scandal, prison sentences for white-collar offenses became more common but, when imprisoned, white-collar offenders do their time in minimum-security federal prisons.

White-collar crimes are often much more costly to society than street crimes, but the public is more frightened of being attacked on the street than of insurance fraud or other white-collar crimes. Yet, in some quarters of our nation, efforts to make upper-class corporatists accountable for exploiting the earth's resources and causing unnecessary illness and deaths are increasing; more people have begun to recognize that environmental hazards are a class and race issue, as so many poor minority communities deal with polluted areas.

Ironically, some of the clearest voices on the intersection between poverty, race, and environmental hazards come from prisoners living in highly polluted facilities. One example is inmate Jonathan Jones-Thomas who exposed a scandal about massive sewage spills in Washington State's Skykomish River near the Monroe Correctional Complex. While pointing out that acting as a whistleblower about this public health hazard landed him in solitary confinement, he says his efforts did result in *Seattle Weekly* reports on the condition of Skykomish River. Unfortunately, the river, that flows into Puget Sound, is now so full of sewage spills that the dike holding the sewage lagoon is failing.[10]

Another inmate, Bryan Arroyo, revealed his pollution story on Prison Radio, a media outlet broadcast on independent radio stations around the country. Arroyo has spent many years at Mahoney prison in southeastern Pennsylvania where he joined environmental groups in the free world to fight a coal gasification plant near his facility. Arroyo says he never planned to be a "jailhouse environmentalist," but, after becoming aware of this danger, he encouraged 400 fellow inmates to write letters to the Mahoney Township Supervisors. The coal gasification plant was not built, but Arroyo was transferred to another prison, ironically named Frackville.[11]

Following in his mother's footsteps, Robert Gamez became an environmental activist at the Florence prison complex in the Arizona desert. His mother, Linda Almazan, had organized an environmental group because her family was impacted by the Trichloroethylene Groundwater Contamination Area, a military Superfund site in Tucson, Arizona. When Gamez realized his cell was surrounded by a military Superfund site and a proposed copper mine waste pit, he took his mother's advice to apply for the Environmental Protection Agency's (EPA) Environmental Small Grants Program and generate resources for advocacy work inside his prison walls. Both Almazan and Gamez are concerned about the isolation of prisons from mainstream society, as well as the lack of participation by prison staff at environmental conferences and workshops.[12]

The Human Rights Defense Center (HRDC), a 26-year-old advocacy group led by former prisoners, has begun the Prison Ecology Project (PEP) in which prisoners write to HRDC about assorted problems, including black mold infestations; contaminated water; hazardous waste and sewage overflows; risks of floods and extreme heat; and illnesses due to living in overcrowded, toxic facilities. HRDC, located in Florida, reported that the mid-Atlantic sector of the EPA cooperated with inmates and initiated actions against prison pollution in that part of the country. While mid-Atlantic EPA was concerned, other EPA regional offices did not join in the effort and no progress was made.[13]

Inmates who have engaged in protesting environmental problems in their prison systems have often been punished. An example of this occurred at Norfolk prison in Massachusetts when inmates complained about poor physical conditions, including brown and black drinking and bathing water. Frustrated by lack of attention to their complaints, they organized the Deeper the Water campaign. When descriptions of the pollution were sent out into the free world through the prison pipeline, the *Boston Globe* Spotlight team started an investigation. Journalists reported that the drinking water at the prison was full of harmful chemicals, including high levels of manganese and iron, while the guard dogs received purified bottled water. For their action, the men involved in the Deeper the Water campaign were labeled political prisoners, the subject of the next essay.[14]

Notes

1. Interview with parole officer in Chicago, Illinois
2. Governor Rockefeller had national political ambitions, perhaps a reason for his advocacy of harsh drug laws. Previously, the governor had recommended addicts be treated for their drug problems.
3. After the Watergate debacle, advisors wrote that Nixon's drug war had ulterior motives. The President's negative feelings about the African-American civil rights movement influenced him to advocate severer punishment for the sale and possession of heroin and cocaine, thought to be favorites of African-American drug users; Nixon's dislike of pot-smoking hippie protestors against the Vietnam War led him to include marijuana in the War on Drugs.
4. The gap in sentencing guidelines between the use of crack cocaine and powder cocaine has been narrowed in the past years due to federal reforms, but is still not completely even.
5. Victoria Law, "New York Supermax Report Reveals Brutality, Neglect, and Prolonged Solitary Confinement at Southport State Prison," https://www.solitarywatch.org/2017/12/14
6. Ibid.
7. Gene Demby, "Why Does Wisconsin Lock Up More Black Men Than Any Other State?," https://www.npr.org/sections/codeswitch/2013/04/24/178817911/wisconsin-locks-up-more-of-its-black-men-than-any-other-state-study-finds
8. Alexandra Natapoff, *Punishment Without Crime*. New York: Basic Books, 2018
9. "PART 2 of COINTELPRO 25 Years Later: NYC Settles with Former Black Panther Who Was Wrongly Imprisoned," https://www.democracynow.org/2000/12/8/cointel_pro_25_years_later_new
10. Released from Monroe Correctional Complex in 2014, Jones-Thomas found employment as a wastewater manager, and he teaches classes to inmates on how to obtain work in this field.
11. "A Visit with Bryan Arroyo," Prison Radio
12. "Incarceration, Justice and the Planet," http://www.sfbayview.com/2016/05
13. "HRDC's Prison Ecology Project is Cited in a 'Green New Jail,'" https://www.prisonlegalnews.org/in-the-news/2019/hrdcs-prison-ecology-project-cited-green-new-jail/
14. David Abel, "Water at State's Largest Prison Raises Concern," https://www3.bostonglobe.com/metro/2017/06/17/water-state-largest-prison-raises-concerns/xDEkyL3GFwsqag7qvywl3K/story.html?arc404=true

10
The Political Prisoner

On a trip to Ireland, I read the biography of an Anglo-Irish woman, named Constance Gore-Booth Markievicz, who was born in 1868 to a wealthy family in County Sligo and married in 1900 to Polish Count Casimir Markievicz. Besides her role as a wife and mother, Constance was an accomplished artist, actress, and one of Ireland's political heroines.

Constance served five prison sentences in England and Ireland because she opposed the continuation of English rule of Ireland. After her participation in the 1916 Easter Monday nationalist uprising, Constance was imprisoned in Dublin's Kilmainham Jail and condemned to death. However, while fifteen male leaders of the failed uprising were executed, her death sentence was reprieved because of her gender and her aristocratic family connections. Constance was incarcerated in England's Aylesbury prison as a traitor.

After rising at 6 AM, Constance ate a breakfast of six ounces of bread and one pint of cold tea before performing daily labor. Her noon meal consisted of two ounces of meat, two ounces of cabbage, and one potato; a supper of a cup of cocoa or tea and six ounces of bread was served at five o'clock. Prison authorities allowed her one book a week and permission to write one letter a month.[1]

Constance tried to be an obedient prisoner because she knew that those who complained were certified insane and sent to a lunatic asylum. This practice is reminiscent of Lawrence Pope and the seven other Texas jailhouse lawyers who were placed in the Texas mental illness unit in order to discourage their legal activities. In many ways, Lawrence Pope's conditions of incarceration were not that different from those of Constance's. In her letters to her sister, pacifist and poet Eva Gore-Booth, she spoke of the filth and poor food and she stressed that prison only bred criminals and should be abolished. Constance told her sister that the majority of the inmates were insane and she attributed much of their condition to their solitary existence.[2]

As a result of their firsthand knowledge of prison life at that time, the Gore-Booth sisters and their close friend, actress Maud Gonne, became vocal advocates of humane treatment of inmates. All three were also involved in the women's suffrage movement in England and Ireland. The women's movement in America and in England split between those who advocated diplomacy and those who engaged in marches and civil disobedience action. The latter were frequently arrested and abused in the jails in which they resorted to hunger strikes and were force-fed many times a day.

In 1921, after being imprisoned several times, Constance Markievicz's leadership helped bring about independence from Great Britain for most of Ireland's counties, but Irish men and women continued to be incarcerated for protesting the division of Ireland, as well as the unjust treatment of Catholics by the Protestant majority in Northern Ireland. Some, such as famed Bobby Sands, participated in hunger strikes in the 1980s because they were not given special status as political prisoners after their arrests for their Irish Republican Army actions.

Constance Markievicz used her time in prison for moments of renewal and writing. In this way, she provided a model for other courageous disciplined political prisoners, such as Nelson Mandela, Martin Luther King Jr., and Dietrich Bonhoeffer.

Dietrich Bonhoeffer was a Lutheran pastor in Germany who early on opposed Adolf Hitler and, in particular, the Nazi policies of euthanasia and genocidal persecution of Jews. He was active in helping Jews escape to Switzerland and for this he was arrested in 1943 and sent to Tegel prison where he began writing *Letters and Papers from Prison*. A sympathetic guard smuggled his writings out of Tegel.

Bonhoeffer was in touch with German military officers who planned the attempted assassination of Hitler in July of 1944. Despite considering himself a pacifist, the pastor had come to believe that Hitler was so dangerous that he needed to be stopped. While the imprisoned Bonhoeffer could not have participated in the failed assassination attempt, he was sentenced to death for his association with the assassins and for being aware of their plans. In April of 1945, shortly before the collapse of the Nazi regime, the pastor was hung by wire, to increase his suffering.

Dietrich Bonhoeffer's most famous work is *The Cost of Discipleship*, written before his imprisonment. In his book, he denounced what he called "comfortable Christianity" and urged the followers of the Confessing Church movement to have compassion and act in the world against Nazism and other evils. Bonhoeffer is considered a "modern-day martyr" by many Christian churches.

African-American Reverend Martin Luther King Jr. was an admirer of Dietrich Bonhoeffer, as well as of Indian leader Mahatma Gandhi, from whom he adopted his nonviolent approach to fighting for civil rights for minorities in America. Having participated in sit-ins and marches throughout the South, Reverend King of the Baptist church was arrested in Alabama in 1963. In a solitary cell, King penned *Letter from Birmingham Jail* in which he laid the moral basis for the civil rights movement. After his release, he gave his famous "I Have a Dream" speech to 200,000 marchers at the National Mall in Washington, DC.

By 1968, Reverend King had expanded his minority rights movement to include his opposition to the Vietnam War, as well as his support of workers' rights. Because of his stand on justice in so many areas, he was the subject of Federal Bureau of Investigation (FBI) surveillance. In April of 1968, he was speaking in Memphis, Tennessee, to a crowd supporting a sanitation workers' strike when he was assassinated. Americans celebrate King's life each year in January and he remains the iconic spokesman for the civil rights movement in our country, as well as in the world. The Solidarity movement in Poland and the end to apartheid movement in South Africa owe a debt of gratitude to the work of Martin Luther King Jr.

Nelson Mandela, the future leader of South Africa, was strongly moved by the life of Martin Luther King Jr. and he also found hope in literature. Mandela often recited an English poem, "Invictus" in which his favorite line was "I am the captain of my soul." Enduring 27 years at Robbin Island prison for his opposition to the apartheid regime in South Africa, Mandela used his time, after long hours of physical labor, to meditate and to study the Afrikaner language and history in an effort to understand his oppressors. Mandela looked to the future when he would be free to help his countrymen, both black and white, live together. His use of prison time is remarkable and holds a key: if prisons promoted programs that offered some notion of alternative futures to inmates, less violence and mental illness might occur.

Besides Nelson Mandela, many other persons have been incarcerated for their opposition to colonial rule. Filipino Emilio Aguinaldo led a resistance movement against the American takeover of the Philippine Islands after the Spanish-American War of 1898 and was tortured and imprisoned. Historians have cited the American war in these islands as the beginning of the national security state because the country that freed the Filipinos from Spanish rule began using spying, data management, and torture to keep control of the Philippine Islands until after World War II.

One of the most famous opponents of colonialism was Indian leader Mahatma Gandhi, who like Constance Markievicz, stood against British rule. When the Irish won their war of independence in 1921, Gandhi took notice and stepped up his protests. He went to prison on many occasions, but the English, fearing reprisals from his supporters all over India, released him after short periods.

Unlike Constance Markievicz, Gandhi advocated a nonviolent approach, emulating the ideas of Russian Leo Tolstoy and American Henry David Thoreau. Long before Mahatma Gandhi walked to the sea to protest the British tax on Indian salt, nineteenth-century writer, Henry David Thoreau of Massachusetts, engaged in civil disobedience. Opposed to the 1840s Mexican–American War, Thoreau refused to pay his taxes, because, like other northerners, he viewed this war as a southern attempt to increase the territory in which slavery could exist. After a relative paid his taxes and he was released from jail, Thoreau wrote his essay, "Civil Disobedience."

Henry Thoreau's example has guided many American political protesters. One of them, Eugene V. Debs, founded the American Railway Union in the 1890s and organized a boycott of Pullman cars over the issue of pay cuts to the company's workers. As a result, Debs was convicted of defying a court injunction and, after serving six months in prison, he became committed to the international socialist movement. He ran for the US presidency five times on the Socialist Party of America platform and, as a skilled orator, Debs made speeches encouraging young Americans not to volunteer in their country's participation in World War I.

. President Woodrow Wilson denounced Debs as a traitor and he was convicted in federal court under the Sedition Act of 1918. When Debs was sentenced to 10 years in a federal prison, he stated that, while there was one soul in prison, he was not free. Eugene Debs appealed his sentence to the Supreme Court, but the justices supported the Sedition Act of 1918 and Debs's incarceration. In 1920, Debs ran for the presidency of the United States from his prison cell, mirroring Constance Markievicz's election to a seat in the British Parliament on the Sinn Fein ticket while she was incarcerated in an English prison. While Debs's sentence was commuted by Republican President Warren G. Harding in 1921, four years later, he died of cancer, the result of the unhealthy conditions he endured in prison.

When World War II broke out, conscientious objectors, many of them Quakers, spent time in prison for their opposition to the war. However, the most well-known political prisoners during this period were the Japanese Americans who were moved from their homes to internment camps in various parts of our country. At the time, they were seen as possible enemy combatants, conspiring with the imperial government in Japan that had ordered the attack on the American naval base at Pearl Harbor in Hawaii. The US Supreme Court in *Korematsu v. United States* upheld President Franklin Roosevelt's order to create these military internment camps for national security, but this decision was later decried by much of the American public and their representatives.

In the aftermath of World War II, the rise of the Soviet Union led to a strong anti-communist feeling in our country. Americans, mainly Hollywood figures, were called to testify at congressional hearings about their prior memberships in the Communist Party; most were blacklisted and some received prison sentences.[3]

America's engagement in Vietnam created more political opposition. In 1969, a group of activists entered a draft board location in Catonsville, Maryland, and removed records of young men about to be shipped to Vietnam. The group, including two brothers, Catholic priests Daniel and Philip Berrigan, took the government files outside and burned them in garbage cans. Called the Catonsville Nine, the members were convicted of federal charges of destroying US property and interfering with the Selective Service Act of 1967, offenses that earned them three-year sentences at a federal facility in Connecticut.[4]

After being released, Daniel and Philip founded the Plowshares Movement, referring to the Gospel call to turn swords into plowshares. The atomic bombing of Japan in 1945, plus the nuclear arms race between the Soviet Union and America, had produced the movement called Ban the Bomb. Now, the Berrigan brothers led anti-nuclear protests and they were arrested for entering a General Electric nuclear missile site in King of Prussia, Pennsylvania, where they spilled blood on nuclear warhead nose cones.

While the Berrigan brothers have received the most notoriety about their political actions, thousands of Americans have been arrested for civil actions against nuclear weapons and nuclear energy facilities. Operating on the same principles as the Berrigan brothers, an 82-year-old Roman Catholic nun, Megan Rice, along with two companions, broke into the Y-12 National Security Complex in Oak Ridge, Tennessee in July of 2012. The three activists spray-painted anti-war slogans and splashed blood on the wall of the uranium-enriched facility. They were sentenced under the Sabotage Act, passed in World War II, but an appeals court threw this charge out; Megan Rice served three years in prison for the crime of harming government property.[5]

Several members of minority groups, who have protested the lack of civil rights protections, have claimed political prisoner status. Examples are Leonard Peltier of the American Indian Movement and Mumia Abu-Jamal of the Black Liberation Movement; both men have served long prison sentences for crimes that say they did not commit. Because they were vocal about inhumane prison conditions, the two men were placed in total isolation at Marion Federal Correctional Institute. A grassroots movement, urging their release, has been in existence for several years.

In general, little attention is paid to the plight of American political activists. During President Jimmy Carter's administration, Andrew Young, an important African-American diplomat, pointed to the existence of political prisoners in our country, but he was rebuked for this and stepped back his statements. Nevertheless, it is widely known that most political prisoners in the United States, estimated to be over 100 persons, are housed at Marion Federal Correctional Institute in Marion, Ohio, the only level six prison in our country in which inmates are locked down in isolation for 22 hours a day. If their behavior warrants more freedom, they may go to a pre-release unit in which they manufacture weapons for the US military. Because many political prisoners have been incarcerated for actions against American militarism, it is unlikely that they decide to cooperate.

Returning to Irish history, Maud Gonne's son, Sean McBride, who served time in an Irish jail for his opposition to the division of Ireland into two parts, founded Amnesty International, a group that continues to support political prisoners worldwide. Amnesty has often spoken out about inhumane conditions in American correctional institutions, the subject of the next section of this book.

Notes

1. A recent interview, sponsored by GreeneSpace for their program entitled, *Punishment and Profit*, three American former inmates revealed prison conditions very similar to those suffered by Constance Markievicz.
2. Constance's experience as a political prisoner is recorded in her letters held in Dublin archives. *MarkieviczPrison Letters and Rebel Writings* by Lindie Naughton is a good source.
3. A film entitled *Trumbo* relates the story of Dalton Trumbo, one of Hollywood's top screenwriters, who was active in opposing weapons of war.
4. Daniel Berrigan, poet and Jesuit priest, wrote a play, entitled the *Trial of the Catonsville Nine*, which was later made into a film.
5. A book called *Almighty* about Sister Megan Rice's actions was published by *Washington Post* reporter Dan Zak in 2016, and a film entitled *The Nuns, the Priests, and the Bombs* was produced in 2017.

PART III
MAJOR PROBLEMS IN CORRECTIONS

11
Guard Brutality and Corruption

During our interview in 1981, Texas correctional director George Beto said how difficult it was to hire guards who had common sense and were able to interact well with all kinds of people. Dr. Beto felt that guard behavior was among the most important features of any prison system and that a good officer could provide helpful counseling to inmates. In this, his thinking was ahead of his time. Reacting to calls for reform of the low standards set for corrections officers, George Beto lobbied the Texas legislature to fund more educational programs for guards who worked alongside highly educated counselors and teachers, but the legislators turned him down, citing monetary constraints.[1]

During the 1980 *Ruiz v. Estelle* prison lawsuit in Texas, references to widespread guard brutality by inmate witnesses were disputed by prison officials who said that this behavior was isolated and should not be used as an overall indicator. Director Jim Estelle defended his staff as among the best in the country, adding that, while the public would never support guard brutality, he did not expect his employees to be "somebody else's punching bag." When I raised this issue with jailhouse lawyer Lawrence Pope, he said, "Estelle knows about the guard violence and he promotes the people responsible."[2]

Yet, Lawrence Pope admitted that correctional officers face many challenges. While I was a faculty member at Santa Fe Community College in New Mexico, criminal justice students heard lectures from several correctional figures, among them the director of the New Mexico State maximum-security penitentiary, a probation officer, a chaplain, a juvenile judge, and a corrections officer. The latter guest, about to retire after a long career at the Santa Fe penitentiary, emphasized that men and women in his line of work usually prefer administrators who have prior experience as correctional officers and are sympathetic to the problems involved in overseeing inmates. Our guest asserted that when prison administrators show humanity, guards act accordingly and the opposite is true.[3]

One of this officer's major points was that guards work in unpredictable environments and they resent supervisors who ignore the many roles that they take on each day: social worker, confidante, interceder, medic, and incarcerator. In addition, compared to others in law enforcement, correctional officers' salaries are generally low. California and New York offer the best wages and Mississippi and New Mexico the lowest; in Canada, the western provinces are more generous than the Atlantic coast ones. Good benefit packages, in which correctional officers can retire after twenty years on the job, can compensate, but turnover is frequent, with many guards never collecting a pension.

DOI: 10.4324/9781003280279-14

Our guest brought up several challenges that members of his profession face, most of them not understood by the wider community. For instance, correctional officers' varying work shifts play havoc with their sleep patterns and family members must adjust to the officer sleeping at irregular hours. The officer also said that members of his profession, similar to police officers, endure eight to sixteen hours of boredom and isolation, interrupted by periods of danger. Guards must remain alert because they can be subjected to assaults by angry inmates who can turn common objects into weapons. The threat to these men and women does not stop when they exit the prison because guards have been attacked by former prisoners outside the walls. While they witness violence among the inmates, including killings and suicides, our visitor stated that most officers do not receive counseling.

Due to the conditions of their work environment, correctional officers are at high risk for a variety of problems, including divorce, domestic abuse, and suicide. The number of correctional officers suffering from post-traumatic stress disorder (PTSD) is more than double the amount that military veterans report. Some guards have gone public, admitting that they have endured PTSD, even though acknowledging this condition could jeopardize their jobs.

The COVID-19 crisis of 2020 added to the list of problems facing correctional officers. While our visitor mentioned that correctional facilities are especially vulnerable to disease, he did not address pandemics. Due to COVID-19, many guards have taken ill or have died and many have left their profession. Recently, investigative reporters have focused on the chaos at the Rikers Island Jail in Manhattan produced by COVID-19. Without sufficient staff, the atmosphere at Rikers has become far more dangerous. Officials have tried to alleviate the suffering by moving some women and homosexuals to other facilities. One prisoner sent to a Connecticut jail said that the conditions there were far better than at Rikers.

The officer who addressed the class in 2016 ended his talk by suggesting that certain reforms would help, such as creating competency standards and providing additional training for guards, along with improving the ratio of guards to inmates and addressing the high rate of staff turnover, a problem that existed before COVID-19 made it worse.

Interviews with other guards over the years have indicated that correctional applicants are given little training, generally six weeks to six months, and what they learn often does not help them on the job. In addition, officers are trained to have an attitude of "us against them," encouraging them to look upon inmates with suspicion and even contempt. These men and women are told never to be too friendly with inmates, or even with volunteers who are sometimes seen as posing a security risk. Rather than learning how to handle dangerous situations in a nonviolent manner, most correctional officers are instructed in military combat techniques, escalating situations in such volatile environments. Courses in anger management that could reduce guard brutality toward prisoners are rare.

Numerous lawsuits are brought annually against guards for sexual violence, but Tutwiler prison for women in Alabama holds the record for reported sexual abuse of inmates. Attorney Bryan Stevenson's Equal Justice Initiative investigated this situation at Tutwiler, interviewing over fifty women who claimed sexual attacks by guards, with some women becoming pregnant from the rapes. Between 2009 and 2011, six correctional officers were found guilty of criminal sexual abuse, but only one man served more than five days in jail. The women who came forward to complain were punished with solitary confinement and loss of family visitation rights.[4]

In 2014, the US Justice Department investigated conditions at Tutwiler prison and published findings that denounced the women's prison for its "toxic sexualized environment," in which more than one-third of the staff had intercourse with incarcerated women and several prisoners claimed that they had given birth to officers' children. As a result of the Justice Department's investigation, Tutwiler's administrators installed hundreds of security cameras and hired many more female guards, resulting in a prison mainly run by women.[5]

However, Tutwiler is not the only facility dealing with violence by staff. While writing this essay, a headline referring to sexual abuse at a women's prison at Springer, New Mexico, was emblazoned across the *Santa Fe New Mexican* Sunday paper. Six former inmates had filed lawsuits claiming rape and sexual assault by guards and they indicated that they had waited to file charges until they were released because inmates who complained about rapes were ignored, or worse, punished for coming forward. Meanwhile, Springer's authorities maintained that sexual assault claims were on the rise because of a new atmosphere in which inmates felt more comfortable bringing allegations. Attorneys from the American Civil Liberties Union (ACLU) disputed this change in approach and filed civil rights violation complaints, alleging that Springer's authorities dismiss reports of sexual misconduct by guards.

A similar case against the New Mexico Department of Corrections arose in 2019 at the Western New Mexico Correctional Facility at Grants, a women's prison in which an inmate claimed that two guards sexually abused her and that her grievance notification was destroyed by another guard. Later, she was disciplined for flirting with an officer, an action she denied. ACLU, the accuser's defense, told the *Albuquerque Journal* that the state of New Mexico has failed to protect incarcerated women, but acting cabinet secretary for corrections Alisha Lucero responded that the New Mexico Corrections Department takes accusations of sexual misconduct very seriously.[6]

Today, many more females are working as correctional officers than in the past and they can be subjected to harassment and sexual abuse. In 2010, the Equal Employment Opportunity Commission (EEOC) issued a report stating that the federal Bureau of Prisons ignores sexual harassment claims by staff and retaliates against women who come forward with complaints.

In a *New York Times* article on federal prisons posted in November of 2018, the reporter wrote, "Some inmates do not stop at stares. They grope, threaten, and expose themselves. But what is worse, court documents and interviews with female prison workers show that male colleagues can and do encourage such behavior, undermining the authority of female officers and jeopardizing their safety."

The *Times* reporter used as an example a federal prison in Victorville, California, a hub of abuse against female guards. These women were not only subject to large numbers of prisoners masturbating in front of them on a daily basis, but also to male fellow officers encouraging this behavior and rewarding prisoners for their actions. Nevertheless, correctional administrators did nothing to protect the women, and one guard, a single parent, plans to take early retirement due to the harassment.

The reporter continued with a story of a female correctional officer at the Coleman federal prison in Sumter County, Florida, who, after complaining to authorities about harassment by a high-ranking male officer, was told to play down the episode; refusing to do so, this woman was subjected to a medical exam that involved exposing her breasts to a colleague. Despite a $20 million settlement paid by the Bureau of Prisons to female employees at this Florida facility in 2017, reports continued about sexual abuse by both male inmates and guards.

In addition to the federal prison litigation, several state prison systems, including ones in Colorado, Florida, and South Carolina, have faced costly lawsuits because of authorities' failure to provide protection from verbal and sexual abuse. One female guard involved in a sexual abuse case told the *New York Times*, "Nobody will vouch for me. I'm not trusted with anything. They think, 'If you weren't here, we'd have a man in your place.'"[7]

The widespread abuse of male inmates in American prisons exists as well. In 2005, an Illinois male inmate was beaten to death after being accused of insulting an officer. The prisoner was struck 100 times while pleading for mercy; medical help was denied and he died two days after the beating. In 2006, a suit was filed by prisoners against the state of Illinois because they were forced to live in unsanitary, inhumane conditions. Guards stripped one inmate of his clothing and placed him in a solitary cell for six days without a mattress, sheets, toilet paper, towels, soap, or toothpaste.

That same year, a suit was filed in Wisconsin on behalf of an inmate who, because he slept with his head in the wrong direction, was subjected to "behavior modification" treatment in which he was forced to lie naked on a concrete floor in an unheated cell. The man injured himself and became suicidal, but the officials who ordered observation of the inmate did not change the conditions of his confinement.[8]

In the July 6, 2020 edition of the *Washington Post,* Steve J. Martin, who has worked for 50 years in correctional settings and is now a federal monitor at New York's Rikers' Island Jail, wrote an opinion piece in which he said, "Institutional brutality is deeply ingrained and persistent in this country."

Steve Martin said that, while corrections officers have authority to use force to control dangerous inmates, the employment of gas guns, batons, and attack dogs is way out of proportion, especially against African-American inmates with mental disease. One of the cases that Martin cited concerned a 62-year-old confused man, Nick Christie, who was arrested on a nonviolent misdemeanor offense. When Christie became upset and banged on his cell door, guards sprayed chemicals on him 10 times and then held him in a restraint chair with a mask over his face to keep him from spitting. Christie died from cardiac arrest.[9]

In response to such violence, jailhouse lawyer Lawrence Pope said that prisons made monsters out of people. Other voices have given various reasons for widespread guard violence.

In the 1930s, researcher Dr. Frank Tannenbaum commented on the difficulty of being a guard; he suggested that the routine of numbering, counting, checking, and locking inmates produced a "lock psychosis" in guards. Dr. Tannenbaum said that the endless attempts by staff to prevent collusion among inmates resulted in conflict and were the core of guard brutality.[10]

Daniel Glasser in his 1964 book, *The Effectiveness of a Prison and Parole System*, indicated that there were enormous differences in treatment of prisoners by guards; some were humanitarians, some viewed their work as simply a job, and a third group enjoyed having power over other people. Related to the later group, Donald Clemmer, author of *Prison Community*, suggested that some guards used their profession as an opportunity to fulfill their egos by having dominance over a helpless group.[11]

Shortly before African-American inmate George Jackson was killed during his attempted escape from a California prison in 1971, he wrote that any man who enters prison work will quickly lose his sensibilities or his job. Jackson blamed the atmosphere of the prison for destroying anything that is good or healthy in guards and he said that there were two groups of unbalanced people in prisons, one guarding the other. Jackson also believed that prisons are a microcosm of the worst behavior in the free world, including sexism and racism.[12]

New York's Marshall Project, in an effort to bring attention to dysfunctional officer behavior, created an animated short film, entitled *The Zo: Where Prison Guards' Favorite Tactic Is To Mess With Your Head*. Zo is prison jargon for the Twilight Zone, and the film is based on inmate reports for the American Prison Writing Archives, located at New York's Hamilton College. In this Twilight Zone atmosphere, prisoners endure irrational application of rules, difficulty getting ordinary needs met, and retaliation by administrators against those who report misdeeds by guards.[13]

In addition to systemic brutality, corruption on the part of some correctional officers is a major problem. The United Nations, the Center for Advancement for Public Integrity, the

RAND Corporation, and the University of Denver have studied illegal guard activities that include accepting bribes from prisoners for delivery of drugs, cell phones, and other contraband. This corruption stems from the low salaries earned by correctional officers, making payoffs from prisoners very tempting.

A federal inquiry found that corrections officers at the Rikers Island jail earned from $400 to $900 a day smuggling drugs and other contraband into the complex and that this criminality thrived due to lack of adequate supervision by prison administrators. The investigators also discovered that, of over 100 new hires at Rikers Island Correctional Center, 54 men had red flags on their records that should have precluded them from being employed. Due to rampant corruption at Rikers Island, the New York Department of Corrections ordered the installation of hundreds of new security cameras, along with body scanners at prison entrances and exits; this action resulted in a 20% increase in seizures of contraband.[14]

Widespread corruption in prisons led the Federal Bureau of Investigation (FBI) to address contraband smuggling; Operation Ghost Guard, begun in 2014, involved the investigation of the vast Georgia prison system and resulted in the indictment of 46 officers from nine Georgia prisons for smuggling contraband. As drones flew over prison yards with deliveries, guards were paid between $500 and $1,000 per smuggled phone. FBI agents seized 23,000 phones, some of which were used to commit identity theft and other financial frauds, as well as enabling drug trafficking and a kidnapping.[15]

When the FBI probed abuse in the Los Angeles County jails, they collected information on corrupt officials, including the Los Angeles County Sheriff and Undersheriff, who had initiated a plan to derail the FBI investigation. These officials were convicted of their crimes.[16]

Correctional departments' use of private companies to create prison policy documents related to guard behavior is a factor that prevents transparency and accountability. Written, not to protect inmates, but to protect the institution, these vague policy statements make it very difficult to fire correctional officers who should not be in these positions of authority. In response, major cities, such as Oakland and San Francisco, are writing their own policies regarding correctional officer standards in their jails.[17]

Concerned with the myriad problems related to correctional officers' behavior, Colorado psychiatrist Caterina Spinaris offered her services at Desert Waters Correctional Outreach in Florence, Colorado, site of a Supermax prison. Spinaris claims that officers often suffer from what the military calls "moral injury," a term referring to the practice of guards who, after having seen something or done something wrong, try to forget about it. Guilt and shame are the result and these emotions produce PTSD. Dr. Spinaris advises correctional officers to talk about their issues, and, through counseling and reflection, find reconciliation and peace. In this way, she feels they will conduct their difficult daily duties in a more constructive fashion.[18]

Notes

1. Interview with Dr. George Beto, October 1981
2. Molanphy, Helen Clarke, *Idea of Punishment: Texas Prison System as a Case Study*, p. 187
3. Guest lecture by Santa Fe State Penitentiary corrections officer, Fall 2007
4. "Julia Tutwiler Women's Prison," https://www.themarshallproject.org/tag/julia-tutwiler-women-s-prison
5. The documentary film, *Tutwiler*, was produced by the Marshall Project and PBS Frontline and is available on YouTube.
6. "It's Time for a Closer Look at Treatment of Female Prisoners," *Albuquerque Journal*, February 25, 2021
7. Gaitlin Dickerson, "Hazing, Humiliating, Terror, Working While Female in Federal Prison," *New York Times*, November 17, 2018
8. The Marshall Project, https://www.themarshallproject.org/records/50-prison-abuse

9. Steve Martin, "It's Not Just Policing that Needs Reform, Prisons Need It Too," https://www.washingtonpost.com/opinions/2020/07/06/its-not-just-policing-that-needs-reform-prisons-need-it-too/
10. Frank Tannenbaum also served on Wickersham Committee on Penal Reform in 1931.
11. Molanphy, Helen Clarke, *Idea of Punishment: Texas Prison System as a Case Study*
12. George Jackson, *Soledad Brother: The Prison Letters of George Jackson*
13. "The Zo: Where Prison Guards' Favorite Tactic Is Messing with Your Head," https://www.themarshallproject.org/2020/02/27/welcome-to-the-zo?utm_medium=social&utm_campaign=sprout&utm_source=twitter
14. "'A Stain on New York City': As Council Votes to Close Rikers Island, Some See History Repeating Itself," https://www.washingtonpost.com/nation/2019/10/18/new-york-rikers-island-voted-close/
15. "Major Drug Traffic Ring Operated Inside Georgia Prisons Using Drones, Prison Guards," https://www.wjcl.com/article/major-drug-trafficking-ring-operated-inside-georgia-prisons-using-drones-prison-guards/26754197#
16. "Former L.A. Sheriff Is Ordered to Prison for Obstruction," https://www.nytimes.com/2020/01/16/us/lee-baca-prison.html
17. Greene Space Zoom seminar on Profit and Punishment, February 2021
18. "You Have Heard It Said: Visit the Imprisoned But What About Their Guards?," https://www.americamagazine.org/politics-society/2018/05/31/you-have-heard-it-said-visit-imprisoned-what-about-their-guards

12
Wrongfully Convicted

Despite the European Enlightenment that, in some cases, offered a gentler approach to dealing with human imperfection, the English and Dutch Puritan punitive attitude remained strong, emphasizing a God who was wrathful. Harvard College taught the liberal arts, but Puritan preachers dwelt on hell and damnation; those who veered from the "party line" were the first to be harshly corrected. The Puritan emphasis on a strong work ethic remains part of modern American culture, as does its advocacy of retributive justice.

The Salem Trials museum in Salem, Massachusetts, provides extensive information on the 1692 witchcraft trials of the seventeenth century in which Puritan prosecutors based their evidence on hearsay from accusers who held old enmities against the people who they indicted. As a result, close to 200 people, mostly women, were accused of practicing "devil's magic," and were subjected to torture to obtain confessions. Several of the accused died in jail, while 19 were hung on Gallows Hill and a 71-year-old man was pressed to death with heavy stones. Five years later, with the arrests ended by order of the governor of the Puritan colony, judges confessed their error and the General Court ordered a day of fasting to atone for the tragic events in Salem.

The American invasions of Afghanistan and Iraq in the opening of the twenty-first century were a reminder of the Salem witch trials. Abu Ghraib prison in Iraq, a fortress-like facility used by Iraqi dictator Saddam Hussein to torture his opponents, became filled with Moslem men, arrested after Afghani and Iraqi informers accepted payment from US military officers to name terrorists.[1]

In addition, the Central Intelligence Agency (CIA) paid American psychiatrists James Mitchell and Bruce Jessen $81 million dollars to run a sensory deprivation program directed at the Moslem prisoners at Abu Ghraib. When news leaked out about this torture, both men were condemned by the American Psychiatric Association. Meanwhile, one of the American military guards at Abu Ghraib forwarded pictures of the widespread abuse at the prison that included waterboarding, standing for days on end, interrupted sleep, and a variety of sexual acts, especially offensive to male Moslems. Graphic pictures, showing so-called "enhanced interrogation" were presented by CBS News, CBS *60 Minutes*, and other journalism outlets, such as *Life Magazine*.

Thirty-four American soldiers were convicted of abuse at Abu Ghraib, but the higher-ups who ordered the torture were given immunity through linguistic changes in the legal procedures. While George W. Bush's administration maintained that waterboarding was not tortured, the International Red Cross disagreed, declaring that these practices did constitute a form of torture.

The *New York Times* edition of December 5, 2019, featured a front-page story about the first prisoner, Abu Zubaydah, to endure the CIA's torture program, including being waterboarded 83 times. This man, who claims he was never a terrorist, drew pictures of the various torture methods used on him; his attorney, Mark Denbeauz, a professor at Seton Hall University School of Law in Newark, New Jersey, has included these sketches in a 61-page report, "How America Tortures."[2]

Deceased Republican Senator John McCain of Arizona, imprisoned and tortured during the Vietnam War, denounced the use of waterboarding, stating it should never be used by a democracy. John McCain and several senators questioned to what extent these practices arrived at valuable information because many tortured men stated they gave false testimony in order to stop the painful abuses. Other voices suggested that word about the torture of Muslim men only produced more recruits to terrorist organizations.[3]

It is not only abroad that wrongful convictions occur. Many innocent men and women have languished in our federal and state prisons, resulting in suffering that ranks high among the worst tragedies that can happen to human beings. In author John Grisham's novel, *The Guardians*, the fictional story of several innocent men, the narrator says, "Prison is a nightmare for those who deserve it. For those who don't, it is a daily struggle to maintain some level of sanity. For those who learn that there is proof of their innocence, yet remain locked up, the situation is literally maddening."

Studies indicate that the number one reason for wrongful convictions in our legal system is due to false identification by victims or witnesses to the crimes who are mistaken or who lie. One widely publicized example of misidentification occurred in North Carolina in which a white victim of a rape, Jennifer Thompson, identified her assailant in a police lineup as African-American Ronald Cotton. In court, this young woman testified that she was 100% certain that he was her attacker, while Cotton declared his innocence.

After Ronald Cotton spent 10 years in prison, his attorney gathered information that identified another person as the rapist, and, when DNA evidence established Cotton's innocence, he was exonerated by the governor of North Carolina. Feeling guilty, Jennifer Thompson made overtures to Cotton who agreed to meet with her. When she apologized, Cotton, an amazing individual, said he had long ago forgiven her. The pair began making public appearances in which they spoke about false identification and enabled North Carolina to make advances in the way police lineups are organized. It is currently accepted that police officers administering lineups should remain unaware of the suspect's identity so as not to influence witnesses' decisions. Police should also ask witnesses to assess their level of confidence in their identifications and videotaping of the entire process should be routine.[4]

In addition to mistaken identity, sloppy police investigations and unethical prosecutors also contribute to innocent persons being incarcerated. One of these real-life situations was dramatized in director Errol Morris' *Thin Blue Line*, an Academy award-winning documentary that relates the story of an innocent man arrested for the murder of a Dallas police officer.

The Dallas police and the prosecutor ignored strong evidence pointing to a teenager because, due to his age, he was not subject to the death penalty. The defense attorney for the older accused man also believed that authorities were prejudiced against his client because of his long hair and beard. To guarantee that the "hippie" was found guilty, the prosecutor made deals with witnesses who gave false testimony. Meanwhile, the teenager struck again, committing another murder for which he was finally arrested. This second crime could have been prevented by good police and prosecutorial work in the first case; without the notoriety from Errol Morris's film, the innocent man would have been executed because killing any Texas law enforcement officer carries the death penalty.

A 2005 documentary, *After Innocence*, reveals the plight of various individuals who were wrongfully convicted and served long sentences, sometimes on death row. What was most disillusioning about the cases shown in the film was the reluctance of several district attorneys to admit their fault; in some instances, these officials prevented the release of innocent persons, even after all doubt about their guilt was removed.

Along with filmmakers, many attorneys have participated in efforts to free innocent persons. A good example is Bryan Stevenson, a Harvard law school graduate and an attorney who takes on these cases, often pro bono. Stevenson relates to the inmates in a holistic manner, acting as a guide for their intellectual betterment by providing books for them.

Through his southern organization, Equal Justice Initiative (EJI), Bryan Stevenson has saved many lives, particularly innocents on death row. His book, *Just Mercy*, is based on several cases of wrongfully convicted persons and was turned into a major Hollywood film highlighting Stevenson's tireless advocacy, over a period of 16 years, for the release of Alabama inmate-writer Anthony Ray Hinton.

Hinton was incarcerated for 30 years in an Alabama death row cell in which he kept himself sane by starting a book club among other inmates, only to watch them be executed by the state of Alabama. Authorities in Alabama, embarrassed by their mistake in arresting and imprisoning Hinton, set him free, rather than granting him a new trial as directed by the US Supreme Court. Oprah Winfrey chose Anthony Ray Hinton's book, *The Sun Does Shine: How I Found Life and Freedom on Death Row*, for one of her club selections.

Barry Scheck is another dedicated attorney who has made an impact on wrongful convictions by founding the Innocence Project based at Yeshiva University in New York City. Scheck employs law school students to do the legwork, disputing the charges against inmates. While Barry Scheck has affirmed that the number one reason for wrongful convictions is false identification, his investigative work has also revealed issues of forced confessions by police, lying by jailhouse informants, bad forensics science, incompetent defense attorneys, and unfairness in prosecutorial offices in which important evidence is withheld. Half of our states do not require crime scene evidence to be preserved and evidence is often unavailable for reevaluation once a convicted person is incarcerated. Sometimes DNA proves the inmate's innocence, while other times, the Innocence Project discovers information that the local district attorney or the police overlooked, either deliberately or not.

An example of the latter form of injustice was evident in the case of Darrell Siggers who went to prison at age twenty for the 1984 murder of James Montgomery. After spending 34 years in a Michigan prison, he was found innocent. His attorney, Wolfgang Mueller, has filed a lawsuit against a former Detroit police detective and a crime lab technician, both accused of fabricating the evidence against Siggers.

During the pandemic, Darrell Siggers gave an interview to the Pulse Institute about the effects of COVID-19 on Michigan prisoners. He urged Democrat Governor Gretchen Whitmer to release any prisoners who were vulnerable to the virus because it was spreading so rapidly among inmates and staff. He added that, with only two or three doctors for every thousand inmates, and with corporations in control of prison medical systems, the situation was worsened.

Siggers ended his interview by saying, "This is a teachable moment for us all. This virus has revealed some serious deficiencies in our prison system which can be corrected, especially now that we are aware of them."[5]

Wrongful convictions of hundreds of persons head the list of these deficiencies. The work of independent attorneys, as well as the Equal Justice Initiative and various Innocence Projects, including one in Dallas, Texas, has freed many innocent persons. Many receive some financial compensation from the state that imprisoned them, as over half of US states do provide some amount of money for restitution. The other half do not.

Working off the hypothesis that prosecutorial power is too great and is a major cause of wrongful convictions and of overly lengthy sentencing, Emily Bazelon's book, *Charged: The New Movement to Transform American Prosecution and End Mass Incarceration,* analyzes the past history of American prosecutorial zeal, as well as the issue of overworked public defense attorneys. 90% of those charged with crimes in our country require the services of a public defender, a startling statistic, and one that, due to underfunding, results in public defenders taking on excessive caseloads. A US Department of Justice report has shown that the caseloads of 73% of public defenders exceed the maximum recommended limit: 150 felonies or 400 misdemeanors per year.[6]

In line with this report, a representative from the New Mexico Criminal Defense Lawyers Association (NMCDLA) has requested an increase in funding to hire more attorneys at the Law Office of the Public Defender because he says that lack of sufficient public defenders has led to innocent people being sent to prison. In requesting the funding, the defense attorney pointed to the fact that some Missouri public defenders have refused to continue to take on their enormous client load and are suing their state.[7]

John Pfaff's 2017 work, *Locked In: The True Causes of Mass Incarceration,* also focuses on the rise of prosecutorial power, a result of the campaign for law and order and a major cause of America's swollen prisons. Pfaff points to the War on Crime during which legislators took away discretionary sentencing from judges who they declared "soft on crime," and inadvertently put a great deal of power into the hands of prosecutors whose main goal was to win cases and be reelected. These prosecutors increased the use of plea bargaining and advocated harsh bail laws and longer sentences to satisfy voters reacting to crime.[8]

The issue of prosecutorial severity has reached the popular culture through the efforts of Women's National Basketball Association (WNBA) most valued player Maya Moore who took up the case of wrongfully convicted Jonathan Irons. Moore sees prosecutorial reform as essential to a just correctional system because these persons have so much power over sentencing, bail reform, and racial bias, all leading to mass incarceration. In an interview for *Nation* magazine, Moore said, "I love celebrating good leaders, but I also have high standards for leaders because the impact that we have can be really great or it can be devastating."[9]

Attitudes are evolving in the prosecutorial arena. An example is recently elected Philadelphia Attorney General Larry Krasner who citizens turned to because their city had among the largest number of pre-trial persons incarcerated in the nation. A former criminal defense attorney, Krasner viewed the Philadelphia prosecutors' office as too insular and he was particularly interested in hiring candidates, including former criminal defense attorneys, willing to find ways to avoid prosecution in certain cases.

Krasner is a critic of the vast use of plea bargaining, affecting 90% of cases nationally. In addition, he cites as unconstitutional the prosecutorial practice of threatening higher sentences if accused persons choose to go to trial. Similar to other reform-minded prosecutors, Krasner plans to open a sentence review unit because he contends that too many inmates are over sentenced and that their cases should be reviewed to help eliminate mass incarceration. However, Krasner's work is opposed by the Philadelphia police union as being soft on crime and he is also attacked by those on the left who are disappointed that he has not been able to achieve reforms that they favor.[10]

Other forward-looking prosecutors are facing the same kind of opposition in their cities, but, like Krasner, they ignore the criticisms and continue to work at reforming the system. One of these innovators is Brooklyn district attorney Eric Gonzalez. While journalist Bill Moyers and chief medical officer Dr. Homer Venters drew attention to inhumane conditions at Rikers Island, it is district attorney Gonzalez who has kept alive the movement to close the jail and to create smaller facilities in each of the five New York City boroughs.

Of Puerto Rican heritage, Gonzalez was born into a working-class neighborhood in Brooklyn where, after graduating from law school, he was hired as an aide to Brooklyn's District Attorney Ken Thompson. He participated in Thompson's reforms, encouraging nonprosecution of many low-level marijuana possession cases and the creation of the Conviction Review Unit, a model that employs small groups of lawyers, social workers, and investigators to review past cases of excessive sentencing. As the successor to Ken Thompson, Gonzalez announced his intention to seek probation and community service whenever possible, and, over the last five years, his office has also become known for the exoneration of 25 wrongfully convicted persons.[11]

Another example of the progressive approach to prosecution is taking place in San Francisco where the newly elected district attorney, Chesa Boudin, has stated that he reduced San Francisco's jail population by 40% since March of 2020, with the majority of those released elderly and medically vulnerable, or facing low-level charges. Chesa Boudin added that when public safety allows, his office is delaying filing new charges and is working with the courts to expedite scheduled releases for inmates who have solid reentry plans. The San Francisco district attorney's office also avoids detaining people for technical violations of parole, such as missed appointments.

Chesa Boudin has recommended that inmates over the age of 65, who have served 10 years or more, should be released because holding this category of inmates, who have a recidivism rate of 4%, is expensive in ordinary times and puts them at high risk during this pandemic. Due to the pandemic's effects on inmates, the San Francisco prosecutor urged the public to balance the risks of incarceration against the release of inmates.[12]

In Dallas, Texas, a Conviction Integrity Unit, founded by District Attorney Craig Watkins, investigates claims of innocence. Watkins also heads the Innocence Project that has been highlighted in a book titled, *Guilty Until Proven Innocent*, a memoir by Ronald Eubanks who was wrongfully convicted of rape and served over 10 years in a Texas Department of Criminal Justice unit.[13]

Marilyn Mosby, the district attorney of Baltimore, has also joined the ranks of progressive leaders dedicated to exonerating the innocent. Her office of Conviction Integrity Unit is headed by veteran prosecutor Lauren Lipscomb. Lipscomb was recently successful in getting three African-American men, falsely accused of the murder of another teenager, released after they spent over 35 years in prison. Lipscomb found that misidentification, police bullying, and prosecutorial unethical behavior were all involved in the three cases.

These two women, plus Chesa Boudin, Eric Gonzalez, Craig Watkins, and Larry Krasner, are examples of prosecutors who have been elected by voters with a mandate to dedicate themselves to a fairer, more humane justice system. These officials are far different from the New York City prosecutor who refused to bring Rikers Island teenager Kalief Browder to trial when the 16-year-old declared his innocence and refused to plea bargain.

Notes

1. Mark Fallon, author of a memoir, *Unjustifiable Means*, asked, "What better way to enrich yourself, while resolving old grudges, than to finger a neighbor who was your enemy, regardless of his support for either Al Qaeda or the Taliban?"
2. "CIA Prisoner Sketched Agony of His Torture." *New York Times*, December 5, 2019
3. Several Iraqi and Afghani prisoners, presently housed at Guantanamo base in Cuba, have proclaimed their innocence and have been represented by volunteer attorneys in military trials kept secret from the American public.

4. "Ronald Cotton Celebrates 24th Exoneration Anniversary," https://innocenceproject.org/cases/ronald-cotton/
5. "Wrongfully Imprisoned for 34 Years," https://thepulseinstitute/2020/05/16
6. This situation violates the Sixth Amendment to the US Constitution guaranteeing a speedy trial, as well as the US Supreme Court decision in the *Gideon v. Wainwright*.
7. New Mexico Legislature, Santa Fe, NM, January 2019
8. John Pfaff, *Locked In: The True Causes of Mass Incarceration*. New York: Basic Books, 2017
9. Dave Zirin, "WNBA MVP Maya Moore Takes on the Criminal Justice System," https://www.thenation.com/article/archive/wnba-mvp-maya-moore-takes-on-the-criminal-justice-system/
10. "Philadelphia's Top Prosecutor Pursues 'Social,' Not Actual, Justice," https://www.wsj.com/articles/philadelphias-top-prosecutor-pursues-social-not-actual-justice-11578697582
11. "Took a Plea? Brooklyn's District Attorney Will Support Your Parole," https://www.themarshallproject.org/2019/04/17/took-a-plea-brooklyn-s-district-attorney-will-support-your-parole
12. "I'm Keeping San Francisco Safer by Emptying the Jail," https://www.latimes.com/opinion/story/2020-05-06/mass-incarceration-san-francisco-coronavirus
13. Ronald J. Eubanks and Dawn Lynn Anderson, *Guilty Until Proven Innocent: When A Woman Cries Rape: The Life Story of Ronald Eubanks*. Conneaut, PA: Page Publishing, 2020

13
Treatment of Mentally Ill Inmates

In the 1980s, French sociologist Michel Foucault explored the thesis that a variety of institutions are organized around punishment and social control principles; these include military bases, monasteries, and psychiatric facilities, as well as prisons. At various times voices have been raised calling for transparency in psychiatric institutions. For example, in the early years of the twentieth century, social worker Dorothea Dix campaigned to have mentally ill inmates removed from prison.

As a result, public and private psychiatric institutions emerged. When abuses in these facilities were reported by journalists in the 1980s, a second deinstitutionalization movement began; the number of mental hospitals decreased, but plans for sufficient government-sponsored community facilities did not go forward. Mentally ill persons began wandering city streets, encountering police officers, and were often taken to jails and prisons. Dorothea Dix would decry our present society in which a majority of those incarcerated are suffering from some form of mental illness.

Following in Dix's footsteps, New York based Human Rights Watch has issued a report entitled, "Callous and Cruel Use of Force against Inmates with Mental Disabilities," stating that the number of untreated mentally ill persons in prisons has increased dramatically in the last three decades. These persons struggle more than other inmates to adjust to prison environments and they are incarcerated for far longer periods than free world people with similar illnesses are held in psychiatric wards. The mentally ill are denied food and exercise and endure heckling, chemical spraying, and taser attacks after minor infractions of rules. They are often subject to wrongful convictions and find themselves caught in a revolving door between hospital emergency rooms, homelessness, and corrections.[1]

Human Rights Watch has cited various prison lawsuits regarding the mentally ill. In 2006, the state of Colorado was sued because of excessive use of pepper ball guns, restraint chairs, tasers, and electroshock belts on mentally ill inmates. *Mast v. Donohue*, a 2007 case in Indiana, revealed that three mentally ill inmates were placed in solitary confinement under severe conditions. The Indiana prison also punished those who complained of depression by strapping them in leather restraints for four hours at a time. In Florida, the lawsuit, *Thomas v. McNeill*, highlighted how mentally ill inmates were housed in nine-by-seven foot cells and received their food through a flap in the steel door; they were also sprayed with chemical agents for disruptive behavior.

In his speeches around the country, Dr. Homer Venters, former chief medical director at Rikers Island Jail in New York City, has described patients who react to mistreatment by flooding their toilets and by physically cutting themselves. One of his stories involved beatings of the mentally ill by out-of-control Rikers Island guards; these violators later retaliated against medical personnel who spoke out about their attacks.

Dr. Venters has called attention to serious problems that contribute to the mistreatment of the mentally ill. These include covering up numerous physical injuries in fear of lawsuits or of reprisals by guards; the paramilitary setting that puts nurses and doctors in a position of obedience to the administration, rather than to their code of ethics; sexual abuse; unattended health problems; wide use of solitary for the mentally ill; and lack of attention to stemming contagious diseases. Regarding the latter, Dr. Venters sent out a warning about the coronavirus pandemic, saying that, as COVID-19 spreads in prisons, it overwhelms local health systems.[2]

Dr. Venters supports suggestions for reform from Human Rights Watch. These include: providing more long-term state hospital beds and other housing options for the seriously mentally ill; implementing a "guilty and mentally ill" statute as an alternative to guilty and not-guilty; and a call to pass legislation, preventing guns getting into the hands of the mentally ill, that is supported by the National Rifle Association. In 2014, Dr. Venters wrote a book entitled, *Life and Death at Rikers Jail*, in which he made other recommendations, including lowering the incarceration rate to reduce overcrowding and inhumane conditions; firing brutal guards; creating higher use of improved community corrections; reducing the use of solitary confinement; and employing clinical alternatives for the mentally ill.[3]

Dr. Venters also pointed out how frequently the mentally ill resort to suicide attempts. Addressing this same problem, the Washington State Department of Corrections called in Lindsay Hayes, a scholar at the Baltimore National Center on Institutions and Alternatives and an expert on suicide prevention in prisons. Hayes has his work cut out for him because 4% of deaths in federal prisons, 7% in state prisons, and 35% in jails are due to suicide.

After Lindsay Hayes evaluated four Washington State prisons, he wrote a 47-page report in which he was insistent that those in charge of prisoners be properly trained to pick up warning signs of an impending suicide. Hayes recommended that incoming inmates have privacy when they are asked personal questions, such as, "Have you ever considered suicide?" because it is likely that the inmate will lie if too many people are in the room. While Hayes' assessment did not include creating separate facilities for the mentally ill, as many European countries have done, he did urge the prison authorities to eliminate harsh methods, including stripping inmates of their clothes and putting them in safety smocks, as well as separating the inmates from their belongings and escorting them in hand and leg restraints.[4]

The August 23, 2021 edition of the *New Yorker* magazine describes a tragic case of an inmate who committed suicide in a Louisiana jail. Lamar Franks, a 27-year-old African-American man, was stopped for driving a car with overly tinted windows, and he was arrested when the officer found that Lamar had an outstanding warrant from another parish for an illegal $500 check cashed years earlier. Taken to the East Baton Rouge Parish jail, he was placed in a common room with 100 men overseen by two guards. In this chaotic atmosphere, Lamar became unhinged. Other inmates have suggested that he ingested synthetic marijuana, available in the jail, and became paranoid.

Matters escalated and two prisoners later testified that guards took Lamar to an isolation cell and began to beat and pepper-spray him. When his mother Linda Franks called the jail to inquire about Lamar, she was told he had had an accident, but in reality, Lamar had hung himself in a cell that was supposed to be monitored. In their suit against the East Baton Rouge jail authorities, the Franks family complains that Lamar was never given a mental assessment and that his inhumane treatment led to his suicide. Critics have cited East Baton Rouge jail as one of the deadliest in the country.[5]

In this *New Yorker* article, author Eyal Press says, "The absence of transparency is one reason that the stories of people who die in jails rarely make headlines." A Vera Institute spokesperson, Jasmine Heiss, agrees and adds that families of victims are usually too poor to obtain a lawyer to hold the system accountable.[6]

Judge Steven Reitman of Florida's Eleventh Judicial Court in Miami-Dade County studied statistics showing that one in four police shootings involve mentally ill persons. He was frustrated by failing to help a couple provide, within the existing system, attention to their mentally ill son, as well as by his years of sentencing mentally ill persons to prisons in which they receive little or no care. The judge understood that recovery from mental illness requires therapy, medication, but also opportunities for recreation, as well as employment that responds to the patient's capabilities. In response to his experiences with the mentally ill in his courtroom, Judge Reitman developed a pre-arrest divergence program, called Criminal Mental Health Project (CMHP) that opened in 2000.

Instead of charging the mentally ill with a crime, Miami police are trained to deescalate their encounters and see that these persons receive social services, including food, clothing, and medication, as well as transportation to treatment sessions at the Miami-Dade County Counseling Center, rather than being incarcerated. Some of the persons working at the counseling center had once received mental health treatment and now act as peers to help newcomers navigate the system. At first, the CMHP program only dealt with misdemeanors but, after showing success by saving thousands of jail bed days and millions of taxpayer dollars, Miami police have been able to extend the divergence program to felons.

For his work, Judge Reitman has been awarded the Public Official of the Year by a periodical, called *Governing*, and a Rehnquist Award for Judicial Excellence from the National Center for State Courts. He reminisces that his idea for the divergence project was at first scorned by many in the criminal justice community, but they have since realized CMPH's merits and the project has received many grants, enabling the building of a 200-bed facility in what was once a state hospital. Judge Reitman has recently collaborated with congressional expert Norm Ornstein, who lost his son due to mental illness, to produce a documentary, *Defining Insanity*, that indicts poverty and illness as the major reasons why 1.3 million mentally ill persons are incarcerated in our jails and prisons.[7]

Any discussion of the mentally ill in prisons leads to the subject of solitary confinement as so many mentally disturbed people, including the subject of the *New Yorker* article, Lamar Franks, are placed in this type of cell.

African-American Dhoruba Bin Wahib was held in isolation for 23 hours a day for a wrongful murder conviction. Exonerated, he spoke about this experience at a Yale Law School conference.

> Although supposedly you have a right to one hour of recreation, often you don't get it. You get it if the guard feels like it. If he gets mad at someone on the outside, he may walk in and decide he wants to give you a half hour or he might just forget about you all together. Even within that hour you have to make a choice between making a telephone call or taking a shower. Isolation units are not just about the removal of prisoners, but also about destroying people's psychological and physical integrity.[8]

Somewhere between 80,000 and 100,000 American prisoners are estimated to be in solitary confinement, often for minor offenses. While extended isolation causes the brain to change, leading to hallucinations, paranoia, and self-mutilation, prison officials and guards often favor this method for its efficiency. However, many Americans, noting reports from psychiatrists and other experts, view placing inmates in harsh conditions in solitary units for long periods as a national scandal and a counterproductive technique.

The United Nations in the Mandela Rules has called for an almost total ban on solitary confinement, especially for juveniles and individuals with mental illness. Great Britain has completely abandoned the use of solitary after years of placing members of the Irish Republican Army in strict isolation. When the Peace Accord in Ireland largely eliminated this threat, British authorities changed their solitary policy. The British public found it hard to imagine humans spending years without having regular social interaction, or without full access to basic physical activities, such as showering and exercising.

In my interview with the counselor at the Canon City, Colorado correctional facility, he told me that under Colorado Correctional Director Rick Raemisch's leadership, solitary confinement practices in that state have changed dramatically. Because of his approach, Raemisch was awarded the Tom Clements Better Government Award at a dinner sponsored by the Association of State Correctional Officers. Director Raemisch gave a rousing speech and ended by asking, "When did it become okay to lock someone in a room the size of parking spot for 23 hours a day while their demons chased them around the room?"[9]

Raemisch's efforts were influenced by the murder of warden Tom Clements by a psychotic prisoner kept in solitary for many years and released without any counseling. Ironically, Warden Clements, known for being progressive, had started to reform the use of solitary confinement because he took seriously studies showing that inmates, released suddenly from long-term solitary, were more likely to re-offend.

Today, due to Director Raemisch's leadership, a Colorado inmate placed in solitary must have committed a serious offense. Further, this state is using a step-down program in which solitary inmates are allowed outside their cells for a minimum of four hours a day and he or she can participate in social and recreational activities, as well as in programs that improve problem-solving skills. Colorado's new rules mandate that, after release from solitary, prisoners engage in 10 hours of weekly therapy and 10 hours a week on other activities outside their cells. While a few years ago, over a 1,000 Colorado prisoners were held in solitary, today there are approximately 100 persons housed in this type of confinement. In addition, one supermax prison, filled with solitary cells, has been closed, saving lives and a good deal of taxpayer money.

Director Raemisch recognized how important it was to get the support of staff for this change because guards, involved in dangerous work, might view the new system as insecure. While some officers found employment in other states or retired, after the reforms were in effect for a year, Director Raemisch cited improved relations between prisoners and staff, including fewer assaults on guards. The new policy appears revenue-neutral and should improve long-term public safety.

New Mexico officials, using neighboring Colorado as a model, announced efforts to move low-risk inmates out of solitary; they claimed that 6% of the state's inmates are in solitary, down from 10% two years ago, with no measurable increase in violence. However, the American Civil Liberties Union (ACLU) is suing the New Mexico Department of Corrections on the grounds that these figures are false and that solitary confinement should be limited further.

ACLU pointed to the New Mexico case of Isaiah Cabrales who, after seven months in solitary, hung himself from a light fixture in his cell. New Mexico State Representative Antonio Maestas, who has also highlighted Cabrales's tragic end, sponsored a bill in 2015, banning the use of solitary for juvenile offenders, as well as limiting the use of solitary to fifteen days at a time, with no more than 60 days per year for all inmates. Maestas's bill was killed in committee due to the opposition of corrections officers and administrators who argued that solitary is an important tool to control inmates in a prison system that is understaffed.

In 2017, representative Maestas introduced a less ambitious bill banning the use of solitary for pregnant women, juveniles, and mentally ill inmates. While his bill passed both houses of the New Mexico legislature, it was vetoed by then-Republican Governor Susana Martinez.[10]

As more states begin to consider reforms in which solitary inmates are given ordinary chores and participate in group counseling sessions led by trained staff members, rather than being locked up for 23 hours, they are joining the movement to bring humanity to their institutions. Besides this new approach to the use of solitary confinement by prison administrators, members of the American Architectural Society have agreed that their association will no longer engage in the planning of solitary confinement cells. This action from the architects' association reflects the growing interest of ordinary citizens in bringing more humane treatment to troubled persons locked behind closed doors.[11]

Notes

1. "United States Force Against Prisoners With Mental Illness," https://www.hrw.org/news/2015/05/12/united-states-force-against-prisoners-mental-illness
2. The Rikers Island Jail is swarming with COVID-19 cases according to Democracy Now news program.
3. Homer Venters, *Life and Death at Rikers Island Jail*. Baltimore: Johns Hopkins University Press, 2019
4. Overview of Recommendation of Suicide Prevention Expert, Lindsay Hayes, https://www.sccgov.org/sites/soc/document
5. Eyal Press, "Dying Behind Bars," *New Yorker*, August 23, 2021
6. Dhoruba Bin Wahad, "Speaking Truth to Power: Political Prisoners in the United States," https://openyls.law.yale.edu/bitstream/handle/20.500.13051/7728/08_2YaleJL_Lib35_1991_.pdf?sequence=2&isAllowed=y
7. "POY: Rick Raemisch: Executive Director, Department of Corrections," https://www.governing.com/poy/gov-rick-raemisch-poy.html
8. "Stuck in Solitary: Efforts to Reform Prison Practices in New Mexico," *Santa Fe New Mexican*, October 21, 2019
9. GreeneSpace Profit and Punishment Zoom seminar, February 25, 2021
10. Jeff Proctor, "Legislature Passes House Bill to Restrict Solitary Confinement," https://nmindepth.com/2017/03/18/senate-passes-house-bill-to-restrict-solitary-confinement/
11. Julia Jacobs, "Prominent Architects Group Prohibits Design of Death Chambers," https://www.nytimes.com/2020/12/11/arts/design/american-institute-of-architects-execution.html

14
Prison Labor

After arriving in Huntsville, Texas in 1981 to interview Dr. George Beto, a guard escorted me to the main building at the Texas Department of Corrections. As the two of us walked along a gravel path, I glanced across to a large group of white-suited men, mainly African Americans, picking cotton in a field. When several of the men put down their tools and stared at me, a guard on a large brown horse, his rifle slung over his broad belly, shouted to them; the men picked up their tools and looked away. My escort explained that these inmates were growing cotton, more than 3,500 quarter-ton bales annually, used to make uniforms and linens; other convicts were working in gardens to provide food or were part of the industrial program.

In the old days, Texas prisoners, assigned to farm units, worked from 6 am to 9 pm in the heat and cold. By the 1930s, most farmers were using tractors, but mules and horses were still employed in Texas farm units. Planting and harvesting were performed by inmate hand labor and, at the end of their long day, prisoners were forced to run five miles back to their dormitories, while their guards rode horseback. In Texas and other southern states, whippings in the fields to get the men to work harder had a long life. An official Texas prison history book, housed at Sam Houston State College library, includes the following:

> Everyday a number of inmates got whipped in the fields. The officers whipped the inmates with their bridle reins, bull whips, blackjacks and clubs. I was whipped with the "bat" seventeen times. Several times Bud Barnes whipped me. The whoppings were almost unbearable.[1]

During the 1930s, regular reports appeared in urban newspapers about daily self-mutilations; prisoners, hoping to be assigned a lighter duty, cut their heels and were admitted to the Walls hospital, while Warden Lee Simmons responded by saying, "Bring them more axes, boys!"[2]

Working conditions improved somewhat under directors O. B. Ellis and George Beto because agriculture became more mechanized and the industrial jobs created were not as demanding as working long hours in the cotton fields, although that assignment still existed, especially for unruly prisoners and for African-American and Hispanic inmates.

While many reform groups had recommended the use of work release, during my 1981 interview with Dr. Beto, he expressed no interest in reviving a previous work release program that he viewed incompatible with prison goals. Beto said that when their associates in the workplace went out for a beer, inmates returned to prison to be strip-searched and to eat their dinner without a knife. Other critics dislike work release because these jobs do not provide marketable skills for inmates who must hand their wages over to the authorities.[3]

All southern states have employed working conditions similar to that in Texas. Today, Louisiana, a state known for its high per capita incarceration rate, requires inmates to work for a government-owned corporation, Prison Enterprises. The men are paid between .02 and .20 cents an hour, wages that were set in the 1970s. To survive, many Louisiana prisoners, like others in the South, participate in an underground economy in which inmates barter for various services, including haircutting, book lending, and shirt-pressing.[4]

Harsh labor practices in the southern states have spread nationwide, with northern states forcing inmates to work for low wages for major corporations. Approximately one-half of northern state inmates either run the prison facilities, or make products for the government and the private sector. As an example of the latter, New Jersey inmates receive $1.25 an hour, working for several companies, including Chevron, Motorola, Nordstrom's, and Target, and are often sent to solitary confinement if they refuse to work due to illness. In addition, the state gets a kickback from the corporations, while the prison workers are not eligible for Social Security or other benefits. Another example of inmate costs are payments to New Jersey for a 15-minute deathbed visit or a 15-minute visit to a funeral home. Besides the state's 10% charge on every commissary purchase, New Jersey has 22 fines that prisoners pay when they are sentenced, charges that can result in debts to the state when they are released.[5]

Broad use of cheap prison labor exists in the Southwest region as well. According to Joe Brown, former director of the New Mexico State penitentiary here in Santa Fe, close to $3 million is deposited annually in the New Mexico prison system's coffers due to inmate labor. New Mexico Corrections Industries coordinates prison labor throughout the state, with inmates making chairs and desks for the Nambe pueblo, lockers for the Santa Rosa Fire Department, and pews for Holy Cross Catholic Church in Las Cruces. One hundred companies have purchased products made by New Mexico prisoners and many state agencies, especially district courts, rely on their products. What is rarely mentioned is that these men and women work for a few dollars a week, often under difficult conditions.[6]

Undoubtedly, good results can occur from prison labor. The New Mexico State penitentiary does offer opportunities to work in small industries, including a bakery and a crafts shop, along with a vegetable garden maintained by over a dozen nonviolent inmates whose produce is used in preparation of prison meals. Besides offering educational opportunities tied to the University of California at Berkeley, San Quentin prison administrators in the Bay Area claim to have developed work opportunities that can translate to jobs in the free world. A well-publicized example is an inmate at San Quentin who, after working for years with a free world podcaster, was able to continue broadcasting with her after his parole.

Other less positive stories exist. When California forest fires broke out in November of 2018, many prisoners, including women and youth, were recruited to the CalFire program, making one dollar an hour and receiving two days off from their sentences for each day worked. Because incarcerated workers are not protected under any work safety regulations, these inmates, returning with broken bones, burns, and extreme exhaustion from fighting fires during 24-hour shifts, received little treatment. Despite participating in this dangerous work, as ex-felons, California's inmate firefighters were unable until very recently to obtain a state license to join a fire department.[7]

The idea of the work ethic in prisons has its roots in the Puritan philosophy in which hard labor for the incarcerated was viewed as a proper part of punishment and as a means of preventing what some called "Satan's Mischief." This belief has continued long after society dismissed religious references to a devil. Others thought it inhumane to allow prisoners to be idle, and that, by working, prisoners would remain in good psychological and physical condition. When the work was hard, useless, and monotonous, this discipline was viewed as part of the deterrent purpose of prison, as well as a means of rehabilitation. Those who believed in retribution felt that interesting work meant rewarding those who were sent to prison. In reality, useful or interesting jobs are not that plentiful in prison settings and are only offered to a few select prisoners.

Monotonous work can prevent prisoners from forming ordinary social relations common in free communities, and dull, arduous work, such as picking cotton, may only serve to lessen interest in working after release from prison. For the majority of prisoners, part of the lower class and with few skills, menial work does nothing to enhance their chances of gaining useful employment in the free community. In my interview with a former inmate who had spent years in a Texas prison unit, he said that, because his bricklaying work only involved learning one function of the trade, this experience did not enable him to become a skilled bricklayer on the outside.[8]

While US courts upheld the requirement for inmate labor, labor unions in the northern states fought against this practice because prisoners, receiving low pay, produced an unfair advantage over free world workers. During the Great Depression, Congress forbade industrial work in federal prisons but, at the outbreak of World War II, prisoners were employed making war material.[9]

In 1979, Congress passed the Prison Industrial Act that did away with state labor rules and encouraged prison systems to employ inmates. Under the Prison Enhancement Certification Program, 38 states provide certification for joint public-private industries that can undercut unions and local businesses. Examples are British Petroleum's use of inmates to clean up the Deepwater Horizon oil spill in 2010 and the prison-raised tilapia industry run by Whole Foods, now owned by Amazon. While large corporations have seized this opportunity for cheap labor, representatives of small manufacturers are concerned that their members have to compete with these corporations, as well as with prison workers and foreign laborers who produce less expensive products.[10]

Progressives, such as Charles and Pauline Sullivan of Citizens United for the Rehabilitation of Errants, advocate for more companies to offer work that pays prisoners decent wages and is transferable to the free world, similar to what is available in parts of Europe. However, the dominant attitude towards inmate labor has always been the one held by most prison authorities. For example, Texas prison director George Beto felt that unpaid work was important for the inmates to learn discipline and to make a contribution to their maintenance. At the American Correctional Association conference in 1970, Beto said, "The tax-conscious constituents will demand it."[11]

A major problem with unpaid or low-paid prison labor is that most inmates come from the lowest classes in our country. According to the *Sojouners* magazine of November 2018, the average amount an inmate spends on commissary items is about one thousand dollars annually, while these inmates earn between $200 and $600 a year. Many inmates' families, also in the lower income bracket, find it difficult to help with prison costs, such as expensive telephone calls, medicines, and personal sanitary items.

Sojourners Magazine reported the following: 34% of families with incarcerated loved ones said they went into debt to pay for phone calls or visitations; 18% of families were evicted, or denied public housing once their loved ones returned; 50% of family members had negative health impacts due to the incarcerations. Besides *Sojourners*, two prisoner advocacy groups have researched the costs borne by families who help their incarcerated members. The Prison Policy Initiative (PPI) claims that families spend $2.9 billion a year on commissary purchases and phone calls, while the Marshall Project surveyed 200 families who all said they spend hundreds of dollars a month to help inmate relatives.

These families are finding that, instead of being able to ship items from discount stores to inmates, prison officials are demanding that the items be purchased by the companies operating in the institutions and charging higher prices. In addition, since the Great Recession of 2008, authorities have been increasing the number of items that must be purchased in prison commissaries from corporate entities engaged in price gouging. While free world people can buy a pair of $30 sneakers at a discount store that will last for years, prison-purchased shoes cost $45 or more and only last six months.

Prison authorities maintain that buying internally helps prevent contraband entering the institutions, but family members say the authorities are more motivated by the kickbacks they receive from the corporations. Many officials in government-run prisons not only want their facilities to be self-sustaining, as Texas achieved, but also to be profitable. Their model has become corporately run prisons.[12]

The low wages and the high costs of prison-purchased goods have led to resistance among inmates. An example occurred in the Alabama prison system. The Alabama prison system, housing 24,000 inmates, twice as many persons as its prisons were originally built to hold, is among the most violent and dangerous in the country, with many prisoners armed with cell-made weapons. As an example, in 2016, officer Kenneth Bettis was fatally stabbed by an inmate at the Holman unit for refusing to give him an extra tray of food, an event that led Holman correctional officers to declare a short-term informal strike.

Alabama's Holman unit has also been the locale of three labor protests; inmates went on strike in 2014, 2016, and 2018 against what they termed "modern slavery." Besides asking for better work conditions, these inmates suggested other reforms: improved living conditions to decrease violence by inmates and guards; an end to life imprisonment without parole; the provision of funds for rehabilitation services; and voting rights for inmates while they are incarcerated. Two prisoners, Melvin Ray and Robert Earl Council, who led the Holman work stoppages in 2014 and 2016, released statements to the press before they were placed in solitary confinement in 2018.

Council said, "We will not work for free anymore. Without us, the prisons that are slave empires cannot function.... Prisons at the same time, charge us a variety of fees, such as for our identification cards or wrist bracelets, and impose numerous fines. They charge us high phone and commissary prices."

Ray said, "We do not believe in the political process ... we are not looking to politicians to submit reform bills ... we will rely only on protests inside and outside of prisons and on targeting the corporations that exploit prison labor and finance the school-to-prison pipeline."

Ray went on to plead for a national Stop Campaign against McDonald's because this corporation is accused of exploiting prisoners who process beef and package bread, milk, and chicken products.[13]

Spearheaded by members of Jailhouse Lawyers Speak, the August 2018 work shutdown at Holman unit began on the anniversary of the shooting of Black Panther George Jackson in a California prison and ended on the 47th anniversary of the Attica, New York prison uprising. The Alabama strike was backed by the Industrial Workers of the World and was also supported by the American Civil Liberties Union and the Vera Institute for Justice of New York. These groups pointed out that, despite prison labor amounting to a $2 billion industry, the incarcerated are not properly paid, nor compensated for workplace injuries.

The methods used during the 2018 Alabama strike included refusal to work, hunger strikes, and sit-in protests. A boycott of prison commissaries, known as "Redistribute the Pain," targeted the use of collect phone calls and other purchases that profit both private and state-run companies. This boycott was the most subversive way to make the prisoners' point, while other methods, such as a work stoppage, led to retaliation by prison officials who authorized solitary confinement for the offenders or movement to harsher facilities.

It was unclear how far the strike spread nationwide. Some news outlets claimed that seventeen states participated, but officials acknowledged work stoppages in only four states besides Alabama: Washington, California, South Carolina, and Ohio, as well as in the city of Halifax, Nova Scotia. Nevertheless, unlike previous prison strikes in 2014 and 2016, the media gave wide coverage to the 2018 movement, calling it the largest in US history and one that earned some free world labor union support.

After the strike ended, the US Justice Department released a 53-page report that indicted the Alabama system for "severe, systemic, and exacerbated" violations of the cruel and unusual clause of the Eighth Amendment. According to the Justice Department, the main problems were understaffing and overcrowding in a system in which a limited number of Alabama guards are forced to work for 16 hours shifts, supervising prison units filled to 182% of capacity. Guards, as well as prisoners, had issues over working conditions.[14]

The prison industrial complex grinds on.

Notes

1. Molanphy, Helen Clarke, *Idea of Punishment: Texas Prison System as a Case Study*
2. Ibid.
3. Interview with Dr. George Beto, October 1981
4. "Cheap Inmate Labor Bothers Some Louisiana Lawmakers," https://www.nola.com/news/politics/article_f8dcdb03-98dd-54e9-b058-88230a4e47e0.html
5. Prison Policy Initiative: New Jersey Profile, https://www.prisonpolicy.org/profiles/NJ.html
6. Lecture by New Mexico State Penitentiary director Joe Brown in Santa Fe, Spring 2005
7. More recently, California Governor Gavin Newsom has announced a review of conditions for inmates at CalFire.
8. Interview with prisoner at Texas Department of Corrections, December, 1981
9. Today, federal prisoners represent the largest group manufacturing weapons of war.
10. Chris Hedges, in his book, *America: The Farewell Tour*, points out that prisoners are ideal employees for corporations. They receive low wages, with no benefits such as sick pay or injury protection. They cannot earn pensions or vacation time. If they protest, they are placed in segregation units. In addition, the author says that corporations oppose any reforms that reduce the available labor supply in the prisons.
11. Molanphy, Helen Clarke, *Idea of Punishment: Texas Prison System as a Case Study*
12. Julie Bender, "Who Pays for Prisons?" https://sojo.net/magazine/november-2018/who-pays-prison
13. "Major Prison Strike Spreads Across U.S. and Canada as Inmates Refuse Food," https://www.theguardian.com/us-news/2018/aug/23/prison-strike-us-canada-forced-labor-protest-activism
14. "The Everyday Brutality of America's Prisons," https://newrepublic.com/article/153473/everyday-brutality-americas-prisons

15
Privatization of Corrections

Over 20 years ago, renowned social scientist Eric Schlosser wrote an essay for the *Atlantic Monthly* in which he compared the American reaction to crime to the military expansion of our country after World War II. Schlosser stated that the military-industrial complex, growing out of fear of the Soviet Union, was similar to the prison industrial complex that emerged out of fear of crime. He viewed both reactions as excessive, costing the public trillions of dollars and saddling our country with debt that produced little security. Schlosser pointed out that these military and correctional expenditures were backed by various members of our society who stood to gain, even though the success of the military and the penal programs was questionable.

Economic issues are often at the heart of the dysfunction in our correctional system.

The Rikers Island scandal in New York City shone a light on the issue of money bail that affects the largest population of jail inmates, the poor. Private companies manage the bail industry and, through lobbying and campaign financing, discourage legislators from passing sensible bail reform. Instead, many poor people, who may pose no public safety threat, spend long periods in jails. The companies also oversee probationers and run services, including GPS ankle monitoring, phone calls, and drug testing. At this time, more private money is rushing to fuel artificial intelligence systems that may determine who should be paroled.

Despite the influence of private companies who advocate for strict bail laws, governors in California, New Jersey, and New York have made bail reform a top priority and all three backed legislation that would eliminate money bail for those who cannot afford it, as long as they do not constitute a danger to the community.

Inmate advocacy groups, such as the Southern Poverty Law Center, have also focused on the poor medical care generally provided for inmates by privately-run, profit-driven corporations. Doing time can mean that inmates' health is put at serious risk for economic reasons, despite the fact that mission statements for American prison systems include a clause saying that no inmate should endure physical harm while incarcerated.

In California, the *Plata v. Davis/Schwarzenegger* lawsuit of 2005 revealed that 10 inmates endured severe and unnecessary pain, injury, and needless death from prison officials' indifference to their various health needs. A 2007 Nevada prisoner lawsuit was based on a report showing a shocking lack of medical care for prisoners, including a diabetic who died due to being denied medication for three years and an inmate who, after suffering a stroke, received no care or therapy and became paralyzed. In Alabama, diabetic patients suffer from blurred vision, nervous system failure, kidney damage, dizziness, and pain due to lack of care. One Alabama inmate is confined to a wheelchair because inattention led to the loss of his toes.[1]

In 2013, Tuesday Olson, a pregnant mother of a small child, was brought to the La Plata Jail in western Colorado for failing to appear for a traffic violation. Placed in the jail cell, she began to miscarry, but her cries for help were ignored; as she grew sicker, time was wasted while she was tested on how much blood she was losing. Finally, when Tuesday collapsed, she was brought to the Durango, Colorado hospital in handcuffs. After she lost the baby during a Caesarean operation, Olson was taken back to jail and put in isolation. For days, she suffered intense pain, but was again ignored. When Tuesday Olson threatened a lawsuit, she was taken back to the hospital where she was treated for an erupted fallopian tube and the loss of one ovary.

By the time Olson sought help from the American Civil Liberties Union (ACLU), it was too late to sue La Plata County, but the ACLU began broadcasting her story in hopes of saving other women from such serious neglect. After ACLU members tracked pregnant women in Colorado jails, they contacted the *Denver Post* and reporter Diana Sanchez wrote two feature stories, one about a woman who gave birth in a Denver County cell by herself and the second about a woman whose baby emerged in a toilet at El Paso County Jail in Colorado Springs.

On an Internet site, Tuesday Olson says, "Whether they're there on a murder charge or a traffic violation, nobody deserves to go through what I went through. It's not right, it's not human."[2]

Similar highly inadequate medical treatment led one nurse at a New Mexico prison unit to become a brave whistleblower. In 2014, this nurse was joined by New Mexico Behavioral Health Bureau chief Dr. Blanca McDermott. Dr. McDermott filed a report stating that Corizon Health Services was not providing the contractual care for mental patients in the New Mexico prisons that it had signed up for and that the New Mexico Department of Corrections (NMDC) did not monitor its inmate medical care contract with this private firm that charged over $3 million a month. For revealing these problems, Dr. McDermott was fired from her position on the grounds that she was involved in hiring discrimination and insubordination. The doctor is suing NMDC, seeking reinstatement and twice her lost wages, as well as damages for whistleblower harassment. Dr. McDermott's lawsuit provides a cautionary tale, indicating that the poor state of New Mexico pays health providers a large amount of money, yet the inmates receive inadequate care.[3]

Overcrowding and the depressing circumstances of incarceration add to New Mexico's high rates of drug abuse among inmates and worsen the medical situation. After a drug-related epidemic of Hepatitis C between 2012 and 2015, 138 New Mexico inmates filed lawsuits against Corizon. This medical company, which has prison contracts in 20 states, has been sued approximately 1,000 times by inmates across the country. Medically related lawsuits against other private prison health providers, such as Wexford Health Sources and Centurion, have also increased dramatically.[4]

Corizon has an annual revenue of $1.4 billion but, rather than provide decent care, this corporation has paid millions in lawsuit settlements in states as disparate as Oregon, Florida, Idaho, and Kansas. New Mexico's neighbor, Arizona, with the fifth-highest per capita rate of incarceration in the nation, also employs Corizon as its health provider. Despite the difficulty of having prison lawsuits addressed in the courts, US Magistrate Judge David Duncan is overseeing a class-action suit, regarding the poor quality of Corizon's health care in the Arizona prison system.[5]

Balla v. Idaho State Board of Corrections is a decades-old suit in which several prisoners in that western state claimed that Corizon's health care system violated the cruel and unusual punishment clause of the Eighth Amendment. Then, in 2012, a federal judge ordered Dr. Mark Stern, a medical authority, to make an evaluation of Idaho's prisoner health care. In his 94-page report, Dr. Stern stated that, because Corizon was highly neglectful in all aspects of inmate care, the Idaho prison system was violating the Eighth Amendment by employing Corizon as its health provider. Opposed to transparency, Idaho prison authorities tried to convince the federal judge to keep the report private, but he refused.

In 2017, a new Idaho prison suit against Corizon was brought by inmate Gary Merchant, suffering from Crohn's disease and congestive heart failure. Merchant was diagnosed with a leg infection but, when no improvement occurred, he asked to be taken to a hospital. Because his five written requests and seven oral ones failed to get results, he swallowed a small pencil-sharpener blade to gain attention. Hospitalized, doctors performed an operation to remove the blade and part of his intestines, but, when Merchant acquired a flesh-eating infection in his leg, along with septic shock, doctors were forced to amputate his leg. Back in his prison cell, Merchant waited seven months for Corizon to provide him with a prosthetic device for his leg; when the prosthetic proved to be unfit, Merchant had to resort to a wheelchair. At this time, the Idaho prisoner is suing the Corizon medical staff at the prison for physical suffering that could have been avoided.[6]

New York City's justice advocacy nonprofit, Greene Spaces, advanced the work of investigative reporter Danny Robbins, who broke open a health-related prison case in Georgia. Over a period of nine years, an unqualified doctor, sued for wrongful death in a New York hospital, was allowed to work in two Georgia prison units because authorities at the corporate medical company did not properly vet him. Due to his lack of qualifications and the private company's failure to provide sufficient funds for care of patients, at least nine women in this doctor's care suffered harm or death. While this man was eventually fired for lying on his application to the Georgia medical authorities, he has applied for a license in New Jersey that is still pending. Families of his malpractice victims received two million dollars from the state of Georgia.[7]

Part of the health care problem is that prison administrators, when brought to court, align with the corporate providers and cry poverty as an excuse for lack of basic services. In addition, these authorities have received backing from the courts. The US Supreme Court in the 1976 Texas suit, *Estelle v. Gamble*, held that requiring severely injured plaintiff, J.W. Gamble, to work did not rise to the level of cruel and unusual punishment. Further, the US Supreme Court, in both *Rhodes v. Chapman* (1981) and *Wilson v. Seeter* (1991), ruled that the US Constitution does not mandate comfortable prisons. The judges in the latter case stated that prison fiscal costs can overrule cruel and unusual claims of harsh physical conditions, including insufficient medical care.

In addition to privately-run health services, several American prisons, corporately owned and administered, house approximately 10% of the prison population. New Mexico has a high percentage of private prisons, as do many southern states. Miles away, the state of Hawaii's underfunded prison system led officials to send large numbers of inmates to mainland private prison facilities, far from their families and their accustomed culture.[8]

Begun as overcrowding exploded, these private prisons were expected to provide more efficiency and lower costs, but they are now viewed as more costly to the public and less safe for both prisoners and guards than state-run correctional facilities. While these private prisons incarcerate only a small proportion of prisoners and, to save expense, only those eligible for minimum- or medium-security, their owners have powerful voices and lobby to keep themselves in business by urging the continuation of harsh sentencing, as well as the War on Drugs. This process affects the entire prison system and hampers reform.

However, the recent focus on private prison injustices takes attention away from the political benefits that elected officials of both parties have earned by being tough on crime; the campaign to end private prisons also distracts the public from the large amount of money earned by private contractors and vendors in publicly-run prisons. In addition, lobbying efforts by public correctional officer unions, who often oppose reforms that could reduce the prison population, are rarely revealed to the public. Nevertheless, concern about the negative aspects of privately-operated prisons and jails has become a major focus in America.

A journalist from *Mother Jones* magazine is responsible for bringing national attention to private prisons by going underground and becoming a guard at the Winn facility in Louisiana, owned by Corrections Corporation of America (CCA), now CoreCivic. Shane Bauer's book, *American Prison: A Reporter's Undercover Journey into the Business of Punishment*, based on his feature stories in *Mother Jones* magazine, is explosive and underlines the importance of investigative journalism relative to penal matters.[9]

When Shane Bauer decided to apply for a correctional officer position, he and his editors at *Mother Jones* agreed that, if he was asked about his previous jobs, he would acknowledge being a journalist. Without inquiring about his prior experience, the representatives of the Winn facility offered Bauer a position during his initial interview. After Bauer accepted the $9-an-hour guard job, he was given a brief computer training session to acquaint him with the work of overseeing 352 inmates in chaotic and dangerous circumstances.

In *American Prison*, Bauer tells the reader that each inmate at Winn was housed for $25 a day, far below the national average, while CCA was supplemented by taxpayers for $38 a day per prisoner. This set fee, per detainee per night, is in line with other private detention companies who have fixed long-term contracts with the government in which they are guaranteed payment for a minimum daily headcount. While many critics are most upset by the profits these corporations enjoy, their fixed contractual agreements with the government have the most negative effect because they contribute to mass incarceration.

The extreme profit-taking by private prison companies, in which owners reap revenues of nearly $4 billion annually, does not include proper recompense for guards or humane treatment of prisoners. In addition, recidivism rates in these facilities are high and the taxpayer pays the bill. The large profit-making at the top mirrors business enterprises in the free world in which the ratio of corporate executives' salaries has become many hundreds of times greater than that of their labor force. In order for corporate administrators to enjoy these large salaries, the management at Winn private prison in Louisiana did not provide decent medical care, psychological services, or educational and vocational training; reentry programs were unknown. As a result of the cost-saving measures, Bauer observed cases of severely ill inmates who, because they were not hospitalized, grew worse and, in some cases, died.

Working within this unjust system, Bauer decried the insufficient staff and the minimal amount of security provided. He indicated that guards, mainly young and poorly educated, on their first job after high school, were unable to deal with the harshness; many of them left Winn after a brief time, increasing instability. Others became indifferent to the conditions around them or were tempted to supplement their low-paid jobs with payments from inmates for the receipt of drugs or cell phones. While there was a great deal of enmity between guards and prisoners, Bauer wrote that their one area of mutual agreement was the fact that corporate heads at CCA exploited both groups.

Violence was epidemic at Winn, consistent with federal studies that found a 28% higher rate of inmate-on-inmate attacks in private facilities than at government-run prisons. While the corporation reported five stabbings for the entire year, Bauer witnessed 12 stabbings in his first two months of employment, and, in February of 2016, so many attacks occurred at Winn that the inmates were placed on lockdown. Bauer discovered other documents doctored to conceal the high rate of suicides at the prison, and he was disturbed that inmates placed on suicide watch were left naked and received no decent food, a technique used to discourage other prisoners from seeking help when they became depressed or suicidal.

Despite the suffering around him, during his four-month observation, Bauer found he became less and less caring of prisoners' conditions. Reflecting on this, he compared his behavior to volunteers in the Stanford University Prison Experiment who, acting as guards, grew more and more abusive to people posing as inmates. While Bauer was never brutal, he reported that he did develop a cavalier attitude towards the prisoners who he described as manipulative.

When reports of lack of security and undue cost in privately-run federal prisons made the headlines, the Obama administration initiated a policy of gradually ending these institutions. However, the Trump administration overturned this order, causing stock prices for private prisons to rise. The Biden administration is reviewing federal use of private prisons and some states, such as California and Colorado, have made efforts to end private prisons.

Denver, Colorado, has closed down two privately-run community corrections centers, but the city did not reopen them as publicly-run entities. Instead, inmates from the centers were dispersed to crowded jails. The GEO group, perhaps seeing the handwriting on the wall, has closed down Centennial South, a medium-security prison in Colorado Springs. Once again, the state of Colorado decided not to take over the facility and sent hundreds of prisoners to overcrowded jails. Prisoners from Centennial South now sleep on temporary plastic beds in the hallways of these facilities, hoping the situation will be remedied.[10]

At the end of *American Prison*, Shane Bauer gives the reader an account of the man who owns CoreCivic. Don Hutto began his career as a warden at the Texas Department of Corrections' Ramsey plantation unit in south Texas. In his profit-based centers, Hutto, a billionaire, uses the Texas control model and exercises a bottom-line mentality in terms of services for inmates. During the 1980s, Hutto developed the first private facilities for detaining immigrants; today, these detention centers make up 25% of his business and are concentrated in the South and Southwest of our country.

As calls for decreasing or eliminating private prisons for criminals rise, other private operators are depending on incarcerating asylum seekers from Mexico and Central America. The 1980s Central American poor people's uprisings and resulting civil wars created powerful right-wing leaders who became high-ranking drug cartel members. Along with lack of employment, oligarchic governments and environmental destruction, violence from these drug cartels is a major motivation for thousands of people from Honduras, El Salvador, Nicaragua, and Guatemala to seek asylum in America.

Since 2010, Congress has mandated that the Department of Homeland Security provide 34,000 beds for asylum detainees and the number was raised to 50,000 in 2019. Over the last decade, the immigrant detention network has held an average of 400,000 people each year and, in border states like Texas and Arizona, asylum-seekers are keeping privately-run detention centers filled. The horrendous conditions in these facilities caused one federal judge to order improvements, such as toilet accommodations, and another judge scolded the Trump administration for allowing companies to house immigrants in buildings that were never meant to hold people for such long periods of time.

A 2019 edition of the *Catholic Worker* included a reporter's interview of a 15-year-old El Salvadoran male, living in a border detention center, who said the following:

> A Border Patrol Agent came in our room with a boy and asked, "Who wants to take care of this little boy?" Another girl said she would take care of him but lost interest after a few hours, so I started taking care of him yesterday. His bracelet says he's two years old. I feed the two-year-old boy, change his diapers and play with him. He is sick. He has a cough

and a runny nose and scabs on his lips. He was coughing last night so I asked to take him to the doctor and they told me the doctor would come to our room but the doctor never came. The little boy I am taking care of never speaks. He likes me to hold him as much as possible.[11]

Private detention centers were also in the news for not providing medical assistance for immigrant detainees suffering from COVID-19 and a grassroots movement urging their release built through street protests and pressure on politicians. Using social media, more Americans have joined the call to improve conditions for these detainees who are facing enormous obstacles.

Added to these stories about human abuse, unethical financial arrangements by various private detention companies caught the attention of the media immediately after the Trump administration began separating immigrant children from their parents. A New York Times headline of December 21, 2018, read: "Migrant Shelter Provider is Under Investigation." The article said that the Federal Bureau of Investigation (FBI) had discovered misuse of federal money by Austin-based Southwest Key Programs, a group that detains 5,000 of the 14,000 children in its shelter facilities in California, Arizona, and Texas. One detention center, officially cited for inhumane treatment, holds 1,400 children in a converted Walmart Supercenter in Brownsville, Texas.[12]

The FBI investigation of Southwest Key centered on the fact that the chief executive officer earned $1.5 million, far more than the federal salary cap of $157,000. The owner's wife earned $500,000 and the chief financial officer $1 million, while both the CEO and CFO used personal property for 2 of the 24 shelters. Southwest Key is not the first corporation to be investigated, as International Educational Services also lost its federal contracts for similar reasons.

Greed plays a major role in the retributive approach utilized by the American penal system, as well as in maintaining mass incarceration.

The final essays in this book examine efforts by legislative bodies, court mandates, prisoner protests, changes in penal administration, influences from outside the United States, and the implementation of restorative justice principles to bring much-needed humanity to correctional facilities and to tackle the problem of mass incarceration.

Notes

1. "Profits vs. Prisoners: How the Largest U.S. Prison Health Care Provider Puts Lives in Danger," https://www.splcenter.org/20161027/profits-vs-prisoners-how-largest-us-prison-health-care-provider-puts-lives-danger
2. "Woman Recounts Experience of Lost Pregnancy at La Plata County Jail," https://www.durangoherald.com/articles/woman-recounts-experience-of-lost-pregnancy-at-la-plata-county-jail/
3. "Whistleblowing Doctor Sues New Mexico Prisons," https://www.courthousenews.com/whistleblowing-doctor-sues-new-mexico-prisons/
4. Ibid.
5. "Arizona Federal Court Levies Sanctions Against Corizon Health," https://www.prisonlegalnews.org/news/2019/aug/6/arizona-federal-court-levies-sanctions-against-corizon-health/
6. Audrey Dutton, "Idaho Prison Inmate Sues Corizon Over Infection Treatment," https://www.idahostatesman.com/local/crime/article191707729
7. GreeneSpace Profit and Punishment Zoom seminar, March 2, 2021
8. Hawaii study trip, Summer 1993
9. Shane Bauer, *American Prison: A Reporter's Undercover Journey into the Business of Punishment*. New York: Penguin Books, 2018
10. Phone interview with CURE member in Colorado Springs, November 2021
11. *Catholic Worker*, November, December 2019
12. "Migrant Shelter Provider Is Under Investigation," *New York Times*, December 21, 2018

PART IV
TOWARD ENDING MASS INCARCERATION

16
Legislative Agendas

In the eighteenth century, several Enlightenment era philosophers, known as the fathers of the utilitarian and deterrent purposes of punishment, shook their society with their approach to the newly emerging penitentiary system. One of these men was Milanese aristocrat and legal scholar Cesare Beccaria whose 1764 book, *On Crimes and Punishment*, critiqued the Italian penal system. His book won praise from Thomas Jefferson and John Adams, but the opprobrium of many legal scholars, as well as the Roman Catholic hierarchy who placed his work on the Church's *Index of Condemned Books*.

Cesare Beccaria was disturbed by the brutality he witnessed in a Milan prison, but in addition to decrying these inhumane conditions, as Baron de Montesquieu had done earlier, Beccaria produced a system of thought on penal practice. He advised rulers to eliminate excessive pain, especially the use of torture to obtain evidence, and he opposed the death penalty. Beccaria condemned the existence of debtor prisons, pretrial incarceration, secret accusations, and the severe punishment of minor offenders. Instead, he emphasized ideas of proportionality, clarification, and equality before the law, besides advocating the need for swiftness in applying sentencing. Justice, he said, should not be delayed.

Beccaria favored corporal punishment for some violent crimes, but due to his general opposition to severe punishments, he recommended that penal laws be designed by legislators, not arbitrary magistrates. Beccaria's approach relates to the question of how much trust to put in legislators versus judges. Should we have mandatory sentencing or discretionary judgment in assigning punishment?

Another figure of the Enlightenment, Englishman Jeremy Bentham, produced his *Rationale on Punishment* in 1818, in which he stated that punishment was an intrinsic evil because it caused people to suffer. Bentham viewed cruelty and abuses in the criminal law as self-defeating and he argued for moderation on the grounds that severe punishments led juries to find the party innocent, rather than imposing a harsh penalty. He advocated reducing crime and eliminating as much punishment as possible because he felt retribution caused more evil than good.

If alive today, Bentham, who was concerned about the prevalence of disease in the tight quarters of prisons, would mourn the fact that our modern jails and prisons are hotbeds of communicable diseases, such as HIV, hepatitis, tuberculosis, and COVID-19. Bentham also disliked the fact that inmates lived in humiliating conditions without privacy or the opportunity to do creative work. Because Bentham felt that the existing jails encouraged idleness and other evils, he recommended that all penitentiary inmates be employed in useful labor. He condemned the practice of solitary confinement, saying that it led to insanity, desperation, and suicides. Pointing out the negative aspects of imprisonment, Bentham opposed long sentences because these lessened inmates' mental abilities and social contacts. However, he did concede that certain offenders needed to be confined for lengthy periods, even for life terms, if they continued to harm society.

Many of the ideas of eighteenth-century philosophers have been incorporated into modern penal law, such as the Fourth, Fifth, Sixth, and Eighth Amendments in the American Bill of Rights because our nation's founding fathers were inheritors of European Enlightenment thinking.

While it has been mainly liberals who have advocated humanitarian legislative changes in America's penal codes, recently, leaders on the right of the political spectrum admitted that the American prison system is in serious need of reform, mainly because annual costs of state prisons are unsustainably high and sometimes represent a larger portion of the state budget than do schools. Suggestions for utilizing preventative methods to crime, as well as alternatives to incarceration, have emerged front and center in our country.

In this reform atmosphere, Republican leaders, associated with the "Tough on Crime" movement, joined the national conservative effort for prison reform, referred to as "Right on Crime," a project that was given birth at the conservative Texas Public Policy Foundation. Prominent members included former white-collar offender Charles Colson of Watergate fame, tax reformer Grover Norquist, and the Koch brothers, owners of an energy empire. While cost effectiveness and savings to the taxpayers are the major incentives for prison reform by those on the right, some conservatives with libertarian views advocate retrenching the prison system on other grounds, such as individual liberty, limited government, and a preference for solutions based on family and community. Similar to spokespersons on the left, these conservatives object to the waste of peoples' lives during incarceration and after their release.

This conservative interest in correctional reform means that liberals, engaged in prison reform on moral and public safety grounds, have backing from the right, as both sides have agreed that high recidivism rates indicate that the prisons are not doing the intended job. However, despite their newfound agreement, many reformers have serious doubts that conservatives will use fiscal savings from reductions in the prison population to improve conditions for the remaining prisoners, or provide social services for returning citizens. Those of liberal persuasion are also concerned about the wider use of reentry risk assessment techniques, available through artificial intelligence and run by corporate giants.

While right-wing reformers are depending on fiscal policy to reduce mass incarceration, critics feel that economic considerations alone will not bring about enough of a reduction in the number of persons incarcerated, especially if only nonviolent offenders are released. Further, because salaries make up a large part of prison budgets, entire correctional facilities will have to be closed down in order to provide substantial savings. If states are merely interested in reducing costs, this may mean that conditions for remaining inmates could become worse. On the other hand, if leaders are interested in reducing high recidivism rates, then legislatures will have to allocate money to provide social services for returning citizens.

With annual prison costs in Texas amounting to $3.2 million, Republican Governor Rick Perry decided to reduce the state's prison population and he began this reform by concentrating on changing drug laws. While the state ranked second in the nation for marijuana possession arrests, officials reduced the number of drug-addicted inmates by creating hundreds of beds in treatment programs, instead of locking people up for long periods without access to any addiction programs.[1]

Besides this focus on drug offenders, Texas authorities turned their attention to the treatment of the mentally ill because this class of inmate makes up 15% of the state's prison population.

The Texas legislature began funding pretrial diversion programs for those suffering from mental illnesses because officials found that outpatient mental illness, as well as substance abuse treatment, were far less costly than incarceration. The state now has drug courts, mental health courts, and veterans' courts. A Nurse-Family Partnership was established for expectant mothers and infants that has cut crime. As a result of these changes, the rate of incarceration in Texas state prisons fell by 17% from 2007 to 2015 and the juvenile incarceration rate fell by nearly three-quarters. The crime rate dropped by 27%. Texas closed eight prisons, saving $4 billion of taxpayer money and who knows how many lives.

The Texas legislature also directed its attention to reforms that helped offenders resume life in the free world and that have cut the recidivism rate. As an example, prison administrators were authorized to create a six-month re-entry program to help inmates build on life skills. A recent bill in the legislature would allow some first-time low-level offenders to seal their criminal records and the city council of Austin, Texas, has authorized "Ban the Box," so that returning citizens need not reveal offenses when applying for employment. In addition, the legislature supported a reduction in parole officer workloads to allow better supervision of assignees.

As the interview with the former Texas inmate conveys in "Texas Today" (Chapter 5 of this book), mass incarceration is still a huge problem in Texas as elsewhere. However, Governor Perry and the present Texas Governor, Greg Abbott, have fostered agendas that made it easier for other red-state politicians to enact similar legislative reform efforts in a bipartisan way. A recent example comes from Kentucky where the Republican governor decided to grant parole and pardons to many persons as he left office and the newly elected Democrat governor supported legislation allowing returning citizens to vote.[2]

Another example of the "Right on Crime" movement occurred in the state of Louisiana. With its large number of poor persons, it is no surprise that Louisiana has a record of incarcerating among the highest number of prisoners per capita in our nation; besides poverty, Louisiana's high incarceration rate, similar to other states, is also the result of its adoption of mandatory minimum sentencing and restrictive parole policies.

Due to reform efforts, Louisiana officials claimed that persons imprisoned for nonviolent offenses fell 20% in 2018 and that the overall prison population declined by 7.6%. These changes occurred because the state's attorney generals reduced imprisonment for drug possession by 42% and judges lowered the average sentence for drug crimes by 10%. Joining in a bipartisan fashion, legislators offered alternatives to incarceration that resulted in a savings of $12.2 million, with 70% of this money slated for projects to reduce recidivism and to strengthen victim support programs. Louisiana authorities have expressed pride that, due to sentencing changes, instead of 816 prisoners per 100,000, the rate is now below 700 per 100,000. This gave Oklahoma the distinction of being the state with the highest per capita prison population in our nation, a rate of 1,079 per 100,000 people.[3]

However, there is a backstory that has been replicated elsewhere. Because Louisiana held half of its prison population in jails, the latter were declared unconstitutional due to overcrowding. When many jail inmates were moved to the Angola state penitentiary, 6,000 inmates now occupy that institution, the largest number ever in Louisiana's history. The state appears to be playing musical chairs, not unlike the situation that occurred in California after the implementation of *Brown v. Plata*, a US Supreme Court decision that focused on overcrowding in that state's prisons and will be discussed in a succeeding essay.

Critics say that real change cannot occur without a deeper reduction by legislatures in sentencing because half the growth in prison populations has been the result of long sentences, with one in seven American prisoners serving either a life sentence or its equivalent. Louisiana has the highest number of persons with life sentences, many without a chance of parole.

Blue state Washington in the Northwest is taking aggressive action to reduce mass incarceration and its fiscal costs. The state legislature has sanctioned a new approach to the heroin epidemic by passing the Drug Offender Sentencing Alternative (DOSA) that offers first-time nonviolent heroin offenders medical treatment. Designed by the Seattle district attorney's office, DOSA provides a way to cut back on the incarceration of first-time drug offenders, helping them avoid loss of employment, student loans, and housing benefits.

By putting a dent into the War on Drugs, Washington State is providing a model for other states; its neighbor, blue-state Oregon, has recently decriminalized all drug use. Decriminalization or legalization of marijuana has spread from the Northwest region to many parts of our country, including California, Nevada, Colorado, Illinois, Maine, Vermont, New York, and Hawaii. Besides the relaxation of marijuana charges, some state legislatures have reduced penalties on the use of more serious drugs, and several have initiated drug courts that aim at rehabilitating addicts.

Legislative reformers on the left and the right have also focused on the federal Bureau of Prisons (BOP) that houses 205,700 prisoners, a tenth of the 2.1 million incarcerated. Despite the limited number of inmates, federal prisons require $5.5 billion per year of taxpayer dollars. Maximum-security prisoners cost $95 a day, medium $74, and minimum $59, making BOP facilities an important part of the discussion on prison costs. Even though the federal government can print money at will, the BOP appears starved of funds. Recently, the federal corrections officers' union bought twenty billboards in Los Angeles County that warned about possible budget cuts, leading to increased deaths in federal prisons. The head of the union also denounced moves by Congress to reduce benefits for federal employees, citing how difficult it is to retain enough correctional officers in the overcrowded federal prison system.[4]

The federal inmate population had started shrinking due to the movement away from mandatory minimum sentences for low-level drug offenses. Even so, 16,000 prisoners in BOP were on a waitlist for basic literacy training due to overcrowding, estimated at 25% over BOP's capacity. Under the Trump administration, a 64% growth in the number of guard and supervisory personnel vacancies occurred, a figure that had a greater impact than any reduction in the inmate population. This situation led to an increase in overtime work for correctional officers and the use of untrained librarians, teachers, and counselors for guard duty; prisoners took advantage of the lack of sufficient guards, with more violence and contraband the result. To date, this situation has not been corrected.[5]

Acknowledging these problems in the federal prison system, the US Senate and the US House of Representatives, in a bipartisan effort, addressed the fundamental problems at BOP. Republican and Democrat Senators sponsored a bill, entitled the Sentencing Reform and Corrections Act, while the House of Representatives had its own bipartisan version. After months of negotiation, the Senate and House agreed on a bill called the First Step Act that included many sections of their respective bills. The major reforms involved reducing the disparity between crack cocaine and powder cocaine sentences; granting more discretion to judges in sentencing; reducing the severity of automatic and mandatory minimum sentencing laws; and setting up $375 million in federal funds for vocational training and educational programs in BOP.

While the police unions supported the First Step Act, the National Association of US Attorneys expressed opposition to the legislation on the grounds that reduced sentences would contribute to violent crime. Other conservative opponents of the legislation maintained that the First Step Act mandates could be accomplished without legislation because proposals, such as compassionate release of older prisoners and unshackling of women prisoners about to give birth, were already in existence, but were largely ignored by the BOP. Liberal groups objected to the incorporation of what is termed "e-carceration" because reports were emerging about injuries to persons wearing ankle bracelets, and poor people were complaining about the high fees to rent the bracelets from company manufacturers. Instead, advocates began urging cell phone usage for tracking purposes.

After a large Congressional majority sent the First Step Act to President Donald Trump, known for his law-and-order speeches, Trump decided to sign the bill, giving some inmates, who had never had a first chance, a second chance.[6]

The enactment of the First Step Act led to the reauthorization of the Second Chance Act, originally passed into law in 2008, and establishing federal grants for programs that assist former inmates to fare better in the free world.

The First Step Act has affected a limited number of inmates, as only 3,000 persons have been released by BOP, despite the dire effects of COVID-19 and the deaths of thousands of inmates. In recent Senate hearings, BOP officials were asked why they have not implemented sections of the First Step Act. For example, of the 200,000 federal prisoners, 82% have been given no technical instruction and 50% of addicts have no drug treatment. BOP officials responded to this criticism by pointing to inadequate staffing, a situation that is made worse because of the overcrowding in the BOP units. Due to lack of resources, newly hired guards receive only six months of training and can no longer spend time shadowing experienced correctional officers.

The Senate questioning ended with BOP officials asking for more financial help from Congress. There have been other occasions when Congressional mandates or court decisions have not been backed up by proper funding.

The Breathe Act, emerging out of the murder of George Floyd by a Minneapolis police officer, is among the latest legislative ideas addressing penal reform. The act is sponsored by the group, Black Lives Matter, and proposes moving funds from law enforcement to help finance community resources, such as low-rent housing, better schools, and improved medical facilities, with the stated purpose of driving down crime, providing public safety, and eliminating the mass incarceration of poor people. The Breathe Act is supported by critics who claim that previous "decarceration" efforts were not properly funded.[7]

Some on the left of the political spectrum go even further, arguing that prisons should be totally abolished because they are essentially inhumane and that any new legislation will only cut around the edges of correctional dysfunction. These abolitionists point to the fact that, while our country is experiencing a decrease in crime, our prisons remain overcrowded with the poor, the uneducated, and people from dysfunctional backgrounds housed in horrific environments. This is not the first time that abolition of prisons has been suggested.

In 1887, Russian sociologist Peter Kropotkin wrote *In Russian and French Prisons,* in which he argued that prisons should be abolished. Due to his experience as a political prisoner in both countries, Kropotkin highlighted several issues that he felt were destructive to inmates. Among them were the lack of contact with prisoners' families who might provide healthy influences; forced labor that only degraded the inmates; indeterminate sentences that gave administrators control of individuals; ironclad discipline that made prisoners fearful; and isolation that made them feel like outcasts, unworthy of associating with other humans. Kropotkin decried the idea that prisons could rehabilitate inmates in the midst of brutal conditions and, similar to Jeremy Bentham, he felt that a reordering of society was the way to prevent crime and incarceration.[8]

Peter Kropotkin focused on the marginalized, a perspective important in any study of punishment, as penitentiaries were first proposed for the poor because they could not afford to pay fines. Because legislators aimed at deterrence and fiscal savings, they advocated prison conditions that were even harsher than those that the poor endured in a free society. Kropotkin indicted the designers of the penitentiary for expressing hostility to lower-class groups and for using this new institution as a dumping ground for the poor.

In 1975, French sociologist Michel Foucault published *Discipline and Punish: The Birth of the Prison,* in which he agreed with Peter Kropotkin about the social control purpose of the penitentiary. Foucault interpreted the transition from corporal punishment and torture to the penitentiary as part of a general change in society, rather than simply a focused humanitarian effort on the part of reform groups, such as English Quakers. Foucault maintained that the invention of the penitentiary was one part of a vast system, including monasteries, convents, military academies, hospitals, schools, and mental institutions, that built an oversight society operated by authorities in medicine, psychology, and criminology. These institutions employed social control mechanisms that mandated uniforms, silence, rigorous schedules, and the authoritarian control of the incarcerated.[9]

In his writings, Foucault maintained that the very nature of prisons ensured the continual production of delinquents who needed to be treated, while also encouraging more crime and violence. For this sociologist, the lack of transparency prevented citizens and their representatives from discovering and critiquing cruelty in penal institutions. By punishing offenders in this fashion, Foucault also argued that the carceral state stood in the way of broader political activity and enabled industrial society to foster discipline and regimentation. He pointed out that legislators often used social control instead of providing better social safety nets. Money could always be found to militarize police and to build prisons, rather than investing in early childhood education, better schools, job development and training, addiction treatment, and community outreach to impoverished neighborhoods.

Along these same lines, Jessica Mitford's *Kind and Usual Punishment,* also published in the 1970s, argued for the elimination of prisons because of the many downsides for the inmates, their families, and society at large, with so little return for the money. John Pfaff, author and a law professor at Fordham University in New York, contends that the downsides of incarceration are so great that Americans should consider all kinds of alternatives, even though some serious crimes may result from these changes. His thesis makes sense for tackling mass incarceration, but, unfortunately, when released inmates re-offend, the public demands more retribution.[10]

Most people respond with dismay to the idea of abolishing prisons, and many even question reducing mass incarceration. They ask how society can be protected from dangerous persons without an enormous change in human behavior. Instead of advocating for complete prison closure, compassionate individuals of both conservative and liberal leanings have dedicated themselves to drawing attention to the inhumane conditions in penal institutions and they have focused on eliminating mass incarceration through legislative means. When the incarcerated themselves protest through hunger strikes and lawsuits, members of the Supreme Court and the United States Justice Department have paid attention.

Notes

1. CURE newsletter
2. "Kentucky Governor Grants Voting Rights to 140,000 Felons," *New York Times*, December 12, 2019
3. "Louisiana Elections Shows End of 'Old Tough-on-Crime Stuff'," https://www.politico.com/news/2019/11/24/john-bel-edwards-criminal-justice-reform-louisiana-072952
4. Bob Hennelly, "Federal Prison Union: Trump Privatizing To Endanger COs, Public," https://thechiefleader.com/news/open_articles/federal-prison-union-trump-privatizing-to-endanger-cos-public/article_9b92ca6a-ffc2-11e7-82af-2b41b79e4877.html
5. "Safety Concerns Grow as Inmates are Guarded by Teachers," *New York Times*, June 17, 2018
6. The inside story is that the President's son-in-law, Jared Kushner, was enthusiastic about prison reform because his own father had spent time incarcerated for tax evasion. It is not uncommon for prominent citizens who have been to prison for white-collar crimes to support reform; Charles Colson, a Nixon advisor during Watergate, is one of the best examples.
7. The Breathe Act, https://breatheact.org/
8. Peter Kropotkin, *In Russian and French Prisons.* London: Ward and Downey, 1887
9. Michel Foucault, *Discipline and Punish: The Birth of the Prison.* New York: Vintage Books, 1975
10. John Pfaff, *Locked Up: The True Causes of Mass Incarceration.* New York: Basic Books, 2017

17
The Supreme Court and the US Department of Justice

California is a bellwether state; what happens there has an influence on other states and on the federal government. With its nearly 200,000 inmates at last count, this state has the largest prison system in our country, as well as one of the costliest in the world. Prison systems are expensive to build and maintain due to high-security equipment and steel-filled buildings with toilets and sinks in each cell; in addition, California's correctional officers, similar to guards in New York State, can earn up to $70,000 a year, the highest salaries in our nation for this line of work. The state spends approximately $80,000 a year to house one prisoner, compared to $35,000 a year in many states, including Texas.

The Golden State is trying to undo its reputation as one of the most punitive in our country when it was once touted as the least punitive; California moved from having relatively low per-capita prison statistics, similar to those of European nations, to registering one of the highest per-capita incarceration rates in our nation. Much of this was caused by the passage of laws, such as mandatory minimum sentences and the "three strikes" act, one of the most stringent penal mechanisms introduced during the "War on Crime."

States have always passed habitual offender laws, but the "three strikes" law is more severe as it authorizes life sentences without parole for those who commit a third crime. Results of this law include overwhelmed courts, loss of sentencing discretion by judges, and increased costs for prisons housing these lifers. In addition, from a moral perspective, the "three strikes" law imposes life sentences on offenders whose crimes do not always warrant such harsh punishment.

However, in 2012, California voters approved Proposition 36, supported by prosecutors, judges, and police officers. The Proposition changed the "three strikes" law by imposing a life sentence only when the third conviction is serious, or if the accused had prior convictions for rape, murder, or child molestation. Arguments supporting this change to the law were that the new guidelines fit the crimes and that prisons would have sufficient room for more dangerous felons. With approximately 3,000 convicted felons, who are serving life sentences under the "three strikes" law, becoming eligible to petition for reduced sentences, it is estimated that the state could save between $150 and $200 million a year. Because California, like other states in our nation, suffered from the economic impact of COVID-19, these savings are vital to that state's budget.[1]

While this change in the law helped ameliorate some of the overcrowding, primitive conditions continued; in reaction, California prisoners participated in a number of work sit-downs and hunger strikes organized through the prison pipeline. In the summer of 2013, a group of inmates at Pelican Bay State, a maximum-security facility in Crescent City, California, began a hunger strike after officials did not respond to calls for changes agreed to in a mediation session. The Pelican Bay leaders issued a statement saying: "For the past two years, we've patiently kept an open dialogue with state officials, attempting to hold them to their promise to implement meaningful reforms, responsive to our demands."

The inmates ended by saying that they felt they had no other avenue but to start the hunger strike in response to what they termed "state-sanctioned torture" in which officials often utilized group punishment for control purposes and employed snitching practices to identify suspected gang members. The inmates also cited the need for more housing, better educational and rehabilitation programs, and provision of adequate, nutritious food. Pelican Bay inmates were particularly anxious to see an end to prolonged solitary confinement. In response to the latter, California prison authorities, as well as the California Correctional Peace Officers Association with its 27,400 members, defended the use of isolation as a remedy for the extensive gang violence in these facilities.

At its high point, this multiracial protest involved 30,000 prisoners engaged in hunger strikes at 33 facilities around California. During these strikes, several wardens confiscated inmate property and denied visits from outsiders, or the reception of mail from family members. The hunger strike lasted 50 days, with many prisoners resuming eating as their health worsened. In the last days of the strikes, approximately 100 inmates were still fasting.

While prison officials did not agree to any system-wide reforms, inmates at San Quentin Prison and Calipatria State Prison were able to negotiate verbal settlements with their wardens. Attorneys for the inmates announced they were filing a federal lawsuit against then-Governor Jerry Brown, in which prisoners sought both the institution of due process before they were placed in isolation cells and an end to indefinite solitary detention.[2]

Litigation by California prisoners against Governor Brown had already raised unconstitutional issues. In 2011, after 15 years in the lower courts, the inmate lawsuit, *Brown v. Plata*, was accepted by the US Supreme Court and our highest court, in a 5–4 decision, affirmed a lower federal court by ordering a reduction of the population in California prisons. In *Brown v. Plata*, Justice Anthony Kennedy, who wrote the brief for the majority, acknowledged that prisoners give up their right to liberty, but he maintained that they deserve the human dignity inherent in all of us. He based his argument for the reduction of overcrowding on the Eighth Amendment's prohibition of cruel and unusual punishment.[3]

Plaintiffs maintained that the failure to meet prisoners' basic health needs was widespread, with untreated renal failure and denial of chemotherapy for cancer victims as common occurrences. Inadequate plumbing systems and infestations of rodents were rampant and caused more health problems. Photos shown to the court by inmates' attorneys included ones of suicidal inmates, standing in catatonic states inside telephone booth sized cages, filled with their own urine. The five justices for the affirmative agreed that overcrowding and the resulting suffering violated the Eighth Amendment.

The extent of the overcrowding in California prisons was so great that the US Supreme Court had to compromise on how much of a reduction could take place in prison units that, for over eleven years, had housed twice as many inmates as the facilities were originally built for. The court limited the overcrowding to 137.5% of capacity in order to correct living conditions that included 54 prisoners sharing a single toilet and 200 prisoners living in a gym with two or three guards in charge.

Among the four justices in opposition to sending California inmates back to the free world to solve overcrowding were Justice Samuel Alito and deceased Justice Antonin Scalia. Both men suggested that better conditions could take place without releasing prisoners, a move that they felt would bring dire consequences to the California community. These two judges were backed by victim rights' groups who pointed to the 1980s deinstitutionalization of poorly run mental facilities, along with the failure to replace them with community mental health facilities. Just as this change had led to record homelessness and arrests among the mentally ill, victims' rights groups suggested that releasing California prisoners would have the same negative effects, unless enough community support was provided for the unskilled, uneducated persons who leave prison with a small amount of cash and a bus ticket.

On grounds of harm to the state and to victims of crimes, Governor Jerry Brown appealed the court's decision, asking for more time to put the release of prisoners into action. In an effort to delay the Supreme Court order, Governor Brown negotiated a deal with California legislators to spend $400 million on improved health care services for state prisoners. Also, the governor, who, unlike his peers in most other states, is in charge of parole decisions, increased the number of persons eligible for parole.

Despite Governor Brown's efforts to show good faith with the Supreme Court decision, that court did not agree to extend the six-month period to address the overcrowding. As a result, 46,000 prisoners were released by a variety of methods, including the establishment of more community corrections and the placement of some inmates in existing jails, a method that resulted in overcrowded municipal and county facilities. Overwhelmed jail officials were forced to introduce additional services, all of which required funding from the California legislature.

Since that time, the state's voters have approved, through various propositions, reduced penalties for drug and property crimes, as well as sentencing credits that can lead to early release for inmates who complete rehabilitation programs. Yet, critics have pointed out that, despite the reduction in the number of California inmates, mental patients are still receiving minimal medical care for their chronic diseases and they continue to be placed in small confinement cages in which they are routinely pepper-sprayed.[4]

In 2020, a federal court gave California two more years to reduce the inmate population to 112,000 persons. Besides continuing to shift responsibility to county facilities, the state is looking at other ways to move inmates out of prison, including good behavior credits to shorten sentences and more streamlined parole for those thought to be safe for release. In order to narrow its high recidivism rate of 60%, California authorities have instituted programs to reduce substance abuse disorders and mental illness. In addition, in the fall of 2020, Californians voted "yes" on Proposition 47 that proposed keeping a number of low-risk nonviolent offenders out of prison by reducing felony charges for certain crimes to misdemeanors.[5]

California's response to the Supreme Court's decision in *Brown v. Plata* was in line with movements in other beleaguered states dealing with mass incarceration. As an example, Texas' prison reform began in 2003, eight years before *Brown v. Plata* was decided. Although lagging behind Texas, the California lawsuit may have influenced other states, especially those wary of being placed under court surveillance, such as Mississippi. With the second-highest rate of incarceration in the nation, this state has begun reforms, including alternatives to prison for low-level offenders and interventions to reduce recidivism.

Despite Mississippi's efforts to reform their penal system, National Public Radio aired several reports on the great distance that the state's prison authorities have yet to go. In an interview with Mississippi prisoners, listeners heard about the horrendous conditions in the state's maximum-security prison in which pest infestation and rotting food is common, while gangs control much of the daily life and inmates do not receive medical treatment for serious diseases, including COVID-19.[6]

Brown v. Plata also provided motivation to open discussion about conditions in the federal Bureau of Prisons (BOP). If the US Supreme Court could lay down guidelines for overcrowding in a state, reformers argued that the federal prison system should attend to its own house; this led to the federal prison reform legislation, the First Step Act, discussed in the previous essay.

Along with the courts, the US Department of Justice (DOJ) has been active in bringing transparency to American prisons. When the department's investigators find evidence of systemic violations to the US Constitution, they issue a written report outlining remedial measures that the state's Department of Corrections is obliged to implement. Then, the Department of Justice works with the state officials to find solutions.

In September of 2021, *The Washington Post* posted a feature story about the Department of Justice's investigation of Georgia's prisons after advocacy groups, such as the Southern Center for Human Rights (SCHR), had been urging action as conditions grew even worse due to the pandemic. In August of 2020, a massive riot broke out at the Ware State Prison in Waycross, Georgia. Inmates at two other facilities also rioted after being locked in their cells for weeks or months without sufficient water, showers, food, or medical care. Reports have filtered out that in some units groups of men, carrying machetes, roamed through dormitories.

In early September, SCHR filed a class-action lawsuit in US District Court against Georgia's maximum-security prison for holding people over lengthy periods, even years, in solitary confinement. US Assistant Attorney General Kristen Clarke spoke in a video news conference about the numerous Georgia violations, including homicides, stabbings, beatings, weapons smuggling, and gang violence. Twenty-six inmates were murdered last year, and 19 committed suicide, a rate twice the national average. Attorney General Clarke pointed out that Georgia is operating at a 70% officer rate, adding that understaffing is a nationwide problem. Georgia officials denied that they have violated the rights of prisoners or failed to protect them, this in a system where rodent remains and roaches are found in inmates' food and rodents crawl over sleeping prisoners.[7]

In September of 2021, the US Justice Department filed a lawsuit against the Alabama prison system for longstanding unsafe and unsanitary conditions in the men's prisons in which numerous examples of violence by inmates and sexual abuse and brutality by guards were documented. Deeming this action a last resort after two years of failed negotiations with the state, the Justice Department's complaint read: "The State of Alabama is deliberately indifferent to the serious and systemic constitutional problems present in Alabama's prisons for men."[8]

Republican Governor Kay Ivey said that the news of the lawsuit was "disappointing" because Alabama had been negotiating in good faith with the Department of Justice. The governor added that Alabama is planning to construct three new regional men's prisons as a way of reimagining the correctional system.

In response, the Department of Justice spokespeople indicated that Alabama not only failed to resolve existing problems present during the initial 2016 investigation, but that the state has ignored the increase in homicides, suicides, sexual abuse, and general violence, with more overcrowding, lack of proper sanitation, and fewer guards.[9]

It is not only in the South that the Department of Justice has been working for the constitutional rights of inmates. In August of 2021, the department filed a complaint and a proposed consent decree with the state of New Jersey because of conditions at the Edna Mahan Correctional Facility for Women. The primary issue involved is that New Jersey failed to protect prisoners at Edna Mahan from sexual abuse by the facility's staff.

The consent decree, that followed a two-year investigation, holds the state of New Jersey responsible to make improvements to protect the women at the prison from staff abuse. These include better supervision and improved methods for reporting sexual abuse that includes protection against retaliation. Further, the consent decree mandates that staff who commit acts of sexual abuse be held accountable and that greater transparency be achieved through public meetings with former Edna Mahan inmates, prisoner advocates, and family members of current prisoners. An independent monitor will oversee and assess the state's compliance with the consent decree.

In reaction, the governor of New Jersey, Democrat Phil Murphy, announced that he plans to close the Edna Mahan facility due to the conditions exposed; the Department of Justice replied that the consent decree applies to any New Jersey facility, new or old. Victoria Kuhn, acting corrections commissioner, said New Jersey will be guided by the federal monitor to transform the culture at Edna Mahan.[10]

Actions such as these by the US Department of Justice are a major way that transparency can be achieved and the constitutional rights of inmates can be upheld.

In the next essay, we turn to the high rate of recidivism in our country that many experts say can be remedied by the provision of more resources for those returning to the free world and can serve as one of the most effective ways of reducing mass incarceration.

Notes

1. "Reforming California's 'Three Strikes' Policy," https://www.naacpldf.org/case-issue/reforming-californias-three-strikes-policy/
2. "California Inmates Launch Biggest Hunger Strike in State's History," https://www.theguardian.com/world/2013/jul/09/california-prisoners-hunger-strike
3. *Brown v. Plata* lawsuit information was a result of research for a course on prisoner lawsuits.
4. Interview with former California prison teacher, Fall 2019
5. "Proposition 47: The Facts About the Law and Its Impact," https://myprop47.org/wp-content/uploads/2015/11/Prop47_OnePager_9.21.15v.pdf
6. Debbie Elliott, "Mississippi Pressured To Overhaul Prison System After Inmate Deaths," https://www.npr.org/2020/04/20/838297645/mississippi-pressured-to-overhaul-prison-system-after-inmate-deaths
7. Ibid.
8. "Justice Department to Investigate Georgia's Prisons, after Reports of Violence Deplorable Conditions," https://www.washingtonpost.com/national-security/2021/09/14/justice-department-launches-probe-georgia-prisons/
9. "Justice Department Files Lawsuit Against the State of Alabama for Unconstitutional Conditions in State's Prisons for Men," https://www.justice.gov/opa/pr/justice-department-files-lawsuit-against-state-alabama-unconstitutional-conditions-states
10. "U.S. Department Probe Found Sexual Abuse at New Jersey's Women's Prison," https://www.usnews.com/news/us/articles/2021-08-10/us-justice-dept-announces-settlement-to-address-sexual-abuse-of-prisoners-in-new-jersey

18
Reducing Recidivism

Philosophers from Cesare Beccaria to Jeremy Bentham to Michel Foucault have advocated short prison sentences because the longer the incarceration, the harder it is to overcome the lingering effects of prison, adjust to the free world, and avoid a return to prison.

A major obstacle to achieving shorter periods of incarceration is restrictive parole access. Regarding this problem, Iowa is considering legislation to establish a Lifer Review Committee that will examine parole petitions from inmates who have served at least 25 years of their sentences. The committee could then refer the case back to the court and a judge could re-sentence individuals to terms of 25 years, making them eligible for parole.

Other states are examining their parole methodology. Massachusetts legislators are expanding parole board membership, seeking candidates without law enforcement backgrounds. In Florida and Louisiana committees are studying ways to promote access to parole, and Iowa, Maryland, Mississippi, and Virginia are considering eliminating life without parole sentences.[1]

Several state legislatures are considering reform of technical violations of parole rules, costing taxpayers millions when the individuals are returned to prison. When students at the Santa Fe University of Art and Design attended the January 2017 session of the New Mexico legislature, they heard a representative for the American Civil Liberties Union (ACLU) and members of other justice-focused groups testify on the need for reform of the state's parole rules. Typical of most states, New Mexican former inmates often return to prison for technical violations of parole, such as failing to report for appointments with parole officers, or meeting a curfew.

The New Mexico ACLU member claimed that unnecessary incarceration for minor parole infractions costs the state as much as $40 million per year. To correct this problem, New Mexico's Legislative Subcommittee on Criminal Justice Reform considered amending parole procedures, for example, allowing released inmates more time to meet the requirement of holding a job. However, many New Mexico district attorneys, including the state's Attorney General, expressed opposition to any change in parole rules. Even though both houses of the legislature passed bills amending parole regulations, Democrat governor Michelle Luhan Grisham vetoed them, apparently due to pressure from the Attorney General.[2]

Despite numerous cases of COVID-19, a recent report from the Marshall Project stated that parolees who committed minor violations were returned to jails and prisons during the pandemic and probationers were incarcerated in virus-ridden institutions for minor infractions of rules. The Marshall Project also claimed that 15,000 Texans, who earned parole, remained in prison due to their need to take required courses or to complete paperwork, all held up by the coronavirus crisis.[3]

Most prisoners, approximately 90%, return to the free world at some point. A total of 875,000 adults were paroled from federal and state prisons in 2016, and several million persons were released from jails. How many of them will pursue a crime-free life is a serious question facing American society.

In 2016, the Marshall Project analyzed reports from criminologists about recidivism rates in our country. Older offenders and those with more education are less likely to re-offend. Prisoners released before turning 21 had a rearrest rate of about 68%; those over age 60 had a rate of 16%; the latter statistic supports the calls for compassionate release of the elderly, especially because these inmates are more expensive to house and treat. Medical care of inmates makes up the highest proportion of state's budgets, even when the care is minimal. As for educational factors, inmates without a high school diploma and those without a college degree were more likely to reoffend than college graduates. Overall, recidivists are most likely to reoffend within two years of their release, indicating that society should spend heavily on the newly released.

One of the major indicators of recidivism is the length and seriousness of the offender's criminal record. About 45% of federal inmates, mainly drug offenders and white-collar criminals, were rearrested, whereas 77% of state prison inmates, most often violent offenders, were recidivists. Yet, those who committed property crimes showed a higher rate of recidivism than violent offenders or drug offenders. Murderers often have a low recidivism rate.

Critics say that the high recidivism rates may indicate that cognitive behavioral therapy and other rehabilitation programs are not effective in lowering recidivism, but this may depend on how consistently these programs are offered. Various societal conditions are at play when trying to understand what causes recidivism.[4]

Released prisoners in America receive a small stipend and a set of clothing. Approximately one-half of these former inmates remain jobless for a full year, making their unemployment rate at least equal to that of the Great Depression years. While often a result of pre-incarceration deficits in education and mental health, their lack of employment is also due to the stigma of imprisonment; the loss of job and social skills behind bars; the breakdown of beneficial relationships outside prison; and legal impairments to occupations and various services following a felony conviction.

During a sabbatical at the University of Victoria in British Columbia in 2004, a prison counselor told me that this Canadian province had begun increasing the funds for parolees in order to reduce recidivism. She said that this assistance was due to the advocacy of the John Howard Society of Canada, named for eighteenth-century English prison reformer John Howard who provided inmates with housing and other services. The Society continues to operate on the premise that, if newly released people lose hope because they don't have a place to stay, they will go back to what they know and turn for support and shelter to friends who may be involved in crime.[5]

American parolees without family support often rely on nonprofit groups for assistance. During a Santa Fe community college course entitled, "Probation and Parole," a student discovered two Dallas, Texas, nonprofit programs, the Texas Offender Reentry Initiative and Unlocking Doors, both of which find housing and employment for former inmates and, in some cases, employ them, an excellent way to both provide income and to make use of the person's incarceration experience.

Another student discovery was the Prison Education Program (PEP) at New York University (NYU) in Manhattan, offering an extensive array of college courses for inmates and parolees through the university's Gallatin School. PEP is also associated with Thrive for Life, a nonprofit that finds transitional housing for former prisoners, using facilities, such as Gallatin House in the Bronx; to help parolees navigate New York City, NYU produces Connections 2020, a free guide to services in the city.

Despite the odds, many parolees make new lives for themselves and many are bent on informing the public about prison life and what it means to live in the free world again. One of these courageous persons is African-American Albert Woodfox, author of *Solitary*, a book nominated for both a Pulitzer Prize and the National Book Award, in which Woodfox relates his 44 years in solitary confinement at the state prison in Angola, Louisiana. After being incarcerated for a felony offense, Woodfox was accused of killing a corrections officer, a crime he denies. It appears that Woodfox's attempt to establish a Black Panthers group at Angola may have been the reason that he and two other members of the activist group were indicted for the murder of the guard.[6]

Woodfox spent many of his solitary days writing in his journal that became the basis for his bestselling book. This process, as well as his desire to provide an example to other inmates, enabled him to keep his sanity. Due to a review of his case and the testimony of the widow of the dead corrections officer who came forward to urge Woodfox's exoneration, he agreed to a no-contest plea and was released from prison three years ago.

Albert Woodfox has taken his book around our country and abroad, telling audiences about his experiences in prison, including being gassed by guards on many occasions. He recommends that all states institute independent oversight boards to hold prison administrators accountable. If this is not done, Woodfox says that the brutal conditions in solitary, which he calls torture, will continue.

In his speeches, Woodfox tells audiences about the difficulty of adjusting to the free world after long years of incarceration, including learning to eat when hungry and to adjust his sleeping habits because he often wakes automatically at 3 AM, the time when he was accustomed to writing in his prison cell.

The author says, "I had to learn to use my hands in new ways—for seat belts, for cell phones, to close doors behind me, to push buttons on an elevator, to drive. I had to relearn how to walk downstairs, how to walk without leg irons, how to relax without being shackled." [7]

During the pandemic, Woodfox addressed the effects of the coronavirus on prisoners at Angola where, under ordinary circumstances, inmates are not given adequate medical attention. Woodfox pointed out that those diagnosed with the virus were sent to the harshest unit of Angola, with little or no medical care, and that inmates from other Louisiana prisons, also diagnosed with COVID-19, were placed in the same Angola unit. In addition, prisoners eligible for parole were not released because they were unable to complete necessary exit courses, cancelled because of the pandemic.

Another author/ex-inmate has given us some insight into prison life and the scars it leaves. Former Missouri state senator and doctoral graduate Jeff Smith, from a higher class than Woodfox, was sentenced to prison on campaign finance charges. After being paroled, Smith wrote *Mr. Smith Goes to Prison: What My Year Behind Bars Taught Me About America's Prison Crisis*.

Jeff Smith was disturbed by the lack of educational opportunities at his Kentucky federal prison. For example, his computer class consisted of sitting in front of a monitor with no instruction and his nutrition class was taught by a guard who handed out a meaningless brochure on caloric content of fast-food items and dismissed the class after fifteen minutes. In his book, Smith highlighted other problems, such as the underground prison economy, overly long sentences for drug offenses, and the revolving door of recidivism.

Jeff Smith also addressed the difficulties that former inmates have when they are released. He asked why these men and women are not allowed to occupy government-run low-rent housing or receive food stamps and medical aid. Finally, Smith expressed concern on how deeply incarceration affects inmates' families who may lose their primary caregivers and often carry heavy economic and psychological burdens.[8]

The movement to extend voting rights to returning citizens is a good example of how to help people adjust to the free world. After the Civil War, southern states adopted felon disenfranchisement to prevent African-American men from voting and many northern states joined them. Over the years, 6.1 million persons have been disenfranchised by being imprisoned. Supporters of voting reform see this as a way to give people a second chance and to help them be part of the community once again, while opponents say that voting is a privilege, not a right, and that having the vote taken away is part of the punishment.

Voting in prison is legal in most of the European Union and in countries as disparate as Canada, Kenya, South Africa, and Indonesia. Thirty-eight states and the District of Columbia allow felons to vote after release from prison, while 10 states make it difficult for felons to ever vote again. Mississippi, Alabama, and Alaska have extended the franchise to persons incarcerated whose crimes are not serious. Iowa just joined them. Only two states, Vermont and Maine, permit all incarcerated persons to vote.

A Florida initiative regarding ex-inmate voting rights was held in November of 2018. In a grassroots movement, 1.1 million people petitioned to allow citizens to decide whether former inmates could vote; 65% of Florida voters said yes, except in the case of murderers and sex offenders, and for those who are on probation or parole. A backlash arose as Republican legislators passed a bill that requires former inmates to pay a fee before they can use the franchise, but this legislation is being challenged in Florida courts on the grounds that it is a poll tax. Researchers expect that over one million former Florida inmates could be eligible to vote if obstacles are not employed.[9]

On a related issue, the *Santa Fe Reporter* published a feature story about what criminal justice reform advocates call "prison gerrymandering." One third of New Mexico's state prisoners who resided in Albuquerque prior to their incarceration are counted by census as living in smaller towns and rural areas in which their prisons are located. These inmates are counted for representation purposes, but are not allowed to vote. This situation means that political power is transferred from nonprison towns, such as Albuquerque, while smaller towns with prisons, but fewer people, gain inordinate power.

Critics say that, instead of using the current correctional facility address, the last address that an inmate had, as he or she entered prison, should be used in order to create a more equitable representation process. A number of states have enacted laws ending the unjust gerrymandering process. In New Mexico, the Citizen Redistricting Committee Chair, Edmund Chavez, declared that the committee does not have the last known addresses for individuals prior to their incarceration, as lack of data collecting is a long-time problem in the state. Mario Jimenez, campaign director for Common Cause, a nonprofit dedicated to fostering democracy, testified before the New Mexico Legislature's Courts, Corrections and Justice Committee to denounce prison gerrymandering, stating that the process is "unjust not only to incarcerated people but to all New Mexicans."[10]

During the 2019 session of the New Mexico State Legislature, students heard a criminal defense attorney give a passionate address to the legislators on how to decrease US recidivism that ranks among the highest rates in the world. Referring to New Mexico's relative poverty, he cited the need for better social supports for returning citizens and he maintained that serious legislation must be fiscally responsible and rely on methods that actually work, such as parole reform. The attorney stressed that structural barriers to employment, affordable housing, and physical and mental health care are at the root of the problem. He added that penal reform is complicated and that we need enlightened leadership from all segments of our society to bring innovation and ingenuity to bear on the crisis in our correctional system. The attorney ended by pointing to other nations who provide better public safety, as well as humane conditions in their penal institutions.[11]

Notes

1. State Reform, https://www.Vera.org/stateofjusticereform/2019
2. Attendance at New Mexico legislature, January 2019
3. "A State by State Look at 15 Months of Coronavirus in Prisons," https://www.themarshallproject.org/2020/05/01/a-state-by-state-look-at-coronavirus-in-prisons
4. "Seven Things to Know about Repeat Offenders," https://www.themarshallproject.org/2016/03/09/seven-things-to-know-about-repeat-offenders
5. Interview with counselor in Victoria, BC
6. Albert Woodfox, *Solitary: A Biography.* New York: Grove Press, 2019
7. Ed Pilkington, "The Scars of Solitary: Albert Woodfox on Freedom after 44 Years in a Concrete Cell," https://www.theguardian.com/world/2021/feb/19/albert-woodfox-interview-solitary-confinement-44-years
8. "Jeff Smith Was Supposed to Be in Congress by Now," https://www.washingtonpost.com/lifestyle/style/jeff-smith-was-supposed-to-be-in-congress-by-now-instead-hes-an-ex-con--with-a-story-to-tell/2015/09/21/928b9eda-5bd5-11e5-8e9e-dce8a2a2a679_story.html
9. "How Republicans Undermined Ex-Felons' Voting Rights in Florida," *New York Times*, July 17, 2020
10. Bella Davis, "Counting the Incarcerated," https://www.sfreporter.com/news/2021/09/29/counting-the-incarcerated/
11. Attendance at New Mexico legislature, January 2019

19
Alternative Models

Anna, a psychiatrist at the New Mexico maximum-security penitentiary in Santa Fe, introduced me to the documentary, *Doing Time, Doing Vipassana*, set in India's Tibar prison, an institution that, in 2004, housed 10,000 inmates and was considered a hell on earth. The narrator begins the film by expressing his view that humans are often imprisoned by feelings of anger, fear, and desire, but that criminals commit horrendous deeds when they act on these emotions. The narrator adds that many offenders have endured harsher life circumstances and enjoyed fewer educational and economic opportunities than those who obey the law. Understanding this, some criminal justice students have wondered how they might behave if they lived in a crime-ridden ghetto, with little hope of moving out of poverty, except to be involved in the drug trade or other illicit activities.[1]

Doing Time, Doing Vipassana features former tennis star Kiran Bedi who, as the new Tibar prison director, began a series of humane reforms to reduce violence. However, after a few months, she became convinced that offering better food and other amenities was insufficient to correct the violent atmosphere. Puzzled as to what to do next, Bedi paid attention when a prison guard told her about Vipassana, an ancient meditation practice from Southeast Asia. Shortly after their conversation, thousands of prisoners and a sizable number of guards were practicing Vipassana for 10-day periods.

Doing Time, Doing Vipassana provides a very moving experience as the audience witnesses inmates and guards at Tibar prison sitting together in a tent and participating in the silence of the meditation practice. Inmates who blamed others or society for their criminality gained insight into their own behavior and realized how they had hurt their victims. Many appeared to give up their anger and their feelings of revenge; some inmates broke down in tears, while others hugged their guards who appeared moved by the inmates' remorse.

Pleased that the practice of Vipassana led to a decrease in violence within Tibar and also reduced recidivism, Kiran Bedi spread the word about the practice. Today, Vipassana units exist at many other prisons in India and in New Zealand, as well as in the state of Alabama, otherwise known for its harsh prison conditions. Yoga therapy is also being offered in some American prisons as a way to reduce violence. While supporters have praised these spiritual practices as a means of rehabilitation, they stress that literacy and vocational programs are also needed so that released inmates can obtain work.

Twenty years before this documentary appeared, I and six students from my honors class at Richland College in Dallas were introduced to progressive penal policies when we participated in a University of Wisconsin at Madison study trip, focused on criminal justice systems in London and Paris.

In January of 1985, our middle-class group, fortunate to afford this educational trip, traveled in a double-decker bus to our first event in London, a trial at the Old Bailey. Seated in the back rows of the courtroom, we noticed that the defense attorney and the prosecutor, both wearing the traditional white wigs, compared notes and worked together to see that justice was accomplished. Their approach seemed superior to the adversarial American jurisprudence practices, including not sharing important evidence and employing unethical means to win.

Arriving in Paris, our week in the City of Lights began with a visit to an experimental prison. Men were working on Citroen autos for a salary, and mothers in the prison, when not at their paid jobs, joined traditionally clothed Catholic nuns in the care of their children. In an effort to preserve maternal bonds and to motivate these women to rehabilitate themselves, their youngsters lived in the prison until age two.

As we toured the Paris facility, we noticed that each inmate, male and female, had a private cell for purposes of safety and privacy, rather than because of any notion that solitude would reform them. The rooms, decorated with pictures of family members and other loved ones, held a single bed, facing a desk covered with books and writing materials, because inmates were attending classes to prepare for their release back into society. French prison officials expressed pride about the relatively low recidivism rates among men and women leaving this facility.

However, the constructive methods employed in the model prison did not become more widespread. While French minimum-security prisons try to prepare inmates for their release by offering educational and vocational training, the vast majority of French prisoners, many of them poor Muslim immigrants, spend idle days in overcrowded, dirty, pest-infested maximum-security cement buildings.

Before our afternoon excursions in Paris, our group met for three hours in a large room at our hotel for lectures by Professor Jacques, an erudite French criminologist who taught periodically at the University of Chicago. Jacques's first lecture included an overview of several European countries' progressive approaches to incarceration. For instance, in many parts of Europe nonviolent offenders were fined, performed community service, or were placed on probation, rather than being incarcerated. Prisoners who showed good behavior were entitled to early release programs, weekend furloughs, educational programs, and frequent visitation rights.[2]

Even in more severe European prisons, sentences were shorter than they were in America; a burglar in America typically received a 16-month sentence, compared to England where the sentence was seven months. The average prison sentence in America was 29 years, while, in Germany and the Netherlands, the average was 14 years, and throughout Europe, the longest sentence was no more than 20 years, including those called life sentences.

Jacques's lecture led to a discussion on why America depended on long sentencing practices that contributed to brutal living conditions and were a cause of mass incarceration. The Wisconsin participants, several of them criminal justice professionals, felt that a major reason for oversentencing was American politicians' fear of being labeled soft on crime, or being accused of overtaxing citizens by advocating expensive reforms, such as post-prison services.

Jacques responded that politicians in many European nations employed a hands-off approach, allowing the criminologists, not beholden to the public, to determine penal policies. Decision-makers in Europe, concerned with criminal justice matters, are highly specialized unelected government officials, while, in America, the district attorneys, prosecutors, and judges, go through the electoral process, and are responsible to the public. This means that those in charge of American penal policy are motivated to be "tough on crime" in order to please the public and maintain their offices.

Professor Jacques went on to discuss other differences between the European and American approaches to punishment. Recognizing that social and economic inequality is often at the heart of high crime rates worldwide, Europeans have organized their societies around principles that include social safety nets, resulting in less inequality between the classes. Professor Jacques maintained that European officials do not want taxpayers to shoulder the economic and social costs of high crime rates, or the incarceration of repeat offenders. Instead, recognizing the temptation for people to commit crime, these governments authorized strong social and economic supports and effective policing, all of which aimed at reducing the motivation and the opportunity for committing crimes. Grappling with societal problems may be the chief way to reduce crime and bring a humane and effective approach to corrections, but this path has taken time in our country.

The professor also cited two other aspects of American culture that make it notably different from European attitudes towards punishment. The first is our love of privatization, including much of our prison system in which companies involved in criminal justice administration lobby government officials to retain policies that continue mass incarceration. European prisons are all government-run.

The second distinctive cultural difference relates to religion. Unlike Europe, America has been strongly influenced by the Puritan ethic, as well as by Evangelical Christianity, both of which emphasize the need for severe punishment to redeem sinners. Instead, most European countries use methods that are aimed at providing public safety and reducing recidivism, rather than relying on retributive practices.

Professor Jacques ended his first lecture by mentioning that Europeans only used solitary confinement for the most dangerous inmates who might harm others. In 1984, no American state had begun any reform of solitary confinement and it would take two decades for some states, such as Colorado, to consider doing so.

During his second lecture, Professor Jacques stressed the fact that all European countries offered the same medical care to prisoners that other citizens received. In addition, Holland had adapted a medical approach to illegal drug addiction, treating it as a health problem, not a criminal one. Jacques pointed out that, even compared with the Soviet Union and Singapore, two countries that had a zero-tolerance for narcotics, the United States incarcerated more persons per capita for this type of offense.

This information led to a group discussion on the various downsides of America's War on Drugs. The Wisconsin members pointed out that many judges felt frustrated that, under mandatory minimum requirements, they found themselves sentencing addicts to long sentences, while rarely seeing a drug kingpin come through their courts. Other negatives mentioned about the War on Drugs were the corruption of police and border patrol officers; overcrowded prisons; the loss of privacy due to invasive policies; harsh treatment of minorities; and the economic costs of these laws to the public.

Years after hearing Professor Jacques's lecture, despite drug reform emerging in several states, most legal entities in America continue their harsh drug penalties. Meanwhile, several European countries have followed Holland's example. In 2001, Portugal, inundated with heroin from Afghanistan, decriminalized the use of all drugs. Drug dealers were sent to prison, but persons caught with less than a 10-day supply of any drug received mandatory medical treatment, including methadone prescriptions. Drug counseling and treatment became universal throughout the country, a method that Portugal found less costly to their budget and to their society than incarceration.

The Portuguese government also supplemented incomes to lessen poverty, a move that had a very positive effect on reducing addiction. The benefits of Portugal's approach included a

75% drop in drug use from the 1990s; a drug-induced death rate five times lower than the European Union average; and reduced HIV rates because government workers handed out packets of clean needles and condoms. Portuguese citizens, remembering the heroin epidemic, continue to favor this approach to drug addiction.[3]

In our third session, Professor Jacques discussed how Scandinavian, Dutch, and German prison officials aimed at making life on the inside of prisons somewhat similar to life on the outside in order to prevent institutionalization and recidivism. Correctional officials in these countries assumed that losing freedom, being enclosed without privacy, and following strict daily rules were punishment enough. In contrast to America, European countries offered benefits to former inmates, such as sufficient financial assistance and, if needed, psychological treatment. The most important goals of their penal systems were public safety and rehabilitation, not retribution.

After many years, some American leaders are looking across the Atlantic Ocean to study other approaches to penal practices. The CBS program, *60 Minutes*, reported on the work of Democrat Governor Dannell Malloy of Connecticut who, in the early part of the twenty-first century, made a trip to Germany. The governor was impressed by Germany's low rates of violence and recidivism, attributed to the positive interaction between guards and inmates, as well as to the use of rewards for good behavior, such as increased visitation rights and more access to education.[4]

With crime at a record low, Governor Malloy decided that this was the moment to experiment with the German model. Connecticut was able to cut down on the total number of inmates by diverting millions of dollars into community supervision and re-entry programs; in addition, fewer nonviolent drug offenders were arrested due to decriminalization of marijuana and the repeal of draconian drug sentences. Making it easier to obtain parole became another part of Connecticut's effort to reduce the prison population and to take better care of the existing inmates, including a large number of mental patients. Related to the latter, Governor Malloy worked with prison officials to institute humane methods, rather than solitary confinement, to deal with the mentally ill.

The Connecticut governor turned to the main prison, Osborn Correctional Institution, on the outskirts of New Haven, in which he initiated counseling and educational programs. When trusted long-term inmates were offered the opportunity to mentor young felons, many of them without fathers, these offenders received the benefit of a caring male, while the mentors felt that they were earning redemption and making something of their lives. Violence levels fell.

Governor Malloy also backed a bill that raised the age of juvenile transfers to adult court from 16 to 18 years, and he supported building a facility to house offenders under the age of 22 to prevent these young people from mingling with older career criminals.

Due to Governor Malloy's initiatives, *60 Minutes* viewers witnessed examples of success stories in Connecticut's prisons. Especially interesting was the CBS reporter's interview of correctional officers who, used to an "us against them" mentality, were now acting as counselors to inmates. At first, these guards were hesitant to participate in the more open prison atmosphere, but they stated that they became supporters of Governor Malloy's changes because violence went down as hope was restored to many of the inmates. One officer reiterated the European philosophy that because incarceration constitutes punishment in so many ways, it does not make sense to create conditions so punitive that bad results occur.

Miles from Connecticut, in North Dakota, the director of that state's Department of Corrections, Leann Bertsch, participated in a study group touring Scandinavian correctional institutions, and she was impressed that Norway's program, offering vocational training and liberal arts education, appeared to make their society safer. Prison staffers, running the programs for Norwegian inmates, are largely people trained in psychology, an approach that contrasts with American prisons in which only 6% of staff are hired to run rehabilitation programs; the remaining 94% consist of correctional officers whose focus is military-style discipline.

In addition, Norwegian corrections officers fill both security and rehabilitative roles under "dynamic security," the concept that promotes good relationships between inmates and staff in order to reduce the potential for violence. Officers, after receiving two years of extensive training, dress in navy slacks and light-blue shirts with nametags, and prisoners, even the most serious offenders, wear their own free world clothes. Officers and inmates eat together, work together, and play together in physical fitness classes and at sports events. The philosophy of "dynamic security" protects guards from unnecessary stress and also reduces inmate violence and recidivism.

In keeping with Norway's concept of making prisons resemble the free world as much as possible, recreation rooms have flat-screen televisions, sound systems, and mini-refrigerators for rent. These amenities are affordable because the inmates receive wages that permit them to pay for these services, a financial arrangement that emulates life in the free world. Norwegian officials, acknowledging that this is an expensive way to run a prison system, view the monetary cost as worthwhile because this approach helps reduce drug addiction and recidivism, with their long-term social and economic costs. Norway's policies require courage and monetary investment, but the country has a 20% recidivism rate, as opposed to the United States' average 60% rate.

Responding to critics who cite Norway's traditional mono-culture as far different from our own multi-ethnic culture, the country's officials point out that, due to globalization and migration, Norway has become much more diverse in the twenty-first century, with one-third of Norway's prisoners' non-natives who are given language training. While Norwegians do not have the vast gang problems common in American prisons, correctional officers still work to keep lines of communication open to prevent violence.

Director Bertsch returned to North Dakota determined to employ some of the techniques that she observed while abroad. First, Bertsch added more rehabilitative and educational resources to the state's correctional system, known for its high recidivism rates. Then, she devised ways for inmates to earn certain freedoms, such as shopping excursions, day passes home, and the right to wear civilian clothes on site. In another reform, the director ordered a reduction in the number of prisoners held in solitary; by dropping minor infractions, such as talking back to a corrections officer, a two-thirds reduction in the use of solitary took place and those in isolation were offered therapy during their confinement.

Bertsch's most advanced reform was her introduction of the Norwegian practice of relative closeness between guards and inmates. As an example, North Dakota guards were encouraged to have a least two conversations per shift with those held in segregation units. All of these changes constituted new thinking in a largely "tough on crime" state.[5]

As American reformers express hope in this growing interest in Scandinavian and German models of corrections, they point to significant differences in statistics between our country and Europe. American prisons house twelve times the number of inmates as Sweden, eight times that of Italy, seven times that of Canada, five times that of Austria, and four times that of Poland. While we incarcerate over 700 persons out of 100,000, Russia, an autocratic state, imprisons 450 out of 100,000.[6]

In the mid-1970s, our correctional institutions held approximately 300,000 persons, while, today, the number is over two million. Even considering the growth in America's population over those years, this is a huge increase that various prison administrators, legislators, judges, prosecutors, and citizens view as a crisis. Addressing this are persons who support the implementation of restorative justice principles as an important means of reducing mass incarceration and providing more public safety.

Notes

1. Interview with prison psychiatrist Anna Stevens, Summer 2004
2. Lectures in Paris, France – Professor Jacques on European prisons, January 1985
3. Susana Ferreira, "Portugal's Radical Drugs Policy Is Working: Why Hasn't the World Copied It?," https://www.theguardian.com/news/2017/dec/05/portugals-radical-drugs-policy-is-working-why-hasnt-the-world-copied-it
4. "German Style Progress at a Connecticut Maximum Security Prison," CBS 60 Minutes, March 31, 2019
5. Cinnamon Janzer, "North Dakota Reforms its Prisons, Norwegian Style," https://www.usnews.com/news/best-states/articles/2019-02-22/inspired-by-norways-approach-north-dakota-reforms-its-prisons
6. "North Dakota's Norway Experiment," https://www.motherjones.com/crime-justice/2017/07/north-dakota-norway-prisons-experiment/

20
Restorative Justice

During a visit to Victoria, British Columbia, I learned that the Center for Religion and Society at the University of Victoria offered sabbaticals for academics and community members and I was accepted to be a participant during the summer of 2004. Before leaving my home, I read *Spiritual Roots of Restorative Justice,* edited by Michael Hadley, one of the Center's members and a former Canadian naval officer turned history professor. In his groundbreaking book, Hadley includes essays focused on the major world religions which are all rooted in the restorative justice principles of healing for offenders, victims, and the community at large.

Spiritual Roots of Restorative Justice summarizes the origins of restorative justice within the indigenous populations of Canada, Australia, New Zealand, and the Navajo of the American Southwest. This philosophy of punishment made its entry into the white population of Canada in 1974 when the first program was established in Kichener, Ontario; next, Family Group Counseling became part of both New Zealand's and Australia's juvenile justice programs. By the 1990s, there were 700 programs in Europe and 1,300 in the United States. The restorative justice community is largely populated by people already involved in criminal justice activities, such as conflict resolution, probation and parole, and judicial proceedings, and they view the traditional ways of punishing offenders as ineffective.[1]

During a study session at the Center for Religion and Society, Michael Hadley told our group about a project at Victoria's Episcopal Cathedral in which members of the congregation and trusted inmates from a minimum-security prison built a labyrinth together on the stone plaza of the cathedral. While church members were at first reluctant, they soon realized the wholesomeness of the project and the inmates felt like human beings again.

Michael Hadley told a contrasting story that concerned Ferndale prison, located on the outskirts of Victoria. Near this facility, a nine-hole golf course was used by community members, along with some Ferndale inmates, but public clamor over allowing this amenity for inmates closed the golf course down. Despite offering a healthy outlet for men who had proved themselves worthy and providing them with an opportunity to mingle with free worlders in preparation for their return to society, these positive aspects were ignored. Professor Hadley used these cases as examples of how restorative justice principles of reintegration into the community can be utilized.

Toward the end of my sabbatical, I met with Dr. Conrad Brunk, the director of the Center on Religion and Society, to discuss my project. Because Dr. Brunk had written a supporting essay in Michael Hadley's book on restorative justice, I asked him why he advocated this theory.[2]

As Conrad Brunk set aside a sheaf of papers and sat back in his chair, he said that restorative justice offers a healthy and constructive approach to punishment that involves taking responsibility for actions, a vast improvement over current models. Dr. Brunk listed four goals of any theory of punishment. They are: protect, as much as possible, citizens from engaging in law-breaking; give offenders their just deserts; redress the injustice for the offense by requiring that the offender makes amends; and see that the punishment makes the offender a better person.

Using this model, Conrad Brunk pointed out that, in the retributive form, offenders rely on their attorneys and are not directly confronted with the harm caused by their actions. Dr. Brunk argued that the retributive and deterrence models, and even the current rehabilitative model, do not accomplish the fourth goal of making the offender a better person. He said that the high rate of recidivism confirms this and that only the restorative justice model has a chance of improving offenders' behaviors.

Instead of empty punishment in which criminals place blame on others rather than on themselves, in the restorative justice model, they are held accountable for their actions. Dr. Brunk said that when restorative justice practices bring perpetrators to an understanding of how they have injured victims and society, they often make a turn for the better; recidivism is reduced and public safety improves. Under the restorative justice model, the offenders are given a helping hand to return to the community in which, due to their change of heart, they may be received in a better fashion.

I asked, "How do traditional prosecutors and prison authorities view restorative justice?"

Dr. Brunk responded that the present penal system in North America was designed to deal with the worst criminals, not with the majority of routine offenders. He felt that, because prisons are costly and that there is a high recidivism rate, officials should be open to new ideas, even if they spring from the ground up as restorative practices do. He added that most of the restorative justice programs are administered by private nonprofits, though there are some exceptions to the implementation of this method.

Playing devil's advocate, I asked, "What about people who say this is a 'bleeding heart' approach to justice?"

Conrad Brunk shook his head, and said, "Restorative justice does more for victims than any other theory."

He pointed out that restitution is often involved and a clear moral message about the wrongfulness of the offender's action is put on the table. Dr. Brunk debunked the idea that restorative justice is soft on criminals as it offers compensation and apologies to victims, confrontation with personal immorality, and a rebuilding of a just order.

After taking more notes, I asked, "Have there been any successful outcomes using restorative justice?"

Dr. Brunk reached for a report and read out loud about an experiment employing restorative justice in Vancouver, British Columbia.

"These teenagers involved in a restorative justice program sense that they are being treated as redeemable, that they have dignity. The main purpose of RJ is to awaken the conscience, not humiliate or stigmatize."

Professor Brunk said that, due to a grassroots movement, British Columbia celebrates "Restorative Justice Day" each November. He described an effort by the Church Council for Justice and Corrections (CCJC) to persuade the Correctional Service of Canada and the National Parole Board to work toward enlightened corrections so that offenders, victims, and their communities can be brought together through restorative circles, family conferencing, and just sentencing.

CCJC is also engaging the churches of Canada in rediscovering the foundations of what is known as "transformative justice," in which members of society assist offenders as they return to society. One of the most well-known of these projects, the Victim Offender Reconciliation Program (VORP), has found its way to our country, with one unit located in the small town of Alamosa, Colorado, home of Adams State University, the institution that was my home base at the time.

While attending VORP sessions, I learned that Texas leaders were holding sessions in which juvenile offenders and their victims accomplished discovery of the facts, with confession, restitution, repentance, and reconciliation to follow. In Louisiana, several school districts were employing restorative justice methods after researchers at the Southern Poverty Law Center showed that black youth were being punished more severely than white youth. Louisiana's "whole school" approach involved teachers, students, and parents, all impacted by disciplinary incidents; groups sat in a circle and devised ways to address harms that the incidents had caused, a process that led to a decrease in student suspensions and a reduction in the number of youngsters drawn into the "school to prison" pipeline.

Today, in Los Angeles, a teen court operates under the guidance of David Wesley, presiding judge for the Los Angeles Supreme Court, and a strong supporter of a form of restorative justice, called Stop Hate and Delinquency by Empowering Students (SHADES). The judge maintains that this process is an effective way to prevent future teen offenses.

In New York City, the Center for Court Innovation began employing restorative practices in a community in Brooklyn and this program has begun operating in the other four boroughs of the city. Offenders are sentenced to work on projects in local neighborhoods, while court staff link offenders to drug treatment, health care, and education. Studies show that 79% of participants in this community court system have become responsible, functioning members of their communities.

Even though restorative justice principles have been mainly utilized in juvenile cases of low-level crimes, a New York City nonprofit group has been working with violent adult offenders, offering them the option of working under restorative justice guidelines. Through this experience, it is hoped that even serious offenders can realize the damage that they have done to their victims and to society and can be helped to avoid further criminal behavior.

With this in mind, several prison facilities have begun introducing restorative practices to inmates. At San Quentin prison in northern California, a Victim Offender Education Group (VOEG) aims at the personal transformation of inmates who engage in this program that was started by the Insight Personal Project (IPP). Inmates in VOEG learn new emotional skills and ways to correct anti-social behavior through classes in violence prevention and meetings with victims and survivors.

One former San Quentin inmate agreed to talk to the press about his experience in the VOEC program. Robert Frye, incarcerated for armed robbery, went through a year-long study of the impact of his crime on the victim, the victim's family, and the wider community. He says he became aware of the effects of parental abuse on him, as well as his need to develop emotional regulation and anger management. A study of the results of VOEG programs revealed that a majority of those participating did not re-offend.

The state of Minnesota has been a pioneer in restorative justice principles since 1992 when it established the Office of Restorative Justice Planner. The office director facilitates training in restorative justice practices, provides technical assistance to communities around the state, builds a network of professionals who share knowledge and support, and establishes healing circles for victims and offenders, as well as circles to establish sentencing plans. Offenders are referred to these programs by Minnesota judges who trust the process of victim/offender mediation.

Vermont uses a program called reparative probation in which offenders sign contracts promising not to create more crimes and both adults and juveniles engage in community service, supervised by citizen volunteers. Victims feel a sense of justice because offenders understand the effects of their crimes and learn ways to avoid reoffending as they seek restoration in their communities. While Vermont's program is not a prison diversion program as such, it does ease the number of persons in jails.

In Austin, Texas, district attorney Ronald Earle has been employing restorative justice practices for years, convinced that they help stem the school to prison pipeline. He also led the way for passage of a law authorizing a Community Justice Council and a Community Justice Task Force aimed primarily at juveniles. Earle is predisposed to restorative justice because this model sees crime as an offense against victims and the community, not merely the state of Texas.[3]

Attorney Bryan Stevenson relies on restorative justice principles in his advocacy work at his nonprofit organization, Equal Justice Initiative. The University of Mississippi Department of Legal Studies has engaged inmates from the Mississippi prisons in its program entitled the Common Reading Experience, and the professors involved have used Stevenson's book, *Just Mercy,* as a selection. One inmate participant, after participating in the Common Reading Experience, said, "We have learned through our restorative justice class that the things we did to our victims took away from them the power they once had and instilled fear instead." Another inmate thanked the professors from Ole Miss for helping to change the mindset of how incarcerated persons are viewed.[4]

The philosophy of restorative justice has reached into the general American culture. In her popular TED talk, Deanna Van Buren, a 47-year-old architect, has supported building gathering spaces based on restorative justice principles. Van Buren's group, Designing Justice/Designing Spaces, developed a project, called Restore Oakland, located in a former nightclub. Restore Oakland acts as a hub for social justice nonprofit groups in the San Francisco Bay area and works with the Restaurant Opportunities Center to provide fine dining training for former inmates and low-wage workers.

Another project using architecture for restorative justice purposes is operating in New Haven, Connecticut, where the Yale University School of Architecture has built a studio in which faculty work with a group called Impact Justice to design community justice centers that can minimize the erosion of life in minority communities, often resulting from overly punitive responses to crime.[5]

Restorative justice is becoming more widely appreciated. However, the Council of Europe points to limits on how well restorative justice practices can be used in prisons due to various structural problems. First, offenders have to admit guilt and demonstrate remorse. Second, the very nature of incarceration makes it difficult to arrange the mediation sessions, especially in the time of COVID-19 when so many programs have been eliminated. The fact that record-keeping on the results of restorative justice practices has been limited also discourages prison authorities from utilizing these methods.

The Council of Europe reports that, while many European countries have increased the use of restorative justice either by local entities or by funding it throughout a nation, restorative justice is rarely used to its full potential. In addition, the Council maintains that several rehabilitative programs are placed under the title of restorative justice but do not meet the same criteria.[6]

Finally, worldwide, there is a difference of opinion among restorative justice practitioners; some want to keep the nonprofit community-based model, while others say that restorative justice will never grow unless it is formally incorporated into the overall correctional system. Nevertheless, it is clear that restorative justice principles bring new insights to the subject of punishment and reinforce the idea that reconciliation is a noteworthy path to reducing mass incarceration and to building a humane approach to corrections. Restorative justice emphasizes looking to the future, rather than lingering in the morass of past mistakes and crimes. This approach is the opposite of a penal system that practices mere retribution in a divisive atmosphere in which the public is often in disagreement on how offenders should be treated.[7]

Much of the American public, understandably interested in security, focuses on retributive punishment and can be blind to the possibility of positive outcomes from other approaches. The public's often harsh attitude toward prisoners may be largely due to lack of understanding of what it means to be incarcerated. Transparency into the workings of correctional systems could overcome this resistance to newer models.

As we end this essay, Anglican Archbishop Desmond Tutu of South Africa comes to mind. The Archbishop led the movement to utilize a form of restorative justice, called the Truth and Reconciliation Commission, in order to heal the wounds from years of apartheid injustice in his nation. In an interview by PBS, when asked about the problem of evil, Archbishop Tutu responded: "I do believe that there are monstrous and evil acts, but I do not believe that those who commit such acts are monsters or evil. To relegate someone to the level of monster is to deny that person's ability to change and to take away that person's accountability for his or her actions and behaviors."[8]

Notes

1. Michael Hadley, *Spiritual Roots of Restorative Justice*. New York: State University of New York Press, 2001
2. Interview with director Professor Conrad Brunk, University of Victoria, BC, Summer, 2004
3. Jan Reid, "Ronnie Earle," https://www.texasmonthly.com/news-politics/2-ronnie-earle/
4. "Stevenson's 'Just Mercy' Selected for Common Reading Initiative," https://www.muw.edu/news/7436-stevenson-s-just-mercy-selected-for-the-w-s-common-read
5. A book about this project, entitled *Space for Restorative Justice*, suggests that architecture can define how we seek justice and help to build community. The dean of the Yale School of Architecture, Deborah Berke, has praised the work of Deanna Van Buren for her devoted focus on restorative justice principles in her building sites.
6. Ian D. Marder, "Restorative Justice and the Council of Europe: An Opportunity for Progress," https://www.penalreform.org/blog/restorative-justice-and-the-council-of-europe/
7. Ibid.
8. *Sun Sentinel*, February 26, 2010

Epilogue

During my teaching years, I became aware of the creative work of journalists, artists, writers, and filmmakers that has proved to be an effective way of bringing transparency to our penal system. These dedicated advocates have felt that too much is at stake for inmates, their families, prison administrators, correctional officers, and society at large not to stay focused on justice and humaneness within penal institutions.

One outstanding member of this group of creatives is Sister Helen Prejean, the author of the 1993 book on capital punishment, *Dead Man Walking*, that became the basis for an Academy Award–winning film under the same title. Sister Prejean has written a second book, *The Death of Innocents: An Eyewitness Account of Wrongful Execution*, and she has formed Survive, a support group for murder victims' families.

Prejean's work on the death penalty brings to mind Truman Capote's novel, *In Cold Blood*, based on a true story of two murderers on death row that raised questions about the justification for capital punishment. Capote's southern friend, Harper Lee, wrote *To Kill a Mockingbird*, a best-selling novel that was transformed into a successful film and, a much later, Broadway play. In the film version, actor Gregory Peck plays Atticus Finch, a small-town lawyer, unpracticed in criminal trials, who defends an innocent African-American man and loses the case in front of a white male jury; the guilty verdict leads to tragedy for the accused.

Besides authors who have addressed injustice due to race and class, others have written about discrimination against women. An example is Eve Ensler, author of the play, *Vagina Monologues*, who conducted weekly writing classes for female prisoners in a New York State penal institution at Bedford Hills. Ensler used the women's stories to produce a documentary, *What I Want You to Know*, in which she stressed that strong societal supports for women are needed to halt their increasing incarceration. Ensler's V-Day foundation dedicated 2018–2019 to spotlighting troubling conditions for women in prisons and immigrant detention centers.

Along with these writers in the free world, Shahidul Alam is an example of the many inmates who write to avoid the monotony, the violence, and the bullying that make up prison life. While reading and writing provide an escape for him, Alam is frustrated that few magazines and publishing houses are accepting handwritten work, but he continues on without a typewriter or a computer in the hope that his writing will help the public understand the effects of mass incarceration.

Besides writers, visual artists are a large part of the prison awareness movement. In Connecticut, artist Titus Kaphar created "The Jerome Project," a series of pictures of men imprisoned in conditions similar to that of early Christian Saint Jerome. Artist Hank Willis Thomas joined with New York's John Jay College professor, Dr. Baz Dreisinger, in a collaboration entitled, "The Writing on the Wall," that uses modern hieroglyphics made from essays, poems, letters, and notes to reveal prisoners' experiences.

Chinese dissident and artist, Ai Wei Wei, exposed the plight of political prisoners by displaying portraits of these persons at Alcatraz Island in San Francisco. He had his own experience of political imprisonment when he was incarcerated by Chinese authorities for his artwork that focused on a school building collapse, caused by the use of poor construction materials. Ai Wei Wei has also developed art pieces related to the frightful condition of refugees from Africa and the Middle East who arrive in small boats on the Italian island of Lampedusa.

Photographer Richard Ross offers his visual work, "Juvenile Injustice," along with "Juvie Talk," stories of juveniles from poor backgrounds caught up in the criminal justice morass; his years of work have influenced legislators to take a new look at juvenile detention systems. Recently, professor and activist Ashley Hunt traveled across America to take photos of 250 prisons and jails. Hunt, director of the photography and media arts program at the California Institute of the Arts, entitled his work, "Degrees of Visibility," because so many correctional institutions are hidden from the public, without any transparency. In the February 21, 2018 edition of the weekly *Santa Fe Reporter*, Ashley Hunt was quoted saying, "Maybe the very invisibility of our penal system—the way we punish people by camouflaging them—maybe that's why incarceration in this country has grown so out of control."

Ed Epping of New Mexico has produced the Corrections Project in which he uses mixed media to portray aspects of mass incarceration and over-criminalization. Epping's father served a prison sentence for a white-collar offense and Epping points out that, because his family was middle-class, they did not endure the hardship of lower-class families. His exhibit, in which he aims to put a face on people who have only been a number, is motivated by his father's experience.

Another artist has hosted visual works about punishment at a museum, formerly a prison, in Holmesburg, Pennsylvania, in which drug experimentation on inmates was conducted for decades. When his college education was interrupted by a sentence of four years for a minor drug charge, this artist was troubled to see how many other people were imprisoned for even longer periods on drug charges. Determined to shine a light on this situation when released, he gained backing for his art project from a nonprofit organization dedicated to reform.

James Hough, serving a life sentence in Pennsylvania, has produced a work entitled, "How High House Products Makes Boxer Shorts." This project concerns the fact that a six-pack of underwear from his commissary costs him $3.09, while, as a 44-year-old prison laborer, he is paid a few cents an hour to make the shorts he has to purchase. Influenced by the same economic issue, New York State prisoner Paul Cortez painted a three-panel piece, "Prison Profit-Tears," to express his frustration that relatives are charged $3.95 to listen to prisoners' voice mails. After learning that New York City and San Francisco officials eliminated any charges for inmate telephone calls to family, Cortez felt some hope.[1]

Other artistic projects, such as an exhibit entitled, "Capitalizing on Justice," are calling attention to the industry that has developed around America's mass incarceration. The Corrections Accountability Project in Manhattan accepted artwork from prisoners across our nation, including from an inmate at a Super-Max prison in Florence, Colorado. Concerned about mass incarceration, the Rover Rauschenberg Foundation offered grants of up to $100,000 to artists for projects on this issue.

Theater people are involved. Damon Turner, a hip-hop artist, and dancer Brianna Mims are using the power of their art to ignite change. Along with other artists, the pair gathered a quarter-million signatures to create Measure R, an initiative giving the Los Angeles Sheriff's Civilian Oversight Commission the power to investigate misconduct complaints.

Actor Tim Robbins, director of the Oscar-nominated film, *Dead Man Walking*, founded the Actors' Gang, a Los Angeles theater company that conducts workshops in eight California prisons to help inmates get in touch with their humanity through acting. Actors' Gang has been working for decades to help rehabilitate inmates of all races who Robbins calls "the toughest of the tough." Participation in these workshops is supported by California prison officials who appreciate the behavioral changes of inmates inside the facilities, as well as the lower recidivism rates. Robbins says he was motivated in this work because he grew up in a difficult neighborhood in New York City in which he was mentored by generous people, while several of his peers, who received no guidance, went to prison.

A former Santa Fe colleague, Professor Hank Rogerson, produced a documentary film, *Shakespeare Behind Bars*, set at a Kentucky state prison in which a reform-minded warden welcomed a college professor's project in the arts. The literary scholar, who meets with prisoners each year to direct them in Shakespearean plays, selected *The Tempest* for Hank Rogerson's film. The inmates/actors, who have committed violent crimes, found Shakespeare's message relevant to their own lives and they were able to work out some of their emotions. Through this project, the Kentucky warden and the educator display their humanity and their belief that prisoners are not monsters, even if they commit monstrous deeds.

The documentary, *A Place to Stand*, is a good example of a visual presentation focused on the issue of rehabilitation and features former prisoner/poet Jimmy Santiago-Baca in a version of his memoir by the same name. At age 21, Santiago-Baca faced five to 10 years behind bars for selling drugs. Imprisoned in an Arkansas penitentiary, much of his time spent in isolation, Santiago-Baca was contacted by a minister who, by encouraging him to learn to read literature and write poetry, helped Santiago-Baca transform his life and become a nationally recognized prize-winning poet.

Jimmy Santiago-Baca's story harks back to the medieval epic poem, *Divine Comedy*, by Dante Alighieri. This Italian poet, exiled from Florence and threatened with the death penalty, created a fictional inferno that provides a guide for offenders who want to reintegrate into society. Most intriguing about his poem is Dante's vision of the difference in punishment between hell and purgatory; for this medieval poet, hell is an icy funnel that gets narrower and narrower, a good metaphor for the life of crime and its consequent sufferings.

Opposed to this barbarous state, Dante offers the reader purgatory, a mountain in which the offender ascends to the top with angels as his guide. Here, the focus is on the future, not the past. Just as Dante is helped by angels, Santiago-Baca was assisted by the kind minister and by inmate friends who admired his endurance. Finally, Dante achieves paradise and is redeemed by sharing love; Santiago-Baca followed this same path by mentoring young people.

Besides these writers and artists, journalists play a major role in providing transparency in our prison system. Although humorist Finley Peter Donne remarked that journalists "comfort the afflicted and afflict the comfortable," their path has not been easy, especially for those who report on penal institutions. Mary Beth Pfeffer, a freelance reporter for the *New York Times*, was refused entry to California's Pelican Bay Prison because authorities said she was a researcher, not a journalist. The Federal Bureau of Investigation, at one point in their War on Terror, decided on a complete ban of any media personnel.

Several 1970s Supreme Court decisions. *Pell v. Procunier*, *Saxbe v. Washington Post Co.*, and *Houchins v. KQED* declared that reporters had no special access to prisons. In 2003, the US Supreme Court ruled in *Overton v. Bazzetta* that prison administrators could nullify First Amendment rights of prisoners by barring visitors to prison at will. The state of Rhode Island is an exception, taking pride in its policy of open access to reporters who give their citizens important stories about prison life.

Despite limited access, *New York Times* journalist Tom Wicker wrote *A Time to Die*, in which he described the brutal conditions at the New York State Attica Correctional Facility and its subsequent uprising in 1971. Tom Wicker also acted as a state-appointed observer to help negotiate between the prison authorities and the inmates who had taken hostages in order to demand the end of inhumane conditions at Attica. Tom Wicker's book is considered a classic on the causes of prison rebellions and their consequences and was the reason why so much became known about the Attica uprising, while other prison riots of that time were not as widely covered.

A decade after Attica, when the New Mexico penitentiary in Santa Fe exploded in an inmate riot, journalist Roger Morris exposed the brutality and conflict in this institution, as well as the state's lack of due diligence. His book, *The Devil's Butcher Shop: The New Mexico Prison Riot*, was published because the prisoner pipeline managed to get information to Morris.

Considering this secretive prison atmosphere, *American Prison: A Reporter's Undercover Journey into the Business of Punishment*, the recent work of *Mother Jones'* journalist Shane Bauer, is remarkable. His blow-by-blow account about his four months working as a guard at Louisiana's privately-run Winn prison opened up the subject of private prison conditions.

In an earlier era, Tom Murton also operated underground by posing as a prisoner in an Arkansas unit when he was actually the newly appointed Arkansas director of the state prison. The film, *Brubaker*, starring Robert Redford, shows the viewer the horrendous cruelty that Murton unearthed in Arkansas's prison system, as well as the opposition from political figures who fired him because of his discoveries.

Harry McCormick, Tom Wicker, Roger Morris, and Shane Bauer have given voice to people who do not have one. Also prominent in their ranks is Chris Hedges, a former war correspondent who exposes wrongs in our penal system, as well as teaching writing to inmates in Princeton, New Jersey. Hedges claims that his students are exceptionally hardworking and he has produced a play, called "Caged," written and performed by his inmate/students.[2]

Jennifer Gonnerman has faithfully reported stories of abuse in our criminal justice system and her recent article for the *New Yorker* magazine concerned our broken parole system. Gonnerman's award-winning book, *Life on the Outside: The Prison Odyssey of Elaine Bartlett*, tells the real-life story of a single African-American mother of a large family who spent 16 years in New York's Bedford Hills prison for a narcotics offense.

In a typical case of entrapment, Bartlett was approached by a drug pusher, working for the New York State Police, who offered her money to take a package of cocaine from New York City to Albany. A first-time offender, Bartlett received a 25-year sentence under the Rockefeller drug laws, but Jennifer Gonnerman's book helped Bartlett be released earlier. A major part of *Life on the Outside* centers on the difficulty that this former inmate experienced when she returned to her community.

Jennifer Gonnerman's November 1, 2021 article in the *New Yorker* concerns a wrongful conviction that took place over 35 years ago in Baltimore, Maryland. Entitled, "The Witness," Gonnerman's piece profiles a man who, as a teenager, was bullied by police into giving false testimony about the murder of his best friend. Gonnerman's outstanding reportage allows the reader to see the extent of the problem of wrongful convictions in our nation.

Reporters from the *East Valley Tribune* in Phoenix won a Pulitzer Prize for "Reasonable Doubt," a series that profiled Arizona Sheriff Joe Arpaio, known for his dogged pursuit of Latino immigrants. Due to Arpaio's anti-immigrant fixation, during his tenure, 400 sexual violence and rape cases were not investigated; as a result, the family of a 13-year-old rape victim received a $3.5 million settlement. When the award to the *Tribune* was presented, the Pulitzer committee praised the reporters for using their limited resources to expose how Sheriff Arpaio failed to investigate violent crimes at the expense of public safety.

Recently deceased investigative journalist, James Ridgeway, devoted many years to the issue of solitary confinement. At 73 years of age and on a walker, he dug into his retirement funds to cover startup costs for a website, called Solitary Watch. Ridgeway's nineteenth book, entitled *Hell is a Very Small Place: Voices from Solitary Confinement*, utilized primary source material in the form of letters from those held in Special Housing Units or SHUs, a term frequently used for solitary. In an interview for the *New Yorker* in February of 2019, James Ridgeway indicated that the inmates who wrote to him just wanted to have some contact with the outside world.

The *New Yorker* magazine edition of June 22, 2020, carried an extensive article by journalist Rachel Aviv, entitled "Punishment by Pandemic." Through testimony from nurses working in the Arkansas prison system, readers learned about the total lack of care from the corporate medical company for the numerous inmates suffering from COVID-19. Rachel Aviv's work reveals a house of horrors, filled with needless suffering.

Inmate journalists also provide valuable transparency, producing perceptive, real-time sources of information on living conditions in prison facilities. By the 1950s, most states had at least one prison-operated newspaper and some of them drew readers and advertisers from outside audiences. However, as budgets for educational programs were eliminated in order to attend to the costs of the swelling prison population, prison newspapers were closed.

Plaintiffs in the 1974 *Martinez v. Procunier* Supreme Court case demonstrated that the number of magazines and newspapers, written by inmates, had fallen steadily. The remaining papers included *The Angolite* at Louisiana State Penitentiary at Angola, nominated for a National Magazine Award; *The Echo* at Huntsville Prison in Texas; and *The Prison Mirror* at Stillwater Prison in Minnesota that billed itself as an important outlet for discussion of prison reform. In *Martinez v. Procunier*, originating out of California, US Supreme Court Justice Thurgood Marshall ruled that, under the First Amendment, prisoners were free to develop such periodicals.

Despite resistance, several prisons in California have witnessed the revival of inmate newspapers; one of the most well-known is the *San Quentin News*, founded in 1940, but shut down in the late 1980s. The paper, known for training inmates to become journalists, was reopened in 2008 by Warden Robert Ayers Jr. who believed the project would bring dignity to the news staff and to the entire inmate population. After Robert Ayers recruited outside journalists to guide inmates, a four-page newspaper was delivered to 5,000 inmates. Since then, the *San Quentin News* has received several Best Prison Newspaper awards and continues to have administrative support.

On the other coast, New York University's Prison Education Program works with the University's Gallatin School Writing Program to foster writers and journalists in the prison population. The students, mainly from New York's Wallkill Correctional Facility, produce an annual creative writing journal that interested readers can access by going to the Prison Education Program website. NYU's *Broken Silence* publication of 2017 offers poems and essays written by inmates who express the idea that they want to be thought of as human, even though they have made mistakes.

Besides journalists, nonprofit organizations advocate for prisoners. One of these groups is the Marshall Project, an online journalism organization, based in New York City, that covers criminal justice issues and invites inmates to send their stories for publication. Named for Chief Justice Thurgood Marshall, the project was founded in 2014 by hedge fund manager Neil Barsky and executive editor of the *New York Times* Bill Keller.

Neil Barsky wrote an editorial for the December 18, 2019, *New York Times*, entitled, "How to Fix Our Prisons? Let the Public Inside." In it, Barsky maintained that, despite widespread interest in prison reform, not enough change has occurred inside the walls. As a supporter of the Vera Institute of Justice's report, "Reimagining Justice," calling for human dignity, Barsky recommended that the president of our country declare mass incarceration a failure. Stressing that too many people are in prison for too long and at a high cost to them, their loved ones, and the taxpayers, Barsky suggested that citizens volunteer to teach skills to prisoners in a program that he entitled, "Let Us In."

The nonprofit, Prison Fellowship International, was founded by long-time advocate of rehabilitation, Charles Colson. Shortly before beginning his prison sentence at Maxwell Correctional Facility in Alabama for covering up the Nixon-era Watergate burglary, Colson turned to Christianity. As a result of his conversion, Colson founded Prison Fellowship International that aims at bringing transgressors to Christ. This group has had success in their conversion approach, but has not been involved in advocacy work on systemic matters, such as sentencing reform or "three strikes" laws.

The Los Angeles–based group, Mothers Reclaiming Our Children (Mothers ROC), is an example of a grassroots effort aimed at penal reform. Mothers ROC originated in 1992 because of a neighborhood criminal case and is now an established multi-racial nonprofit that focuses on bringing change to a system that has incarcerated so many of the members' children. Their mission statement includes the phrase, "to be seen, heard, and felt in the interest of justice."

Ben and Jerry's ice cream company, known for its public service, has spent millions of dollars on ads denouncing mass incarceration and demanding mental health funding in prisons, while also advocating for the reduction in the number of persons entering the prison system. Ben and Jerry's has partnered with two penal reform advocacy groups, Color of Change and the Advancement Project, to produce their latest ice cream flavor, Justice Remix'd.

Charlie and Pauline Sullivan, founders of Citizens United for the Rehabilitation of Errants (CURE), have dedicated their lives to prisoners and their families. Today, the Sullivans reside in a one-room office/apartment in a drug-ridden neighborhood near the US Capitol in Washington, DC. At 80 years of age, they make the rounds of Congress, arguing that legislation for prison reform is both a social and moral necessity.

Recently, the Sullivans persuaded congressmen to sponsor legislation on juvenile justice and to endorse both the Second Chance Reauthorization Act and the Addiction Recovery and Expansion Act. Besides working with CURE groups that they have organized in every state, the Sullivans sponsor biannual international conferences focused on the subject of criminal justice reform. In between their foreign trips, the couple participates in panel discussions at the United Nations headquarters in New York City.

Charlie and Pauline hope to see a day when far fewer persons wind up behind steel bars. They are joined by the many people who work for humane prison conditions, including former inmates who remember those left behind in America's gulag.

The Sullivans are joined in these hopes of reform by Pope Francis I. In 2016, almost 40 years after my visit to the Cerezo jail, Pope Francis toured Juarez and spent time at the jail, a newer and far larger facility than the 1980s model. Known today as the most dangerous of Mexican correctional institutions, Cerezo, still afflicted with gang violence, is now controlled by drug cartel members and has a reputation for widespread corruption by the guards and the administration. A moving film on YouTube shows Pope Francis extending love and forgiveness as he walks among hundreds of Cerezo inmates who reach out and offer him small gifts.[3]

Francis's essential message to the prisoners is that they can have a new life, if they give up their violence and use their sufferings to help heal others. His words to the men at the jail, asking them to turn their lives around, reminds one of the theme in Fyodor Dostoevsky's *Crime and Punishment* that people who commit ugly violent crimes against innocent victims can express remorse.

After Pope Francis left the Cerezo prison grounds, he addressed church and political leaders at a town hall, and said:

> The problem of security is not resolved only by incarcerating; rather it calls us to intervene by confronting the structural and cultural causes of insecurity that affect the entire social framework.[4]

In his talk, Francis I put his finger on an important structural cause of crime and incarceration when he decried the amount of greed among the wealthy and the amount of desperation among the poor. His words were reminiscent of Victor Hugo's novel, *Les Misérables*, in which the author focused on the connection between poverty and criminal offenses by picturing his principal character, Jean Valjean, imprisoned for stealing a loaf of bread.

In a later interview for *America* magazine, Pope Francis said:

> You cannot talk about paying a debt to society from a jail cell without windows. There is no humane punishment without an horizon. No one can change their life if they don't see a horizon. And so many times we are used to blocking the view of our inmates. Divine mercy reminds us that prisons are an indication of the kind of society we are. In many cases, they are a sign of silence and omissions which have led to a throwaway culture, a symptom of a culture that has stopped supporting life, of a society that has abandoned its children.[5]

Through his continuing emphasis on human rights, Francis I offers a path of transparency and reconciliation. The next step is action. Simone Weil, twentieth-century French philosopher/activist, maintained that our purpose here on earth is to reach out to one another, particularly toward people who rank among those she called the "disaffected." Weil, referring to social injustice, said that it was not so much a question of the rights of the downtrodden but of the obligations that functioning societies must meet in order to prevent a hell upon this earth.

With serious consideration of penal reform occurring today for humanitarian reasons, as well as to provide better public safety and to lower financial costs, we should remember that, despite obstacles, positive change has occurred when citizens have a grasp on reality and the moral will.

Notes

1. Two companies, Securus and GTL, control more than 70% of the market for prison phone calls; they charge exorbitant rates and award kickbacks to jail and prison authorities. According to *Guardian* magazine, while some reform of telephone rates was begun under the Obama administration, President Donald Trump's Federal Communications Commission reversed this policy. However, the city of San Francisco is also providing free phone calls from local jails, turning a spotlight on the exorbitant cost of telephone access for prisoners, and prisoners in New Jersey have received a monetary settlement from a phone company for their excessive rates after a successful court battle. The state of Connecticut is considering making calls to prisoners free.

2. In Chris Hedges's book, *America: The Farewell Tour*, he writes: "Prison has become a rite of passage for poor people of color. And the conditions in prison are a model for the corporate state."
3. "Pope Francis Speaks of Mercy at Juarez Prison," https://www.elpasotimes.com/story/news/local/juarez/pope/2016/02/17/pope-francis-speaks-mercy-jurez-prison/80436620/
4. Ibid.
5. Cindy Wooden, "Pope Francis on Prison Systems: 'We Will Be Judged on This'," https://www.americamagazine.org/politics-society/2019/11/08/pope-francis-prison-systems-we-will-be-judged

Bibliography

Abbott, Jack Henry. *In the Belly of the Beast*. New York: Vintage Books, 1991.
Alexander, Michelle. *The New Jim Crow: Mass Incarceration in the Age of Colorblindness*. New York: The New Press, 2010.
Baca, Jimmy Santiago. *A Place to Stand*. New York: Grove Press, 2001.
Barnett, Brittany. *A Knock at Midnight: A Story of Hope, Justice, and Freedom*. New York: Crown Publishing, 2020.
Bauer, Shane. *American Prison: A Reporter's Undercover Journey into the Business of Punishment*. New York: Penguin Books, 2018.
Bazelon, Emily. *Charged: The New Movement to Transform American Prosecution*. New York: Random House, 2019.
Bentham, Jeremy. *Rationale of Reward*. London: J. & H. Hunt, 1825.
Berger, Dan. *Captive Nation: Black Prison Organization in the Civil Rights Era*. Chapel Hill: University of North Carolina Press, 2014.
Berrigan, Daniel. *The Trial of the Catonsville Nine*. New York: Fordham University Press, 2004.
Braly, Malcolm. *On the Yard*. New York: NYRB Classics, 1967.
Bunker, Edward. *Education of a Felon*. New York: St. Martin's Press, 2000.
Capote, Truman. *In Cold Blood*. New York: Random House, 1965.
Carter, Reuben. *Hurricane: The Miraculous Journey of Reuben Carter*. New York: Mariner Books, 2000.
Charriere, Henri. *Papillon*. Paris, France: Robert Laffont, 1969.
Chase, Robert. *We Are Not Slaves: State Violence, Coerced Labor, and Prison Riots in Postwar America*. Chapel Hill, NC: University of North Carolina Press, 2020.
Conover, Ted. *Newjack: Guarding Sing Sing*. New York: Vintage Books, 2001.
Davis, Angela. *Are Prisons Obsolete?* New York: Seven Stories Press, 2003.
de Beaumont, Gustave, and Alexis DeTocqueville. *On the Penitentiary System in United States and Its Application to France*. Philadelphia: Carey, Lea & Blanchard, 1833.
Earley, Pete. *The Hot House: Life Inside Leavenworth Prison*. New York: Bantam Books, 1993.
Echols, Damien. *Life After Death*. New York: Plume, 2013.
Eisner, Alan. *Gates of Injustice: The Crisis in America's Prisons*. Upper Saddle River, NJ: FT Press, Pearson, 2006.
Eubanks, Ronald. *Guilty Until Proven Innocent*. Conneaut, PA: Page Publishing, 2020.
Fallon, Mark. *Unjustifiable Means*. New York: Simon & Schuster, 2017.
Ferguson, Robert. *Inferno: An Anatomy of American Punishment*. Boston: Harvard University Press, 2018.
Forman, James, Jr. *Locking Up Our Own: Crime and Punishment in Black America*. New York: Farrar, Straus and Giroux, 2017.
Foucault, Michele. *Discipline and Punish: The Birth of the Prison*. New York: Vintage Books, 1975.
Garland, David. *Culture of Control: Crime and Social Order in Contemporary Society*. Chicago: University of Chicago Press, 2001.

Gilmore, Ruth Wilson. *Golden Gulag: Prisons, Surplus, Crisis, and Opposition in Globalizing California*. Berkeley: University of California Press, 2007.

Gonnerman, Jennifer. *Life on the Outside: The Prison Odyssey of Elaine Bartlett*. New York: Farrar, Strauss and Giroux, 2005.

Gottschalk, Marie. *Caught: The Prison State and the Lockdown of American Politics*. Princeton, NJ: Princeton University Press, 2016.

Graves, Anthony. *Infinite Hope: How Wrongful Conviction, Solitary Confinement, and 12 Years on Death Row Failed to Kill My Soul*. Boston: Beacon Press, 2018.

Grunewald, Jill. *Reading Behind Bars: A True Story of Literature, Law, and Life as a Prison Librarian*. New York: Skyhorse, 2019.

Hadley, Michael. *Spiritual Roots of Restorative Justice*. Stony Brook: State University of New York Press, 2001.

Harper, Hill. *Letters to an Incarcerated Brother*. New York: Avery, 2014.

Hayes, Christopher. *A Colony in a Nation*. New York: W. W. Norton, 2017.

Hinton, Anthony Ray. *The Sun Does Shine: How I Found Life and Freedom on Death Row*. New York: St. Martin's Press, 2018.

Hinton, Elizabeth. *From the War on Poverty to the War on Crime: The Making of Mass Incarceration in America*. Boston, MA: Harvard University Press, 2017.

Hugo, Victor. *Les Misérables*. Brussels, Belgium: A. Lacroix, Verboeckhoven & Cie, 1862.

Jackson, George. *Soledad Brother: Prison Letters of George Jackson*. Chicago: Chicago Review Press, 1994.

James, Erwin. *A Life Inside: A Prisoner's Notebook*. London: Atlantic Books, 2005.

Kant, Immanuel. *Metaphysical Elements of Justice*. Indianapolis: Hackett Publishing Company, 1999 (translation of German originally published 1797).

Kerman, Piper. *Orange Is the New Black: My Year in a Women's Prison*. New York: Spiegel and Grau, 2010.

Kilgore, James. *Understanding Mass Incarceration*. New York: The New Press, 2015.

Kropotkin, Peter. *In Russian and French Prisons*. London: Ward and Downey, 1887.

Kunzel, Regina. *Criminal Intimacy: Prison and the Uneven History of Modern American Sexuality*. Chicago: The University of Chicago, 2008.

Lee, Harper. *To Kill a Mockingbird*. New York: J. P. Lippincott, 1960.

Lynd, Staunton. *Lucasville: The Untold Story of a Prison Uprising*. San Francisco: PM Press, 2011.

Marakawa, Naomi. *The First Civil Right: How Liberals Built Prison America*. Oxford, England: Oxford University Press, 2014.

Maschi, Tina, and Keith J. Morgen. *Aging Behind Prison Walls: Studies in Trauma and Resilience*. New York: Columbia University Press, 2020.

Miller, Reuben. *Halfway Home*. New York: Little, Brown & Co, 2021.

Mitford, Jessica. *Kind and Usual Punishment*. New York: Vintage, 1974.

Molanphy, Helen Clarke. *The Idea of Punishment: Texas Prison System as a Case Study*. Dallas: University of Texas at Dallas, 1982.

Morris, Roger. *The Devil's Butcher Shop: The New Mexico Prison Uprising*. Albuquerque: University of New Mexico Press, 1988.

Morton, Dannie, and Sussman, Peter. *Committing Journalism: The Prison Writing of Red Hog*. New York: W. W. Norton, 1995.

Nagel, William. *New Red Barn: A Critical Look at the American Prison System*. New York: Walker & Co, 1973.

Natapoff, Alexandra. *Punishment Without Crime*. New York: Basic Books, 2018.

Oshinsky, Daniel. *Worse Than Slavery*. New York: Free Press, 1997.

Parenti, Christian. *Lockdown America: Police and Prisons in the Age of Crisis*. New York: Verso, 2000.

Paton, Alan. *Cry the Beloved Country*. New York: Scribner, 1948.

Pfaff, John. *Locked In: The True Causes of Mass Incarceration*. New York: Basic Books, 2017.

Prejean, Sister Helen. *Dead Man Walking*. New York: Penguin Random House, 1993.

Reiman, Jeffrey. *Rich Get Richer and Poor Get Prison*. Portland: Book News, 1979.

Richie, Beth. *Arrested Justice: Black Women, Violence, and America's Prison Nation*. New York: New York University Press, 2012.

Ridgeway, James. *Hell Is a Very Small Place: Voices from Solitary Confinement*. New York: The New Press, 2016.

Roth, Alisa. *Insane: America's Criminal Treatment of Mental Illness*. New York: Basic Books, 2018.

Sharkey, Patrick. *Uneasy Peace: The Next War on Violence*. New York: W. W. Norton, 2018.

Simmons, Lee. *Assignment Huntsville: Memoirs of a Texas Prison Official*. Huntsville, TX: University of Texas Press, 1957.
Senghor, Shaka. *Writing My Wrong: Life, Death, and Redemption in an American Prison*. New York: Penguin Random House, 2013.
Smith, Jeff. *Mr. Smith Goes to Prison: What My Years Behind Bars Told Me About the Prison Crisis*. New York: St Martin's Griffin, 2017.
Stevenson, Bryan. *Just Mercy: A Story of Justice and Redemption*. New York: Spiegel & Grau, 2014.
Swanson, Cheryl. *Restorative Justice in the Prison Community*. Washington, DC: Lexington Books, 2010.
Thompson, Heather Ann. *Blood in the Water: The Attica Uprising of 1971 and Its Legacy*. New York: Pantheon Books, 2016.
Travis, Jeremy. *But They All Came Back: Facing the Challenges of Prisoner Reentry*. Washington, DC: Rowman & Littlefield, 2005.
Venters, Homer. *Life and Death at Rikers Island*. Baltimore: Johns Hopkins University Press, 2019.
Western, Bruce. *Homeward: Life in the Year After Prison*. New York: Russell Sage Foundation, 2018.
Western, Bruce. *Punishment and Inequality in American Prisons*. New York: Sage, 2006.
Whitehead, Colson. *Nickel Boys*. New York: Penguin Random House, 2019.
Wicker, Tom. *A Time to Die: The Attica Prison Revolt*. Chicago: Haymarket Books, 1975.
Wilson, James Q. *Thinking About Crime*. New York: Basic Books, 1975.
Woodfox, Albert. *Solitary: A Biography*. New York: Grove Press, 2019.

Index

Page numbers followed by "n" denote notes.

Abbott, G. 91
Abel, D. 51n14
Abu Ghraib prison, Iraq 65
Abu-Jamal, M. 55
ACLU of New Mexico v. The New Mexico Children, Youth and Families Department et al. 38
Adams, J. 89
Adams State University 39
advocacy groups 39–40, 78, 81
African-American civil rights movement 46–47, 51n3
African-American inmates 46; brutality against 62; children 37; confinement of youths 37; religious freedom of Muslims 12n5; in Texas Department of Corrections (TDC) 8, 76–77; and voting reforms 103; women 42, 43, 45n7; *see also* people of color
Afrikaner language 53
After Innocence (documentary film) 67
Aguinaldo, E. 54
Ai Wei Wei 117
Alabama prison system 67, 79, 98; medical negligence in 81–82; Vipassana in 105
Alam, S. 116
Albuquerque Journal 61, 63n6
Alcatraz Island in San Francisco 117
Alexander, M. 33
Alice Project 43
Alighieri, D. 34, 118
Alito, S. 96
Almazan, L. 50
Almighty (Zak) 56n5
Amazon 78
America: The Farewell Tour (Hedges) 80, 123n2
America (magazine) 122
American Architectural Society 75

American Civil Liberties Union (ACLU) 37–38, 61, 74–75, 79, 82, 100
American Correctional Association (ACA) 14, 18, 78
American Indian Movement 55
American Prison: A Reporter's Undercover Journey into the Business of Punishment (Bauer) 84–85, 119
American Prison Writing Archives 62
American Railway Union 54
Amnesty International 55
Anderson, D. L. 70n13
Angola state penitentiary 91, 102
The Angolite 120
Anna (psychiatrist) 36
Annie E. Casey Foundation 37
Anti-Drug Abuse Act 47
apartheid movement in South Africa 53
Arkansas prison system 118, 120
Arpaio, J. 119–120
Arroyo, B. 50
Association of State Correctional Officers 74
Atlantic Monthly 81
Atonement Project 34
Attica, New York prison uprising 79
Auburn, New York 14
Austin, restorative justice practices in 114
Aviv, R. 120
Ayers, R., Jr. 120
Aylesbury prison, England 52

Balla v. Idaho State Board of Corrections 82–83
Baltimore National Center on Institutions and Alternatives 72
Ban the Bomb movement 55
"Ban the Box" 91
Barsky, N. 120–121
battered women's syndrome 42

Bauer, S. 84–85, 86, 119
Bazelon, E. 68
Beccaria, C. 39, 89, 100
Bedford Hills women's prison in New York State 44
Bedi, K. 105
Bentham, J. 89–90, 100
Berke, D. 115n5
Berrigan, D. 55, 56n4
Berrigan, P. 55
Bertsch, L. 108–109
Beth (inmate) 41–43
Beto, G. 9–10, 11, 15, 18–20, 24, 27, 28, 43–44, 45n4, 76–77; on changing working conditions in Texas Department of Corrections (TDC) 76–77; educational programs for guards 59; education plan for Texas Department of Corrections (TDC) 31–32; on unpaid work for inmates 78
Bettis, K. 79
Biden administration and prison reforms 32, 85
Bill of Rights 38, 90
Bin Wahad, D. 75n6
Bin Wahib, D. 49, 73
"Birth of a Nation" (movie) 46
Black Code misdemeanor offenses 46
Black Liberation Movement 55
Black Lives Matter 93
Blue state Washington 92
Bonhoeffer, D. 53
book banning in prisons 33–34
Booker, C. 43
Boston Globe 51
Boudin, C. 69
Boyle, G. 38
Breathe Act 93, 94n7
British Petroleum's use of inmates 78
Broken Silence publication 120
Brorby, D. 24
Browder, K. (inmate) 37, 69
Brown, J. 23n9, 96, 97
Brown v. Plata 91, 96, 97, 98
Brownwood State School 37–38
Brubaker (film) 119
Brunk, C. 111–112
Bureau of Prisons (BOP) 31, 92, 98
Buren, D. Van 114, 115n5
Burns, K. 33
Bush, G. W. 25, 26, 28n5, 65–66

Cabrales, I. 74–75
CalFire program 77, 80
California Correctional Peace Officers Association 96
California correctional system 20–21, 40, 42
Calipatria State Prison 96
Campaign for Youth Justice 39
Canon City facility 40
"Capitalizing on Justice" (artistic project) 117
Capote, T. 116
Carey, H. 47
Carter, J. 55
Carter, R. "Hurricane" 34
Catholic Worker 85
CBS *60 Minutes* 65, 108
censorship of educational programs 33–34
Center for Advancement for Public Integrity, United Nations 62–63
Center for Court Innovation 113
Central Intelligence Agency (CIA) 65
Centurion 82
Cerezo jail 121
Charged: The New Movement to Transform American Prosecution and End Mass Incarceration (Bazelon) 68
Chavez, C. 9
Chavez, E. 103
Chevron 77
Chicano movement 9, 47
Chico, California prison 40
children in prison 37
Christie, N. 62
Church Council for Justice and Corrections (CCJC) 112–113
Citizens United for the Rehabilitation of Errants (CURE) 8, 25–26, 78, 121
civil disobedience 54
civil rights movement 53
civil war 46–47
Clarke, K. 98
Clements, B. 17
Clements, T. 74
Clements, W. 14, 25
Clemmer, D. 62
Clinton, B. 32
Close, G. 44
Clubine, B. 42
cognitive behavioral therapy 101
Coleman federal prison in Sumter County, Florida 61
"College Behind Bars" 33
Colorado jails 82, 85
Colson, C. 90, 94n6, 121
Columbia University educational program 34–35
commissary purchases 78–79
Common Reading Experience 114
community-based initiatives 39
Community Justice Council 114
Community Justice Task Force 114
Confessing Church movement 53
Connecticut jail 60
contraband smuggling in prisons 63
Convicted Women Against Abuse 42
Conviction Integrity Unit, Dallas, Texas 69
Cooper v. Pate 9
CoreCivic 84, 85
Corizon Health Services 82, 83
Cornell University's Center on the Death Penalty Worldwide 43
corporate crimes. *see* white-collar crimes

Correctional Association of New York 48
correctional officers/guards: brutality by 15, 61–63; challenges faced by 26, 59–60; and COVID-19 crisis 60; dysfunctional behavior in 62; females 61–62; guards to prisoners ratio 15; illegal activities by 62–63; "lock psychosis" in 62; moral injury among 63; post-traumatic stress disorder (PTSD) 60, 63; and prison policies 63; salaries 59; sexual abuse by 60–61; training of 60
Corrections Accountability Project in Manhattan 117
Corrections Corporation of America (CCA) 84
corruption in prisons 59–63
Cortez, P. 117
The Cost of Discipleship (Bonhoeffer) 53
Cotton, R. 66
Council, R. E. 79
Council of Europe 114
counseling of mentally ill inmates 73
COVID-19 crisis 40, 72, 97, 100–101, 102; Arkansas prison system 120; and correctional officers 60; and deaths of inmates 93; and immigrant detainees 86; on Michigan prisoners 67; and misdemeanor policies 49; in Rikers Island Jail 75n2
Crime and Punishment (Dostoevsky) 122
Criminal Justice Reform 100
Criminal Mental Health Project (CMHP) 73
Cruz, F. 9–10, 47
Cruz v. Beto 9
culture and criminal justice system 107
custodial convenience 19
#Cut 50 34

Dallas County Jail 42
Daniels, J. 34–35
Danville Correctional Center 34
Dead Man Walking (film) 118
Dead Man Walking (Prejean) 116
The Death of Innocents: An Eyewitness Account of Wrongful Execution (Prejean) 116
Debs, E. V. 54
Deeper the Water campaign 51
Deepwater Horizon oil spill, cleaning by inmates 78
Defining Insanity (documentary film) 73
deinstitutionalization 97
Demby, G. 51n7
Denbeauz, M. 66
Denver Po 82
Department of Justice (DOJ) 95–99
Desert Waters Correctional Outreach 63
Designing Justice/Designing Spaces 114
The Devil's Butcher Shop: The New Mexico Prison Riot (Morris) 119
Dickerson, G. 63n7
Discipline and Punish: The Birth of the Prison (Foucault) 93–94
Divine Comedy (Alighieri) 34

Divine Comedy (poem) 118
Dix, D. 71
Doing Time, Doing Vipassana (documentary film) 105
Dole, B. 34
domestic violence and crime 41–42, 44
Donne, F. P. 118
Dostoevsky, F. 122
Dreams from the Monster Factory (Schwartz) 45n11
Dreisinger, B., Dr. 117
drug-addicted inmates 90–91
Drug Offender Sentencing Alternative (DOSA) 92
Dubois, W. E. B. 34
Duke, D. 34
Duncan, D. 82
Duran, D. 22
DuVernay, A. 46–47

East Baton Rouge Parish jail 72–73
Eastern State penitentiary, Pennsylvania 14
East Valley Tribune 119
e-carceration 92
The Echo 120
economic inequality and racism 49
Edelman, M. W. 40
Edna Mahan Correctional Facility for Women 98–99
Ed (prison inmate) 25–28
educational opportunities in San Quentin prison 77
education in prisons 31–35
Education Justice Project (EJP) 34
The Effectiveness of a Prison and Parole System (Glasser) 62
Eighth Amendment 80, 82–83, 96
elderly prisoners 39–40, 69
Eleventh Judicial Court, Florida 73
Ellis, O. B. 18–19, 24, 76–77
Ellison, K. 26, 27–28
Ellis Unit 20
Elmira Correctional Facility, New York 48
El Paso County Jail 82
English Quakers 94
Enron corporate scandal 50
Ensler, E. 116
environmental problems in prison systems 50–51
Environmental Protection Agency's (EPA) Environmental Small Grants Program 50
Epping, E. 117
Equal Employment Opportunity Commission (EEOC) 61
Equal Justice Initiative (EJI) 36, 60, 67–68, 114
Estelle, E. 14, 22
Estelle, J. 20–21, 59
Estelle v. Gamble 83
Eubanks, R. J. 69, 70n13
European criminal justice system 106–107
European Enlightenment thinking 90
Evangelical Christianity 107

Index

Fallon, M. 69n1
false identification and wrongful convictions 67
Families against Mandatory Minimums (FAMM) 33
family visitation 22, 60
female guards 61
female inmates 41–45; African-American inmates 42, 43, 45n7; giving birth in prison 44; in Oklahoma 41; sexual abuse of 60–61; at Springer 61
Figueroa, E. 11
fines on prisoners 77
First Amendment 9–10, 120
First Step Act 44, 92–93, 98
fiscal costs of mass incarceration 92
Florida inhumane juvenile detention center 39
Florida prison 71
Floyd, G. 93
food for inmates 16, 20, 22, 28, 39, 49, 52, 71–73, 76, 85, 96–98, 102–103, 105
Foucault, M. 71, 93–94, 100
Francis, P. 121–122
Franks, L. 72–73

Gallatin House 102
Gallatin School Writing Program 120
Gamble, J. W. 83
Gamez, R. 50
Gandhi, Mahatma 53, 54
Gatesville prison 41
GED certification 31–32
General Educational Development (GED) program 27
Georgia prison system 63, 83, 98
Gideon v. Wainwright 70n6
Gill, H. B. 32
"Girls Embracing Mothers" 45n4
Glasser, D. 62
Global Tel Link 33
Gonne, M. 52, 55
Gonnerman, J. 119
Gonzalez, E. 68–69
Gonzalez, J. 14
Good Conduct Time (GCT) 48
Gore-Booth, E. 52
Governing (periodical) 73
Graham v. Florida 36
Great Britain, banning solitary confinement 74
Greene Spaces 55, 83
Greene State Correctional Institution 22
Griffith, D. W. 46
Grisham, J. 33–34, 66
Grisham, M. L. 22, 100
GTL 122n1
Guantanamo base in Cuba 69n3
Guardian (magazine) 122n1
The Guardians (Grisham) 66
guards. *see* correctional officers/guards
Guilty Until Proven Innocent: When A Woman Cries Rape: The Life Story of Ronald Eubanks (Eubanks and Anderson) 69, 70n13

Hadley, M. 111
Harding, W. G. 54
Hayes, L. 72
Hedges, C. 80, 119, 123n2
Heiss, J. 73
Hell is a Very Small Place: Voices from Solitary Confinement (Ridgeway) 120
Hinton, A. R. 67
Hispanic inmates 37, 48, 49, 76–77; *see also* people of color
Hitler, A. 34, 53
Holland, medical approach to illegal drug addiction 107
Holman unit, Alabama 79
Home Boys Industries 38
Home Girls Industries 38
Houchins v. KQED 118
Hough, J. 117
Howard, J. 101
Hugo, V. 122
Human Rights Defense Center (HRDC) 50
Human Rights Watch 71–72
Hunt, A. 117
Huntsville Prison 120
Hussein, S. 65
Hutto, D. 85

Idaho's prisoner health care 83
Idea of Punishment: Texas Prison System as a Case Study 22
"I Have a Dream" speech 53
immigrant detention network 85
Impact Justice 28
In Cold Blood (Capote) 116
Index of Condemned Books 89
Indiana prison 71
Industrial Workers of the World 79
inmates: advocacy groups 39–40, 78, 81; deaths 11, 14, 15, 19, 20, 22, 37, 39, 48, 62, 98, 119; difficulty of adjusting to free world 102; elderly 39–40, 69; food for 16, 20, 22, 28, 39, 49, 52, 71–73, 76, 85, 96–98, 102–103, 105; medical care for 40, 49, 81–84, 97–98, 101, 102, 107; Mexican American 47; New York City 34–35; political 52–55; relatives, helping 79; writing by 8–12, 21, 34, 50, 53, 67, 102; *see also* African-American inmates; female inmates; Hispanic inmates; juvenile offenders
Innocence Project 67, 69
In Re Gault 38
In Russian and French Prisons (Kropotkin) 93
Insight Personal Project (IPP) 113
Institute of Contemporary Corrections 19
institutionalization 108
International Rights of the Child 38
Irish Republican Army 74
Irons, J. 68
Ivey, K. 98
Ivins, M. 13

Jackson, G. (inmate) 62, 79
Jacques 106–107
jailhouse lawyers 8–12
Jailhouse Lawyers Speak 79
Jalet-Cruz, F. 10, 11, 13, 24
Japanese Americans as political prisoners 54–55
Jefferson, T. 89
Jerome, Christian Saint 117
"The Jerome Project" 116–117
Jessen, B. 65
Johnson, L. 47
Johnson v. Avery 9
1974 Joint Committee on Prison Reform 16
Jones-Thomas, J. (inmate) 50, 51n10
JPay 33
Justice, W. W. 13–16, 17, 24–25; appointee for the implementation of the Texas reforms 23n9; on power of private prison corporations 25
Just Mercy (Stevenson) 67, 114
"Juvenile Injustice" (visual work) 117
juvenile offenders 113; detention centers 36, 38; justice systems 39; literacy programs for 34
"Juvie Talk" (visual work) 117

Kaphar, T. 116–117
K.C. v. Nedelfoff 37
Keller, B. 120
Kellogg Foundation 34
Kennedy, A. 96
Kentucky state prison 118
Kilmainham Jail, Dublin 52
Kind and Usual Punishment (Mitford) 94
King, M. L., Jr. 9, 53
Koch brothers 90
Korematsu v. United States 54–55
Krasner, L. 68, 69
Kropotkin, P. 93
Kuhn, V. 99
Kushner, J. 94n6

labor practices in southern states 77
labor unions 78
Lawrence 15
Lee, H. 116
Lee, M. 43
Les Misérables (Hugo) 122
Letter from Birmingham Jail (King) 53
Letters and Papers from Prison (Bonhoeffer) 53
Librium 10
Life and Death at Rikers Jail 72
Life Magazine 65
The Life of Ruben Carter (Carter) 34
Life on the Outside: The Prison Odyssey of Elaine Bartlett 119
Lifer Review Committee 100
life sentences in Europe 106
Lippman, J. 37
Lipscomb, L. 69
literacy program for juveniles 34
literacy training 92; *see also* education in prisons

Locked In: The True Causes of Mass Incarceration (Pfaff) 68, 70n8
London, prisons in 106
Los Angeles County jails 63
Louisiana jails 72, 77, 91, 120; overcrowding in 91
Lucero, A. 61

Maestas, A. 74–75
Mahoney prison, Pennsylvania 50
Malcolm X 9
Malloy, D. 108
"Man Alive" program 44–45
Mandela, N. 53–54
Mandela Rules 74
Marion Federal Correctional Institute 55
Markievicz, C. G.-B. 52–53, 56n1
Markievicz Prison Letters and Rebel Writings (Naughton) 56n2
Marshall, T. 8, 120
Marshall Project, New York 62, 63n8, 79, 100–101, 120
Martin, S. J. 62
Martinez v. Procunier 120
Marymount Manhattan College 32
Massachusetts Institute of Technology (MIT) 34
mass incarceration, efforts to end: alternative models 105–110; legislative agendas 89–94; reducing recidivism 100–104; restorative justice 111–115; Supreme Court 95–99; US Department of Justice 95–99
Mast v. Donohue 71
Maxwell Correctional Facility 121
McBride, S. 55
McCain, J. 66
McCormick, A. 31
McCormick, H. 20, 25, 119
McCotter, L. 24
McDermott, B. 82
McDonald 79
Measure R, 118
Medicaid/Medicare 40
medical care for prisoners 40, 49, 81–84, 97–98, 101, 102, 107
medical parole 25
mentally ill inmates, treatment of 71–75
Merchant, G. (inmate) 83
Mexican American inmates 9, 47
Mexican–American War 54
Miami-Dade County Counseling Center 73
Michigan prison 34, 67
Milan prison 89
Miller v. Alabama 36
Mims, B. 117–118
Minnesota, restorative justice principles in 113
minor children in prison 37
misdemeanor charges 49
Mississippi prisons 114
Missouri Youth Services 39
Mitchell, J. 65
Mitford, J. 94

Monroe Correctional Complex 50
Montesquieu, B. de 89
Montgomery, J. 67
Moore, M. 68
moral injury 63
Morris, E. 66
Morris, R. 119
Mosby, M. 69
Mother Jones magazine 84, 119
Mothers Reclaiming Our Children (Mothers ROC) 121
Motorola 77
Moyers, B. 37, 68–69
Mr. Smith Goes to Prison: What My Year Behind Bars Taught Me About America's Prison Crisis (Smith) 102
Murphy, P. 99
Murton, T. 119
Muslim immigrants in Paris prisons 106

Nagel, W. 17
Natapoff, A. 48–49
Nathan, V. 17, 23n9
National Black Women's Justice Institute 43
National Public Radio 97
National Rifle Association 72
Nation (magazine) 68
Native Americans, confinement of 37, 49
Naughton, L. 56n2
Nevada prisoner lawsuit 81
New Jersey prison system 33, 77, 98–99
The New Jim Crow: Mass Incarceration in the Age of Colorblindness (Michelle) 33
Newman v. Alabama 9
New Mexico Criminal Defense Lawyers Association (NMCDLA) 68
New Mexico Department of Corrections (NMDC) 22, 36, 59, 61, 82, 119; officials 74; overcrowding 82; penitentiary riot in Santa Fe 17; plaintiffs 38; prison labor in 77; snitching system in maximum-security penitentiary in 22, 23n9; violent crime in 49; voting rights of inmates 103
New Red Barn: A Critical Look at the American Prison System 17
Newsom, G. 40, 80
New York Bard College's program 33
New York Bedford Hills College Program 32
New York Department of Corrections 63
New Yorker (magazine) 72–73, 119, 120
New York State corrections administrator 33
New York Times 61, 66, 86, 118, 119, 120–121
New Zealand, prisons in 105
Nickel Boys (Whitehead) 39
Nixon, R. 47, 51n3, 94n6
Nixon-era Watergate burglary 121
Nordstrom 77
Norfolk prison in Massachusetts 51
Norfolk State Prison Colony, educational system at 32

Norquist, G. 90
North Dakota Department of Corrections 108–109
Norwegian corrections officers 109
Novak, R. 9
Novak v. Beto 9
Novick, L. 33
The Nuns, the Priests, and the Bombs (film) 56n5
Nurse-Family Partnership 91

Obama, B. 32, 40, 43, 85
Office of Restorative Justice Planner 113
Ohio prisons, banning book donations 33
Oklahoma prison 16, 41
Olson, T. 82
On Crimes and Punishment (Beccaria) 89
O'Neil, G., Sister 41–43, 44
Operation Ghost Guard 63
Ornstein, N. 73
Osborn Correctional Institution, New Haven 108
overcrowding in prisons 14, 25, 92, 96–97
oversentencing in American prisons 106
Overton v. Bazzetta 118

Paris, prisons in 106
parole 15, 19, 22, 25, 36, 38–40, 43–44, 69, 77, 79, 91, 95, 97
Pauline, C. 8
PBS 115
Peck, G. 116
Pelican Bay State 96
Pell Grant funding 32
Pell v. Procunier 118
Peltier, L. 55
people of color: on death row 43; poor 46–51; *see also* African-American inmates
Perry, R. 90, 91
Pew Charitable Trust 33
Pfaff, J. 68, 70n8, 94
Pfeffer, M. B. 118
Philippine Islands, American takeover of 54
phone calls, charges for 78–79
A Place to Stand (documentary film) 118
Plata v. Davis/Schwarzenegger 81
Plessy v. Ferguson 46
Plowshares Movement 55
police lineup 66
police shootings 73
political prisoners 52–55
polluted facilities 50
Pope, L. 8, 10–11, 13, 16–17, 52, 59, 62
Portugal, drug counseling and treatment in 107–108
Prejean, H., Sister 116
Press, E. 73
pretrial diversion programs in Texas 91
prisons: chaplaincy program 43–44, 45n4; deaths 11, 14, 15, 19, 20, 22, 37, 39, 48, 62, 98, 119; labor 76–80; library budgets cut 33; overcrowding in 14, 25, 92, 96–97; oversentencing in

American 106; population, surge in 21–22; rape 26; violence in 61–62, 84–85, 102; work ethic in 77–78; *see also* correctional officers/guards; inmates
Prison Community (Clemmer) 62
Prison Doula Project 44
Prison Ecology Project (PEP) 50
Prison Education Program (PEP) 101–102, 120
Prison Enhancement Certification Program 78
Prison Enterprises 77
Prison Fellowship International 121
Prison Industrial Act 78
The Prison Mirror 120
Prison Policy Initiative (PPI) 78–79
Prison Radio 50
prison-raised tilapia 78
Prison Rape Elimination Act 26
prison systems, environmental problems in 50–51
private detention centers 86
privatization of corrections 81–86
"Probation and Parole" 101
Procunier, R. 24
Project Gutenberg 33
Public Broadcasting Service (PBS) 33, 38
Puget Sound 50
Pulse Institute 67
Punishment and Profit 56n1
Punishment Without Crime 49
Puritan ethic 107
Puritan philosophy 77–78

Raemisch, R. 74
Ramsey plantation unit 85
RAND Corporation 63
Rationale on Punishment 89
Ray, M. 79
Reagan, R. 21, 22
recidivism: among elderly inmates 69; and educational system 32–33; in European jails 108; in juvenile detention centers 38; reducing 90–91, 100–104
Redford, R. 119
"Redistribute the Pain" 79–80
rehabilitation programs 34, 101
Rehnquist Award for Judicial Excellence 73
Reitman, S. 73
religion and criminal justice system 107
Reno, J. 32
Republican leaders on crime 90
Research and Development (RAND) Corporation 33
Restaurant Opportunities Center 114
restorative justice 111–115
Restore Justice 40
Restore Oakland 114
Rhodes v. Chapman 83
Rice, M. 55, 56n5
Richards, A. 25
Ridgeway, J. 120

"Right on Crime" movement 91
right to religious freedom 9–10
right-wing reformers 90
"Rikers: An American Jail" (documentary film) 37
Rikers Island Jail 37, 60, 62; corrections officers at 63; COVID-19 cases in 75n2; inhumane conditions at 69; mentally ill inmates at 72; scandal 81
Ring, K. 33
Rizer, A. 33
Robbin Island prison 53–54
Robbins, D. 83
Robbins, T. 118
Rockefeller, N. 47, 51n2
Rockefeller drug laws 119
Rockefeller legal system 47
Rogerson, H. 118
Roosevelt, F. D. 54–55
Roper v. Simmons 36
Ross, R. 117
Roulet, E. 44
Ruiz, D. 10, 11, 25, 47
Ruiz v. Estelle 13–17, 59

Sabotage Act 55
Salem Trials museum 65
Sam Houston State 38
Sam Houston State College 18, 19, 76
San Bruno jail 44–45
Sanchez, D. 82
Sands, B. 53
San Quentin News 120
San Quentin prison 40, 77, 96, 113
Santa Fe New Mexican Sunday paper 61
Santa Fe penitentiary riot 22
Santa Fe Reporter 103, 117
Santa Fe University of Art and Design 100
Santiago-Baca, J. 118
Saxbe v. Washington Post Co. 118
Scalia, A. 96
Scheck, B. 67
Schlosser, E. 81
school-to-prison pipeline 38, 79, 113, 114
Schwartz, S. 44–45, 45n11
Seattle Weekly 50
Second Chance Act 93
Second Chance Pell pilot program 32
Securus 122n1
Sedition Act of 1918 54
Selective Service Act of 1967 55
self-education 34
Senghor, S. 34–35
"The Sentence" (movie) 43
Sentencing Project 43
Sentencing Reform and Corrections Act 92
Seton Hall University School of Law 66
sexual abuse 60–61, 98–99
Shakespeare Behind Bars (documentary film) 118
Shank, C. 43

Siggers, D. 67
Simmons, L. 76
Simmons, W. L. 19
Sixth Amendment 70n6
Skykomish River sewage spill 50
Smith, J. 102–103
Sojouners (magazine) 78
Solidarity movement in Poland 53
solitary confinement: African Americans in 48, 102; after work stoppage 80; at Alabama's Holman unit 79–80; banning of 74–75; at Colorado correctional facility 74; effect of 73–74; in European prisons 107; females in 37, 60; Fred Cruz in 10; at Georgia's maximum-security prison 98; harsh conditions in 9; Hispanics in 48; Lawrence Pope in 8, 15, 24; mentally ill inmates in 71, 73, 74, 90, 108; at Michigan prison 34; for minor offenses 73; at Monroe Correctional Complex 50; at New Mexico Department of Corrections 74; at Pelican Bay inmates 96; reducing the use of 72; at Rikers Island Jail 37; at TDC 16, 20, 25, 27; youth in 36
Solitary (Woodfox) 102
The Souls of Black Folks (Dubois) 34
Southern Center for Human Rights (SCHR) 98
Southern Poverty Law Center 81, 113
Southport Correctional Facility, New York 48
Southwest Key Programs 86
Space for Restorative Justice 115n5
Spanish-American War 54
Spinaris, C. 63
Spiritual Roots of Restorative Justice 111
Springer prison, New Mexico 61
Stanford University Prison Experiment 40, 85
Stern, M., Dr. 82–83
Stevenson, B. 36, 60, 67, 114
Stillwater Prison 120
Stop Campaign 79
Stop Hate and Delinquency by Empowering Students (SHADES) 113
Stowe, H. B. 34
street offenders vs white-collar offenders 50
strikes by inmates 79–80
suicide: prevention in prisons 72–73; rates among youth in detention 36
Sullivan, C. 8, 10, 14, 25–26, 78, 121
Sullivan, P. 78, 121
The Sun Does Shine: How I Found Life and Freedom on Death Row (Hinton) 67
Supermax prison 63, 74, 117
Sutherland, E. 49–50

Tacoma College Program 32
Tannenbaum, F., Dr. 62
Target 77
Tegel prison 53
The Tempest (play) 118
Texas control model 3–7

Texas Department of Corrections (TDC): effects of COVID-19 on inmates 27–28; heat-related deaths and illnesses in 26; intelligent classification at 15; jailhouse lawyers 8–12; prison administrators 18–23; ratio of guards to prisoners at 15; reforms in 24–28; religious freedom at 12n5; *Ruiz v. Estelle* 13–17; sexual violence in 15; solitary confinement at 16; Texas control model 3–7; working conditions in 76–77; writ-writers at 16
Texas Department of Criminal Justice (TDCJ). *see* Texas Department of Corrections (TDC)
Texas Jail and Prison Coalition 10
Texas legislature 90–91
Texas Observer 27
Texas Offender Reentry Initiative 101
Texas Public Policy Foundation 90
"Texas Today" 91
Texas Youth Council (TYC) 37
Thin Blue Line (documentary film) 66
Thirteenth Amendment 46
13th (DuVernay) 46
Thomas, H. W. 117
Thomas v. McNeill 71
Thompson, J. 66
Thompson, K. 69
Thorazine 10
Thoreau, H. D. 54
"three strikes" law 95
Thrive for Life 101–102
Tibar prison, India 105
A Time to Die (Wicker) 119
To Kill a Mockingbird (Lee) 116
Tolstoy, L. 54
Tom Clements Better Government Award 74
"Tough on Crime" movement 90
Trial of the Catonsville Nine (play and film) 56n4
Tribune 119–120
trichloroethylene groundwater contamination area 50
Trumbo, D. 56n3
Trumbo (movie) 56n3
Trump, D. 85, 93, 122n1
Truth and Reconciliation Commission 115
Turner, D. 117–118
Turner, W. B. 10
Tutu, D. 115
Tutwiler (documentary film) 63n5
Tutwiler prison for women, Alabama 60–61

Uncle Tom's Cabin (Stowe) 34
United Nations International Covenant on Civil and Political Rights 38
University of Denver 63
University of Illinois 34
University of Mississippi Department of Legal Studies 114
University of Victoria 101
Unjustifiable Means (Fallon) 69n1
Unlocking Doors 101

Vagina Monologues (play) 116
Valdez, R. 43
Venters, H. 69, 72
Vera Institute for Justice 73, 79, 121
Vermont, reparative probation in 114
Victim Offender Education Group (VOEG) 113
Victim Offender Reconciliation Program (VORP) 113
Victoria Law 51n5
Victorville prison, California 61
Vietnam War 51n3, 53, 66
Violence Against Women Act (VAWA) 44
Violent Crime Control and Law Enforcement Act 32
visitation rights in Paris prisons 106
visitations charges 78–79
voting rights of inmates/ex-inmates 103

Walker, A. 33
Wallace Pack unit 26, 27–28
Wallkill Correctional Facility 120
Ware State Prison 98
War on Drugs 47, 51n3, 92, 107
The Washington Post 62, 98
Washington State Department of Corrections 72
waterboarding 65–66
Watergate 51n3, 90, 94n6
Watkins, C. 69
Weil, S. 122
Wesley, D. 113
West Virginia prison system 33
Wexford Health Sources 82
What I Want You to Know (documentary film) 116
White, M. 17
white-collar crimes 49–50, 94n6
Whitehead, C. 39
Whitmer, G. 67

Whole Foods 78
Wicker, T. 119
Wilson, W. 46, 54
Wilson v. Seeter 83
Windham School District 31
Winfrey, O. 67
Winn facility in Louisiana 84
Winn prison 119
Wisconsin facilities 48
witch trials in Salem 65
Wolff v. McDonnell (Nebraska court case) 15
Women's National Basketball Association (WNBA) 68
women's suffrage movement 52
Woodfox, A. 102
work ethic in prisons 77–78
workplace injuries 79
work stoppages 79–80
World War II, political prisoners post 54–55
Wright, J. 48
writing by inmates 8–12, 21, 34, 50, 53, 67, 102
Writing My Wrongs: Life, Death, and Redemption in an American Prison (Senghor) 34
writ-writers in prison 8–10, 16, 21
wrongful convictions 65–69
Wyoming state prison 20

Yeshiva University in New York City 67
yoga therapy 105
Young, A. 55
young offenders: decline in 38; in detention 36–37; sexual and physical abuse of 37–38

The Zo: Where Prison Guards' Favorite Tactic Is To Mess With Your Head (film) 62
Zubaydah, A. 66